USA
PHRASEBOOK

Colleen Cotter
Eagle/Walking Turtle

USA phrasebook
2nd edition – August 2001
First published – October 1995

Published by
Lonely Planet Publications Pty Ltd ABN 36 005 607 983
90 Maribyrnong St, Footscray, Victoria 3011, Australia

Lonely Planet Offices
Australia Locked Bag 1, Footscray, Victoria 3011
USA 150 Linden St, Oakland CA 94607
UK 10a Spring Place, London NW5 3BH
France 1 rue du Dahomey, 75011 Paris

Cover illustration
whatever by Patrick Marris

ISBN 1 86450 182 0

text © Lonely Planet Publications 2001
cover illustration © Lonely Planet 2001

Printed by The Bookmaker International Ltd
Printed in China

ACKNOWLEDGEMENTS

About the Authors

The second edition of the *USA Phrasebook* was compiled by coordinating author Colleen Cotter, who is an American and assistant professor in the Linguistics Department and Communication, Culture and Technology Program at Georgetown University in Washington, DC, with the dedicated assistance of Aida Premilovac. Colleen, who received her PhD in linguistics at the University of California at Berkeley, is a former resident of the Upper Midwest, West Coast, England and Thailand.

Kate Burridge, BA (Hons) (UWA), PhD (London) FAHA, wrote the section on Amish communities. Kate is a regular presenter of language segments on ABC Radio, Australia

From the Authors

Colleen Cotter acknowledges that this phrasebook is a collaboration of many, whose generosity, good humour and ability to see how language provides truly awesome glimpses into culture were gratefully received and are deeply appreciated.

The following writers contributed in ways great and small to various sections of the book: Jeff Deby (hockey and Canadian insights), Greg Tennant (Los Angeles, its subcultures and the film industry), Bill Jewell and Harris Dillon (music), Pam Morgan (US Spanish and African-American English), Wadee Deeprawat (Asian-American languages), Mike Brown, Kim Echols, Eric Gustafson and Nicholas Morehead (sports), L Carol Christopher (hunting, gambling), Joe Cutbirth (politics), Mindy McWilliams (tech lingo, Ultimate Frisbee), Matthew Tinkcom (television), Stacy Rosenberg (clubs, meeting people, sports), Aida Premilovac (festivals, theme parks, and colloquialisms), Naomi C Losch (Hawaiian English), Jim Crotty (asides), Rolf Samuels (country music), Joe Grady (US English grammar), Natalie Schilling-Estes (speaking like Shakespeare), Shrona Sheppard (family), David

Widelock (jazz), Rachel Loya (California), Ahava Leibtag (Jewish), Wendy AFG Stengel (Pacific Northwest), Mary-Denise Tabar and Karen Mitchell (the South) and Rachael Lille (Boston).

Contributors and consultants include: Rachel Adelson, Zena Barakat, Alan Breznick, Mary Cotter, Hugh Curnutt, Corey Eagan, David Fischer, Alkisti Fleischer, Melanie Fox, Maria D Garcia-Pastor, Mindy L Glover, Steven Grady, Perrin Grayson, Nick Hales, Toshi Hamaguchi, Leanne Hinton, Alex Houston, Ignatius Hsu, Kelby Johnson, Benjamin Kaplan, Carolyn Kinney, Dainora Kupcinskas, Philip Levine, Daniel Loehr, Joe Lough, Alison Mackey, Jo Mackiewicz, Dan Marschall, Lisa A McClelland, Bruce Morén, Nicholas Onofrey, Charlene Polio, David Robinson, Mónica Sanjur, Otto Santa Ana, Louis Scavo, Debby Schiffrin, Adrienne Scott, Jesse Smith, Kirsten Spalding, Angela L Stahle, Dorcas Billings Taylor, Chad Thevenot, Adrienne Tony and Katherine Watier.

Eagle/Walking Turtle dedicates the Native American section to his grandson, Elvin. For more information on Native Americans see *Indian America, A Traveler's Companion* (1989, John Muir Publications, Santa Fe). The publisher wishes to also thank Anthony P Grant for his assistance with research.

This Book

There are many languages in the USA and, in compiling this book, we were only able to include a sample of vocabularies, accents, dialects and Native American languages. For example, Spanish, Spanglish and many other community languages play a huge part in modern American culture, as does Hawaiian Pidgin English in Hawaii and American Sign Language in the deaf community. Discover more for yourself as you travel through this country.

From the Publisher

This book was joyfully edited by Fleur Goding and assisted by Haya Husseini and Emma Koch. Lou Callan proofread the book and edited it down to a portable size. Sarah Curry made it even more 'schleppable' during layout with editorial assistance from more 'schleppable' during layout with editorial assistance from Karina Coates. These pages were artfully laid out by Patrick Marris with Fabrice Rocher supervising design. Patrick also provided the wonderful illustrations and Natasha Velleley provided the accurate maps. Yukiyoshi Kamimura designed the fonts for the Native American sections. Many thanks to staff of the Lonely Planet US office for their humorous contributions and assistance and to Karin Vidstrup Monk for her invaluable advice. Thanks to Sally Steward, Peter D'Onghia and Ingrid Seebus for tirelessly coordinating the project. And lastly, a huge thanks goes to the author, Colleen Cotter, for always being there for us.

CONTENTS

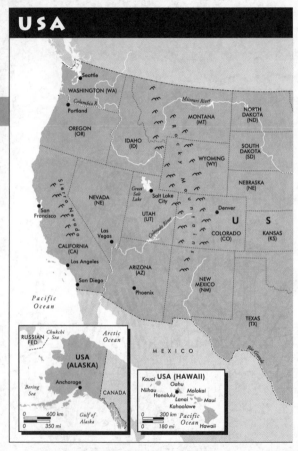

USA

Seattle
WASHINGTON (WA)
Columbia R.
Portland
OREGON (OR)
IDAHO (ID)
Missouri River
MONTANA (MT)
NORTH DAKOTA (ND)
SOUTH DAKOTA (SD)
WYOMING (WY)
NEBRASKA (NE)
Sierra Nevada
San Francisco
NEVADA (NE)
Great Salt Lake
Salt Lake City
UTAH (UT)
Colorado River
Denver
COLORADO (CO)
U   S
KANSAS (KS)
Las Vegas
CALIFORNIA (CA)
Los Angeles
San Diego
ARIZONA (AZ)
Phoenix
NEW MEXICO (NM)
TEXAS (TX)
Pacific Ocean
MEXICO
Rio Grande

Chukchi Sea
RUSSIAN FED.
Arctic Ocean
USA (ALASKA)
Bering Sea
Anchorage
CANADA
Gulf of Alaska
| 0 | 600 km |
| 0 | 350 mi |

Kauai
USA (HAWAII)
Oahu
Niihau
Honolulu
Molokai
Lanai
Maui
Kahoolawe
| 0 | 300 km |
| 0 | 180 mi |
Pacific Ocean
Hawaii

Map 13

A SHORT HISTORY

INTRODUCTION

You can travel through the great expanse of the USA, over the Rocky Mountains, across the wide Mississippi River, down to the humid bayous, up to the cool pine woods, and in and out of cities and small towns, without seeing a single famous sight or reading a single historical marker, and still have a great time – just by listening to the language of the people around you. What you get for free is one of the most entertaining, accurate, idiosyncratic and insightful glimpses of this contradictory country.

The manner in which people talk, the words they use or don't use, the pauses they take, whether they interrupt, whether they use slang or another language, whether they drop their 'r's or not, all contribute to the cultural mosaic that defines the USA; so does what their bumper stickers say ('my wife yes, my dog maybe, my gun never' versus 'don't bear arms, arm bears'), or what you'll read on their T-shirts and billboards.

As you move around the country, you'll find language usage to reinforce the cliches. The slang ('and I'm like, that's *so* last year'), the geekspeak ('message me about your stock options'), the media catch phrases ('is that your final answer?') are all there, as well as hick talk, slick talk, rap talk, back talk, gang talk, slang talk, funny accents and strange conversational styles.

But you'll also find features that characterise a particular region, or define a group, or reflect certain values; features that can add texture, breadth and understanding to a travel experience. By reading menus, listening to local radio stations or reading local papers, overhearing conversations or hanging out in cafes, campgrounds, coffee shops, bars, taverns, hot dog stands, lunch counters and bookshops, you'll be in the linguistic trenches and well prepared to bring back something more curious than a Mickey Mouse hat or an Empire State Building thermometer.

Don't be misled by the fact that you already know English. Or that you've already been thoroughly indoctrinated by Hollywood-exported movies and TV shows. The USA really is a foreign country, even to many of its inhabitants, who may be geographically or ideologically bound to one viewpoint. In fact, travellers have the advantage – of distance and of mobility – especially if they familiarise themselves with some of the information in this language guide.

One of the problems – or challenges, depending on how you look at it – is the country's physical size; the USA is too big to be one monolithic, English-speaking culture. As the 20th century progressed, the old notion of the melting pot – America as a stew in which individual differences are lost in a tasty new uniformity – has given way to the salad bowl or mosaic idea, in which the individual pieces still retain their flavour while contributing to the whole. Or we see cultural syncretism, a compromise between the two views, in which different components combine to form something new and unique, as in Cajun music or California cuisine.

Americans often like to think they are 'plain vanilla', without artifice, and as simple and wholesome as 'mom and apple pie', the phrase that stands in for these important national values. But the truth is that the picture is complicated, messy, rich in flavour and variety, and not without malice – all expressed in the language history of the USA and its contemporary stylings.

THE BEGINNINGS OF AMERICAN ENGLISH

The war against the British during the American Revolution of 1776 extended to language. Several notable founding fathers proposed ways to differentiate American talk from British English as a way to underscore the new country's independence. Noah Webster published his now-famous dictionary, saying that Great Britain 'should no longer be *our* standard'. Statesman John Adams suggested founding a language academy to set official standards for American English (but his contemporaries saw no need to legislate language choice and his proposal foundered).

The efforts of Connecticut-born lexicographer Noah Webster, after the United States won its independence from Britain, are generally credited with the evolution of American spelling, although a host of other ideological and patriotic factors came into play. Besides arguing for a system that would take into account American pronunciation, Webster became a spelling reform advocate, which led to the deletion of 'u' (as in humour) and 'k' (as in publick) in certain words. Some of the reforms laid down in his classic 1790 *Compendious Dictionary of the English Language* became standard, and others did not. The 'u' in humour or the 's' in practise indicate a British or Canadian affiliation.

Despite the battle being waged against the Mother Country in the linguistic realm, the larger issue for political leaders was unity of the new country, and language was a factor only to the extent that they made use of each immigrant language to get the word out. Some members of the Continental Congress, including Thomas Jefferson and Benjamin Rush, promoted the use of languages other than English for practical and educational reasons. The attitude toward language was pragmatic and not ideological (as it has been since the 1980s with still-active 'English Only' movements and since the 1990s with 'politically correct' language).

The country's political history and geographic features, the immigration patterns of several centuries, the realities of social and economic class differences, and the influence of the media, entertainment industry and youth culture in recent decades have all contributed to the unique regional characteristics of American English; from 'y'all' in the South to 'youse guys' in the North and East. What Americans speak now is a far cry from the languages spoken when the country was settled.

Contributing Languages

When the first European colonists and explorers arrived in eastern North America in the 17th century, there was a great deal of mixing of languages, as well as learning of the indigenous languages. This open attitude toward other languages, undertaken for utilitarian and economic reasons, has not lasted. While many Americans may have a language other than English as their mother tongue or language spoken at home, few Americans set out to learn a language other than English. This is mainly due to the lack of emphasis in US schools.

The mixing process that goes on when diverse languages are in contact – as occurred in 17th-century North America – results in a particular, systematic variety of language known as a creole in which features of the contributing languages are evident in the new variety. Unlike a pidgin – a simplified mixed language developed by people who don't speak the same language – a creole has native speakers, and is ultimately the result of the social force of colonial domination. What is known as a 'mixed language', such as Spanglish (Spanish and English) or Japlish (Japanese and English), does not have the colonial component.

Several languages developed or took root in the USA from the time of European settlement. Some are now dying out, others continue to be spoken daily. All have had an influence on the development of American English. (For further discussion of the languages mentioned in this chapter, see The Melting Pot on page 247.)

French Influences

From the 17th century we get Cajun French, spoken by the French-speaking Acadians (the name was reduced to 'Cajuns') from Canada who were forced by the British to relocate to Louisiana. Here, they mingled with African, West Indian and American Indian speakers. Louisiana French Creole (different from Cajun French) developed from the language of the Free Men of Color from Haiti, who spoke a French-based creole upon their arrival in Louisiana. The French-based languages had been separate languages until the middle of this century – now evidence indicates that they're merging. The Cajun language has been eroding over the last century, although Cajun music (zydeco) and cooking (red beans and rice, blackened fish) have increased in popularity.

Mitchif, a mixed language spoken to this day in southern Canada and the northern USA, came about through Cree Indian contact with the early French traders and explorers. It uses Cree verbs and French nouns in its system.

Creoles

Plantation Creole, an English-based creole with African language features, was spoken by Black slaves on the great plantations of the South in the 18th and 19th centuries. Many Plantation Creole features have been integrated into Southern white speech, occurring because slaves were often primary caretakers for white children and because white women, who did not leave the plantation for schooling, were not exposed to other varieties. One particular creole, Sea Islands Creole English, or Gullah, spoken especially on the Sea Islands off the Georgia coast, survived in relative isolation until WWI, and remains linguistically robust today because it is in limited contact with English.

Hawaiian English (also known as Hawaiian Creole English) has a long history of development. Through the sandalwood trade Hawaiians picked up Chinese Coast Pidgin, an English-based pidgin that developed in 17th-century Canton for the purposes of business and trade. The missionaries of the early 19th century influenced the creole, as did the Japanese, Koreans, Spaniards, Russians and Filipinos – the labour force imported to work the sugar plantations. Today Hawaiian English, now being taught in Hawaiian schools, is gaining status in Hawaii as a symbol of native identification. (See page 247 in the Melting Pot chapter, and Hawaiian on page 305.)

German & Dutch

By 1750 the American colonies were peopled by Dutch, English, Spanish, German and French immigrants, each of whom contributed uniquely to the language history of the USA. When Englishman William Penn established Pennsylvania, touting free religious and free economic rights, he advertised in the Dutch and German press as he needed their numbers for his colony to succeed. The Germans were so well represented in Pennsylvania that American founding father Benjamin Franklin (one of the early 'good guys' that every American student learns about) voiced undue concern with their numbers in 1753 and came off sounding like a xenophobic and reactionary 'bad guy'.

Many of the settlers of the Amish and Mennonite faiths spoke a dialect of German that is now known as Pennsylvania German or Pennsylvania Dutch (from *Deutsch*, meaning 'German'), which is still spoken in parts of Pennsylvania, Ohio, Indiana and other Midwestern states. (See page 247 in The Melting Pot .)

Yiddish

Yiddish, a language closely related to German, became a major immigrant language from the 1880s to the 1920s as Eastern Europeans, many of them Yiddish-speaking Jews, immigrated to the USA and settled in East Coast cities like New York. Yiddish is considered an endangered language and is learned less and less (half of the speakers of Yiddish were killed in the Holocaust). Nonetheless it has influenced English, mostly through food items and through the entertainment industry in the middle part of the 20th century. Americans may eat breadstuffs like bagels and bialys and sup on beet-studded borscht or potato knishes; enjoy schmaltzy music when they're feeling sentimental; and feel like a klutz when they do something clumsy.

Spanish

The history of Spanish is a rich and varied one. Early Andalusian-speaking Spanish explorers first settled areas that include New Mexico, California, Colorado and Arizona, giving the American Southwest its particular flavour – in cuisine, place names, vocabulary and regional history. Many residents of the Southwest are bilingual in Spanish and English. Speakers of Castillian-based Spanish from Puerto Rico and Cuba settled in New York City and Miami respectively, influencing speech on the East Coast.

Another variety, Border Spanish, is spoken along both sides of the USA-Mexico border. Spanish speakers from the Dominican Republic are among the more recent immigrant groups. 'Spanglish' is the term for the variety spoken by people fluent in both languages, for whom both languages hold sway.

African-American

African-American Vernacular English (AAVE), also referred to as Black English Vernacular (BEV) or Ebonics, is recognised by certain educators, speakers and linguists as a unique variety of English. It is a speech form that has its own rules and procedures. AAVE sounds different from standard English because of regular patterns like dropping the verb 'to be' ('He sick' instead of 'He is sick'), contracting words ('more' becomes 'mo', 'gonna' becomes 'gon'), or using multiple negation (as they do in French). It is considered an oral variety, one which doesn't have a history of written contexts.

Because it varies from the standard, and because its speakers are generally members of a minority that has suffered a history of slavery and prejudice, its use is simultaneously stigmatised and valued as a marker of ethnic identity and pride. It's important to differentiate AAVE from 'street talk', which is rapidly changing and fluid, and closely tied to street culture. AAVE is the vernacular, used by the wider culture at one time or another. Not all African Americans speak AAVE; it depends on where they grew up, who they speak with and what the particular situation requires linguistically. The variety retains some discourse features from African languages whose speakers value oral tradition and eloquence in speaking. There are call-and-response patterns in which the audience participates in the event, as in a church service, or ritual insults like 'the dozens' (also stylin' and signifyin'). Anything that begins with 'Yo mama ...' will clue you in to the interactive language display of the ritual insult. Don't take it personally.

RECENT HISTORY
American Sign Language

American Sign Language (ASL) was developed in the 19th century by Thomas Gallaudet, an American, and Laurent Clerc, a fluent French Sign Language speaker. ASL, based on French Sign Language and on 19th-century American deaf students' own native schoolyard signing system, is a primary reflex of deaf culture in the USA today.

Most deaf people are bilingual, their second language being written English. For the past 100 years, there has been an often impassioned debate about sign language versus 'oralism', basically lip-reading and using English oral speech. This debate has been updated as medical technologies have advanced to the extent that cochlear implants can help to restore hearing.

Most researchers agree that learning ASL as a native language (it is a real language with grammar rules, regular word endings and word shapes, and the capacity for conveying creativity, innovation and abstract thought) gives a deaf person the linguistic capacity to acquire other languages. There are interesting regional differences in ASL which parallel the spoken language. For example, New Yorkers sign faster than ASL speakers in Mississippi, where Southern speech patterns are slower.

Native Language Loss

Members of the deaf culture, many punished for signing as children, have a few things in common with Native Americans, who were also sent away to boarding schools and punished for speaking their native tongues. The result has been a rapid loss of dozens of native languages; it's thought that 90% will die out in this century (compared to an estimated loss of half the languages world-wide). However, attitudes have changed in the past couple of decades on both sides and Native Americans now are learning and reclaiming their lost linguistic links.

The Native American Language Preservation Act of 1990, although largely symbolic, officially heralded the new move toward language preservation and maintenance. Over the past decade or so, a number of successful revitalisation programs have developed within native communities from Hawaii to Alaska and throughout the mainland.

Asian Immigration

The immigration laws of the USA over the past 150 years have influenced attitudes about foreigners and their languages. Speakers of Asian languages in particular were once excluded from immigration.

The Chinese came to California during the 1849 Gold Rush but were excluded by law from staking claims. Although their labour played a role in the economic development of California, the 1882 Chinese Exclusion Act took care of any further impact.

The Japanese were not excluded by law but were the targets of discrimination, especially during WWII when they were forced to give up their property and their livelihoods and relocate to internment camps throughout the West. The 1965 Immigration Act removed barriers to Asian immigration. In 1979 a presidential directive allowed immigrants from countries such as Vietnam, Korea, Taiwan, Hong Kong and China.

While Asian immigrants follow the typical pattern of English language acquisition in this country – becoming monolingual English speakers by the second or third generation – there are also strong ties to the countries of origin. Saturday language schools operate for young people in many parts of the country, very much like the European immigrant pattern of a hundred years ago.

English-Only Debates

Relevant since the 1980s are the powerful debates about making English the national language of the USA (it is not so designated at present) or legislating English-language use in public contexts. This roughly parallels the change in immigration law, which has allowed many new faces into this country. By now, census reports indicate that one out of every four people over the age of five speaks a language other than English at home. Another social consequence is what is known as the 1.5 Generation. Individuals who come to the USA as older children, fluent in their language of origin but young enough to become fluent in English and US culture, are members of this group who at best feel bicultural and, at worst, that they have no culture.

BORROWING

While English has itself been hospitable to borrowings from other languages for centuries, American English has been equally open to borrowing terms from other languages – particularly when the words have described a new item or activity, or when repeated contact with non-English speakers resulted in influence from that language. These words aren't foreign or unusual at all anymore, and many of them define or evoke quintessentially American memories or experience.

AFRICAN LANGUAGES		
banana	nitty gritty	voodoo
banjo	OK	
goober (peanut)	to tote (carry)	

AMERICAN INDIAN LANGUAGES		
(See the Native American languages section for some more words.)		
moccasin	persimmon	toboggan
moose	racoon	woodchuck
opossum	skunk	
pecan	squash (the vegetable)	

AZTEC TO SPANISH TO ENGLISH		
chili	chocolate	coyote

CHINESE

gung ho	kowtow	tycoon
ketchup	tea	

DUTCH

coleslaw	sleigh	waffle
cookie	snoop	

FRENCH

chief	levee	saloon
chowder	prairie	

GERMAN

check (from *zeiche*, a drinks bill)	glitch	smearcase
cobalt	hamburger	snickelfritz
cottage (cheese)	hex (a spell)	(hobgoblin)
	kindergarten	
	noodle	

IRISH

galore	spree	shanty

ITALIAN

cupola	umbrella	piccolo

SPANISH

alligator	canyon	ranch
barbecue (from Native American via Spanish)	Florida	rodeo
bonanza ('fair weather')	guerilla	San Francisco ('St Francis')
California ('earthly paradise')	lasso	stampede
	Los Angeles ('the angels')	tornado

TAGALOG (FILIPINO)

boondocks	yo-yo

YIDDISH

bagel	knish	schmooze
chutzpah	kvetch	
fin ($5 bill)	to schlep (carry)	

FURTHER READING

American Heritage Dictionary of the English Language, 2000, Houghton Mifflin Company.

Atwood, EB. 1962, *The Regional Vocabulary of Texas*, University of Texas Press, Austin.

Avery, J & J Stevens. 1997, *Too Many Men on the Ice: Women's Hockey in North America*, Polestar, Victoria, BC, Canada.

Bluestein, G. 1998, *Anglish/Yinglish: Yiddish in American Life and Literature*, University of Nebraska Press, Lincoln.

Brecht, RD & C Ingold. 1998, *Tapping a National Resource: Heritage Languages in the United States*, ERIC Digest, Washington, DC.

Caponi, GD (ed). 1999, *Signifyin(g), Sanctifyin' & Slam Dunking: A Reader in African-American Expressive Culture*, University of Massachusetts Press, Amherst.

Conklin, N & M Lourie. 1983, *A Host of Tongues: Language Communities in the United States*, The Free Press, New York.

Crystal, D. 1997, *The Cambridge Encyclopedia of Language*, Cambridge University Press, Cambridge.

Davidson, J. 1997, *Hockey for Dummies*, Hungry Minds Inc, Chicago.

Do, HD. 1999, *The Vietnamese Americans*, Greenwood Press, Westport, Connecticut.

Duignan, P & LH Gann. 1998, *The Spanish Speakers in the United States: A History*, University Press of America, Lanham.

Ferguson, C & S Brice Heath (eds). 1981, *Language in the USA*, Cambridge University Press, Cambridge.

Hendrickson, R. 1994, *Happy Trails: A Dictionary of Western Expressions*, Facts on File Inc, New York.

Hendrickson, R. 1996, *Yankee Talk: A Dictionary of New England Expressions*, Facts on File Inc, New York.

Hendrickson, R. 1998, *New Yawk Tawk: A Dictionary of New York City Expressions*, Facts on File Inc, New York.

Hinton, L. 1994, *Flutes of Fire: Essays on California Indian Languages*, Heyday Books, Berkeley, California.

Kurath, H. 1949, *A Word Geography of the Eastern United States*, University of Michigan Press, Ann Arbor.

Leap, WL. 1993, *American Indian English*, University of Utah Press, Salt Lake City.

Leonard, KI. 1997, *The South Asian Americans*, Greenwood Press, Westport, Connecticut.

McCrum, R, W Cran & R MacNeil. 1993, *The Story of English (revised edition)*, Faber & Faber, London.

Munro, P. 1991, *Slang U: The Official Dictionary of College Slang*, Harmony Books, New York.

Olson, JS. 1988, *Dictionary of the Vietnam War*, Greenwood Press, New York.

Raymond, G. 1990, *New Words and a Changing American Culture*, University of South Carolina Press, Columbia, South Carolina.

Reed, C. 1977, *Dialects of American English*, University of Michigan Press, Amherst.

Rickford, JR et al. 2000, *Spoken Soul: The Story of Black English*, John Wiley and Sons, New York.

Shakespeare, W & M Okrand. 1992, *The Klingon Dictionary*, Klingon Language Institute, Flourtown, Pennsylvania.

Smitherman, G. 1999, *Talkin' That Talk: African-American Language & Culture*, Routledge.

Smitherman, G. 2000, *Black Talk: Words & Phrases from the Hood to the Amen Corner*, Houghton Mifflin Company.

Spears, RA. 1998, *NTC's Thematic Dictionary of American Idioms*, NTC Publishing Group, Lincolnwood, Illinois.

Tabbert, R. 1991, *Dictionary of Alaskan English*, The Denali Press, Alaska.

Tannen, D. 1986, *That's Not What I Meant! How Conversational Style Makes or Breaks Relationships*, Ballantine Books, New York.

SPEAKING AMERICAN

PRONUNCIATION

There are certain pronunciation features distinctive to the different regions of the USA, such as 'r-lessness' in parts of the East, lengthened vowels in the South, and 'singsong' intonation patterns in the far North. Natives of certain parts of the USA, mainly the West, can be identified by their pronunciation of 'cot' and 'caught' – the vowels sound the same, whereas elsewhere people say 'caht' and 'cawt', distinguishing between the two vowels. Even more region-specific is the pronunciation of 'merry', 'Mary', and 'marry' – speakers closer to the East Coast will differentiate between them all, while speakers closer to the West Coast will pronounce them all the same. Rate of speech is also a factor, with a quicker rate predominant in the East and in urban areas, and slower speech prevalent in the West, South and rural areas.

You'll probably also hear what has turned into a characteristic American intonation pattern. Colloquially it's known as 'speaking in questions' or 'sounding like a question'; technically it's called a terminal rise and it sounds like this: 'So I was doing my taxes? And was about to get them in the mail? And I had this problem? And I called the IRS?' It is similar to Australian English intonation.

While a great deal of pronunciation has been standardised through the education system and in the media, there's plenty of variety in each part of the country. With this variety comes less-than-obvious pronunciations of local names:

Nevada	second 'a' pronounced as in 'cat'
Oregon	ORyg'n not oryGON

In the Southwest and California, Spanish place names are generally pronounced as they are in Spanish. For example, **ll** is pronounced as y; **j** is pronounced as **h**:

La Jolla	la HO-ya
San Jose	san hose-AY

With many Indian-origin town names, the main stress or accent is on the second syllable:

Kaukauna	kuh-KAW-na
Oconomowoc	oh-KON-uh-mah-wok
Pewaukee	pee-WAW-kee

Others you may come across include:

Albuquerque (New Mexico)	ALbuh-kerkee
Arkansas	ARk'nsaw
Louisville (Kentucky)	LU-ahv'll
New Orleans	new ORI'ns
Pierre (South Dakota)	PEER (by locals);
	pee-AIR (by outsiders)
Quincy (Massachusetts)	KWIN-zee
Tucson (Arizona)	TOO-sahn
Willamette Valley (Oregon)	wuh-LAM-ett

When to Follow Local Pronunciation

Your pronunciation will mark you as an outsider. So it's best to think about when you want to capitalise on this and when you want to minimise it. Most Americans love foreign accents, especially British, Irish, Scottish or Australian (whether they can tell the difference is another matter).

If you use the local terms and pronunciations for regional landmarks, names of towns or landscape features, transportation and food, you'll get points for knowledge of the area and you'll be regarded as someone who knows their way around.

However, copy *what* people say, not *how* they say it; in other words, use the regional pronunciation of a word, but don't use the regional accent. Say 'Gren-itch' not 'Green-witch' Village, but don't say 'Noo Yawk'. Some people might think you're making fun of how they speak and won't take it for the friendly gesture you intended. Some things will happen naturally as you spend time in a place; you'll modify your speech, possibly throw in a 'y'all'.

SPEAKING AMERICAN

Just be careful; some US terms sound OK coming out of a visitor's mouth, but others may give the impression you're mocking the speaker.

When in doubt, use your own way of speaking. You might also disappoint the natives if you use the slightly crude American 'butt' instead of the endearingly charming British 'bum'. We have our stereotypes to maintain, after all.

Use slang with caution, for reasons that are relevant also in your own region, unless travelling is your time for trying on a new persona. Then go for it. Have fun. Experiment. See how people react to you. That's what slang is for.

GRAMMAR

Americans may have done more than their share of innovating over the last couple of centuries, but one area where they've done very little tinkering is in the structure of their language. While the American vocabulary has exploded with new terms reflecting developments in technology and lifestyle, the structure of American English has hardly changed since it was imported to the New World in the 16th century. There are a few grammatical points where Americans can claim ownership though – some of which developed on this side of the Atlantic and some that actually carried over from earlier stages of English.

Probably the most often remarked upon point of difference between American and British grammar is the treatment of collective nouns: Americans say Congress is in session, while Brits report that Parliament have left the building; Americans are happy when their team wins, while British fans approve when the team play well. These two approaches to noun-verb agreement don't necessarily lead to miscommunication, but partisans can sometimes become adamant about the logical superiority of one system or the other.

Some American verbs also have forms that are unfamiliar on other English-speaking shores. For instance, it is fine in the States to say that a child 'dove' into a pond. British speakers react with

SPEAKING AMERICAN

amusement (or horror, depending on their level of linguistic fussiness) at this apparent vestige of an earlier irregular form of the verb. Americans are also happy to ask whether a friend has 'gotten any new CDs lately'. Elsewhere in the English-speaking world the participle has the simpler form 'got'. The American form has been used at least since the 13th century, though it has fallen out of currency in the Queen's English.

Prepositions are another grammatical area where Americans occasionally distinguish themselves. You will hear about the American students 'taking a course', for example, while their British counterparts are 'on a course'. (Both are references to classes, not golf.) Americans have also invented at least one preposition of their own: 'in back of', as in 'My truck is parked in back of the house'. This is an expression unheard of in Britain, where things are located behind other things. And speaking of being located, American medical patients are to be found 'in the hospital', while British patients apparently get along fine without 'the' in such expressions.

There are various other ways to tell what continent you are on by paying close attention to grammar. The pronoun 'y'all' and its variants (yous, ya's, you all) is distinctively American. And Americans may be more eager to create new verbs from nouns (such as 'to courier a package') but overall, grammar is not the area where American English is most apt to set itself apart. For more flavour, we turn to the regional variations in the grammar, features of language structure that are often of long-standing history themselves.

MISS MANNERS

Many major metropolitan newspapers carry a column by Miss Manners – the estimable Judith Martin who responds to readers' questions about social etiquette and behaviour. She is an excellent observer of culture and custom, linguistic and otherwise, and her columns are worth reading for that insider scoop on US ways.

BODY LANGUAGE

Not all communication or miscommunication happens verbally. Body language is a silent but potent component. It includes your proximity to someone while talking (one arm's length is average in America) and how you make eye contact (direct eye contact can be viewed as friendly or challenging, indirect eye contact as deference or lack of interest).

Some gestures can only be interpreted as insulting. These include the forearm jerk and 'the finger', in which the middle finger is thrust at someone. It is demonstrated most often in traffic. Not to be used in polite company.

Other rules Americans follow: elbows off the table when dining; wink to be friendly or flirtatious; pointing with the index finger is acceptable. Body language expert Roger Axtell says that whistling is not derisive as it is in Europe; a crowd will 'boo' or 'hiss' to voice disapproval. V-for-victory (the peace sign) and thumbs up are frequently used to register general enthusiasm.

Etiquette and Interaction

Remember (even when you return home) that most people evaluate the behaviour of others – linguistic and otherwise – through the rules and requirements of their own system or code. Someone who interrupts a conversation may be rude in one locale, but friendly and involved in another. Most miscommunication is actually a misinterpretation of an individual's speaking style.

Once again, the regional differences of the USA pertain to something as seemingly cut-and-dried as politeness. On the West Coast, saying 'let's get together sometime' when you have no intention of doing so is considered polite, although an Easterner would view this as dishonest if the promise didn't materialise. Linguist Robin Lakoff, who grew up and got her PhD in the East and who has been teaching and writing most of her adult life in the West, has observed that politeness systems usually fall into one of three categories which correspond roughly with region: distance (East), deference (Midwest) and camaraderie (West). The distance style keeps at arm's length all but your intimate friends and family, for whom loud and boisterous disagreements do not mark problems in a relationship, but rather affiliation. On the other hand, the camaraderie style of the West does not interpret conflict as positive. Instead, the impression of agreement is maintained as desirable. In the Midwest is the deference style, whose practitioners do not engage in conflict or excess friendliness and is nicely illustrated by your average Minnesotan.

The fast speech of the typical New Yorker is governed by more than the 'no gap, no overlap' rule of conversational turn-taking, which is typical in the USA. Interruptions are the norm with the New Yorker 'high involvement' style – a stark contrast to other parts of the country where longer pauses between speakers are maintained.

'Getting to the point' or 'beating around the bush' are other speaker options that vary with the individual or the region. In general, stereotypically no-nonsense Americans do not value the characteristics of the indirect style (and for that reason are not considered to be very adept at irony). Something else to figure out: how often is it customary to refuse, say, a piece of cake before it's polite enough to take it (in some regions you have to say 'no' three times before you give in, and in other areas you're out of cake after the first refusal).

When making a request like asking for stamps in the post office, it is often not necessary to end with 'please'. In transactions such as these, people tend to listen to your tone of voice for politeness cues. Too many 'pleases' and you risk being labelled obsequious.

Conducting Conversation

Greetings are fairly uncomplicated with the standard 'hello', 'hi', 'good morning', 'good afternoon', 'how are you?', the more colloquial 'hey', 'hey there' and 'howdy', and the hearty, youthful 'duuuude!' among the options. 'Wassup?' is a popular greeting from African-American vernacular English. There's more variety with a farewell, including 'bye', 'goodbye', 'bye-bye', 'see ya', 'take it easy', 'later', 'take care', 'don't work too hard' and the ubiquitous 'have a nice day'.

While Americans run short on 'please', they say 'thank you' after almost anything. You'll hear 'excuse me' instead of 'sorry'. In a conversation the listener will interject 'mm-hmmm' or 'uh-huh' frequently to let the speaker know they're paying attention and want them to go on. It's a much more enthusiastic style than the judgment-reserving 'mmm'. Agreement with a speaker is signalled (in middle Northern states, anyway) with 'you betcha'. For some talkers the enthusiastic 'uh-huhs' aren't enough, and they will pepper their speech with 'y'know' or 'you hear what I'm saying?', which is not a strictly literal question. If someone says 'say what?' or 'do what?' it simply means 'what?'.

INSULTS & PUT-DOWNS

Put-downs are complex. They're funny. They're creative. They pack in a lot of social information. And they can be deeply, deeply insulting. There's the 'your mother wears army boots' variety, various ethnic slurs, rivalries between towns or states, country and city, and attacks on driving ability or sexual orientation. Some are part of a community's own way of speaking and, like mimicking an accent, might make you stand out if tried (with a rationale equivalent to: I can insult my family, but you can't); and others will mark you, rightly, as insensitive or even racist.

Words that raise ire are: redneck, commie, knee-jerk liberal, bleeding heart, conservative asshole, dufus and Sunday driver. Phrase-length put-downs include referring to people who are one X shy of a Y (eg, one egg short of a dozen). New on the put-down scene is 'dot-commer' – someone who has generally made tons of money or abused power in some way due to an association with the high-tech industry. 'Aggies' (country folk) have always come out on the short end of various jokes, as do blondes and viola players. And there's no shortage of jokes about Texans or Californians or lawyers.

SPEAKING AMERICAN

Some put-downs fall within the acceptable range in general company (state-to-state jokes or those pertaining to politics or profession – unless you're in that state or talking to the politician or to someone in that profession). But it's best to avoid ethnic slurs or slurs against sexual orientation.

Taboo words in American culture revolve more around sex than any other category. The 'f-word' (fuck) is used widely, but not in any context where you want to make a good impression. And note that in some regions of the country, you wouldn't want people to even overhear you using the word. Perhaps the biggest taboo word in the culture is 'the n-word' (nigger) – an extremely offensive slur against African Americans. As with other pejorative terms ('queer' for example), the community itself uses the term to signify solidarity. (See the Regional Variations section, and Pissing People Off in the State to State chapter for a list of geographical animosities.)

LIFESTYLE

Americans like to say they work hard and play hard. Indeed, the standard 40-hour work week has, in practice, stretched out to 50 or 60 hours or more, depending on the job and the region of the country. Internet start-ups and the 'new economy' – which has workaholism built into the social and physical structures of the workplace – are in part responsible for accelerating this growing trend. Americans also say they like their toys. This means they spend money on expensive equipment, vehicles and hobbies – camping, skiing, boating, vacationing, etc.

Besides being active, Americans who can manage it financially spend a lot of time and money on where they live. Gardening and entertaining at home – part of the 'cocooning' trend of the 1990s – are growth activities in the current culture. The family is also a focal point, with children as over-committed as their high-achieving parents; playing soccer, Scouting, taking music lessons – a fact that is causing debate and a philosophical divide among many families and communities.

Americans participate regularly in their churches, at weekend farmers' markets, in their children's schools and activities, and travel to national parks, major cities, theme and amusement parks, zoos and nature areas for their vacations. They are paradoxically often rooted to one locale and on the move.

AMERICAN SOCIETY

FAMILY

The nuclear family ideal of the 1950s has given way to a whole range of partnerships and family living options. There also seem to be labels for every social role and era. You'll still find mention of hippies and yuppies, but 'unwed mother' is a term no longer in use except for specific references.

babysitter, childcare provider
  the 'babysitter' of days past has been upgraded to 'childcare provider' (and 'nanny' or 'au pair' if you're well-off) in some instances. Now working parents bring their kids to 'daycare' or 'childcare', or they have the federal government-approved option of taking unpaid 'family leave' from their jobs for a period of time.

blended family
  when two divorced individuals with children remarry; the 1970s television sitcom *The Brady Bunch* is the quintessential mocked and revered blended family

boomer, baby boomer
  the post-WWII population increase is known as the Baby Boom. Given their numbers, the boomers have social, political and economic clout.

Generation X, Generation Y
  people in their teens and 20s, who are 'so not yuppie' and definitely nowhere near thirtysomething in age or attitude. The term 'slackers', which characterises what Baby Boomers perceived as disaffected behavior, is falling out of usage, perhaps because of their role in the new Internet economy. Gen Xers and Yers tend to look critically at globalisation, leading complex cell-phone-directed protests at World Bank meetings.

mommy track
  women who choose to pursue motherhood and a career simultaneously

Mr Mom
  an informal (non-derogatory) way to refer to a man who stays at home and takes care of the children and house; from an 1980s movie of the same name

seniors, senior citizens, retirees
> various names for individuals who are past the official retirement age of 65

spouse, partner
> don't assume that the other person is a husband or wife; the less value-laden term 'spouse' is preferred in some circles as is 'partner' (also used in same-sex unions)

stay-at-home mom, soccer mom
> since most moms work these days, it's been necessary to qualify what 'mom' means if you want to refer to a woman who has opted out of the workforce while raising her children. Soccer moms are often suburban-based stay-at-home moms who attend and provide transportation to their kids' soccer games.

thirtysomething
> the name of a popular TV show of the late 1980s, early 1990s; now it's a general reference term for someone in their 30s, replacing thirtyish. It's a productive linguistic form; now we have twentysomethings, fortysomethings, etc.

At Mealtime

In the USA, meal times often serve as the focal point of most family gatherings – particularly breakfast and dinner. While the day-to-day pace of life is not always conducive for extended talk and grub sessions, sitting and eating meals together is still customary in most homes.

Generally, it is during conversations at breakfast and dinner that family members become apprised of the events – both big and small – in each other's lives. These occasions function, particularly for parents, as an opportunity to both nurture and nourish. Questions, comments and concern often follow this pattern:

> How was your day?
> Did you get a lot done at work/around the house?
> How was school?
> What did you do for lunch?
> What did you have for lunch?
> How's your friend/boss/colleague?
> Have you finished that project/assignment/chore?

AMERICAN SOCIETY

Faith & Family

Families in the USA are a study in contradictions. While fewer and fewer families attend regular worship services, political candidates who demonstrate strong religious convictions are often looked upon favorably by the general public. It is assumed that such beliefs suggest a strong moral and ethical character.

Generally, the act of worship tends to be more closely adhered to in the South than in other part of the United States. In fact, the Southern states – Florida, Georgia, Arkansas, Alabama and Tennessee – are often referred to as the Bible Belt.

It should be noted that in many social settings it is not acceptable to openly discuss one's religious beliefs. In fact, religion is often considered a private matter not to be discussed in either social or professional settings. It is impolite and impolitic to make public declarations attesting to one's faith.

Friends & Family

The definition of family as a social entity has altered significantly in the past several decades. There is, of course, the traditional definition of people related by blood and marriage. However, increasingly, the American family has taken on the extra-familial presence of friends and others in which the levels of intimacy can sometimes prove greater than traditional familial bonds. This is true, especially, as many Americans find their careers and other pursuits taking them to locales far from their loved ones with whom they are bound by blood.

There are also a sizable number of American couples who choose to live together without getting married. If children are involved, this can establish the kind of bond and intimacy that marks the traditional nuclear family. In fact, the traditional family – often called an 'intact' family – is more idealisation than reality for the vast majority of Americans. There are also increasing numbers of gay men and women who are demanding that their life partners or significant others be recognised as family, both socially and legally.

Family & Identity

Since the family plays such an important role in the construction of identity, people often gauge or form their opinions of each other based on the answers to questions such as:

> Where did you grow up?
> Do you have any brothers or sisters?
> Are your parents still together?
> Are you married?
> Do you have children? What are their ages?

People will answer readily or guardedly, depending on the social circumstance of the inquiry or if they suspect their answers might be considered less than favourable to a listener. In general, it's more complicated than it seems to inquire about marital status, and certainly inappropriate to ask detailed follow-up questions when someone is childless.

EDUCATION

The average American student attends:

elementary school, grade school
> grades one to six (ages six to 12)

kindergarten
> half-day of school for children turning five; features finger-painting, games, music, movement exercises and naptime

middle school, junior high
> grades seven to eight or seven to nine, depending on the local arrangement (ages 12 to 14 or 15)

preschool
> an optional school for very young children (under five)

(senior) high school
> grades 10 to 12 or nine to 12; ninth-graders are freshmen or frosh (ages 14 to 15), 10th-graders are sophomores (ages 15 to 16), 11th-graders are juniors (ages 16 to 17), 12th-graders are seniors (ages 17 to 18)

AMERICAN SOCIETY

This is the end of mandatory schooling. Students who don't finish are derogatorily called 'drop-outs' and can get their GED (General Equivalency Diploma) or high school equivalency later.

business school
> the place where one earns an MBA; they also offer other programs

college
> the majority of high school graduates go on to a four-year college or university, obtaining a BA (bachelor's degree)

community college
> a two-year college; often a transition to a four-year college or university, or you can leave after two years with your AA (associate of arts degree)

grad school
> beyond college is graduate school, where a student can earn an MA (master's degree), MBA (master's of business administration), or PhD (doctorate). Degrees for law, medicine, library science and other professions are also available.

technical college, vo-tech
> a shorter, largely non-academic program teaching technical or vocational skills to high school graduates

An alternative education for children in America is home schooling. This is where children are taught at home, often by parents, as in 'Kelly and Sandy are being home schooled'. Home schooling is often chosen by families with strong religious or moral beliefs which they feel are not adequately addressed in public or even private schools.

School Life

There are some important aspects to US school life. Most high schools and colleges have a 'homecoming' in the fall (autumn), an at-home football game that includes festivals and parades for students and returning alumni. Often, especially in high school, a Homecoming Queen and various attendants are chosen to preside over the activities. The Homecoming Queen and the football team quarterback (or some other male of distinction) also appear together at the Homecoming Dance.

In some areas, cheerleaders are also quintessentially American. Their official role is to rally spectators and uplift morale at sporting events. Cheerleaders also enjoy a relatively high social status which is why making cheerleader tryouts is so important. (In 1991, a Texas mother murdered her daughter's rival.)

At some colleges and universities the Greek system (sororities and fraternities) can have a strong influence on the social scene, with all-night keggers (drinking parties), rowdy or airhead (vapid) behaviour, and celebrated liaisons between frat boys and sorority girls. There are enduring stereotypes associated with the Greek system. The classic 1970s movie, *Animal House*, captures this aspect of Greek life. Fraternities and sororities also undertake service or community benefit projects and, especially at larger universities, provide social contacts, friendships and a home-away-from-home. Different Greek houses cater to students with different interests and inclinations, and most require a certain academic standing to remain a member.

DATING

You could devote an entire encyclopedia to dating language and rituals in America, but there are a few essentials that all friendly travellers should know. While Americans are not famous for their subtlety, the average single person is not incredibly forward either.

As in any culture, dating possibilities depend on the individual and the situation. In big cities and urban centers, people may not be exceptionally friendly while walking down the street, but inside a dark bar or restaurant, many singles are on the prowl (looking for love, checking out the 'merchandise', etc.). If you are looking for this sort of scene, commonly referred to as a 'meat market,' you should expect people to be a little more forward.

If you are sightseeing or visiting friends in a smaller town, however, people are apt to be more friendly and forward in almost every situation (at the grocery store, sporting events and almost any neighbourhood gathering). Every public place offers the opportunity to meet new people and to look a little deeper for possible love interests. Now that most Americans do not get married until well into their 20s, most young people you encounter will be looking at you the same way you may be looking at them.

While body language speaks louder than words in these situations, there are a few phrases and practices that may help you in your search. Some of them are painfully cliched, but classics nonetheless:

PICKUP LINES

The Classics:

Do you come here often?
What's a nice girl like you doing in a place like this?
If I told you you have a beautiful body would you hold it against me?
Your legs must be tired, because you've been running through my mind all night.
Do you believe in love at first sight or should I walk by again?
I lost my number, can I have yours?
Shall I call you for breakfast or nudge you?

College Level:

Nice shoes. Wanna fuck? (believe it or not, a favourite pickup line at some college campuses)
I miss my teddy bear. Can I sleep with you? (also favoured by students living in dormitories)
(Lick finger and touch arm) *Let's say you and me get out of these wet clothes.*
Do you have a mirror in your pocket? 'Cause I can see myself in your pants.
Fuck me if I'm wrong, but haven't we met before?
Remember my name is *John* 'cause you'll be screaming it later.

BOXERS OR BRIEFS?

A cultural 'catchquestion' is 'Boxers or briefs?' – as in, 'Do you wear boxer undershorts (baggy) or briefs (tight-fitting)?' Apparently the preference says a lot about you or about the person doing the asking. Sexual attractiveness is at stake and either choice can be variously seen as sexy.

Saying Goodbye

Dating rituals are hard for anyone to figure out, much less for someone unfamiliar with local customs. Parting ways at the end of an evening is awkward for everyone, so don't worry if you find yourself at a loss for words or wondering if you should leave with a kiss, hug or handshake. Any of these gestures is perfectly acceptable and nothing more should be expected at the end of a first date.

Travellers are also lucky if they choose to keep in touch with new friends. Email makes this task much easier than longhand letter writing, so be sure to exchange addresses before you leave town.

COME HERE OFTEN?

Some public places are very conducive to talking and getting to know someone, to spending leisure time without fear of 'eviction'. Coffee shops and cafes allow long stays. Zoos and museums are good for walking, talking and being distracted by the exhibits when the conversation lags. They also feel safer than parks or trails. Traditional 'meat markets' include bars, clubs and discos. Grocery stores and laundromats should not be overlooked either. Biking or hiking clubs, among others, attract people of like interests.

WEATHER TERMS

When conversation revolves around the weather, it usually makes use of standard terminology, thanks to the Weather Channel on cable and broadcasts on the local news. 'Hot enough for ya?' is a usual comment on the (hot) weather; often used as a greeting or conversation starter. Common replies might be 'It's like a sauna' or 'Hot enough to fry an egg' (on the pavement). Quaint or local terms still persist in some parts of the country:

chinook (various places)
    a warm wind
kissling (Pennsylvania)
    freezing rain, 'It's kissling.'
nor'easters, nor'westers (East)
    winds from the northeast and northwest, respectively

norther, blue norther (Texas)
    unexpected cold (or even colder) wind from the north
open-and-shut day (New England)
    variably cloudy
Santa Anas (California)
    hot, dry winds
toad-strangler, gully-washer (South)
    heavy, intense rainstorm
tornado, twister, funnel cloud (various places)
    violent storm from a destructive, funnel-shaped cloud; occurs
    most often in the Midwest and Plains states

Sometimes the weather becomes a major feature of a region's identity, and is known on a national level. The rainy climate of Seattle, for instance, or the desert heat in the Southwest region. Vocabulary springs up accordingly, but the words are restricted to insiders. For instance, the rains of Seattle have led to the following terms:

sun break
    a brief period of time during which you can actually see sunlight
    through the overcast clouds. A sun break can last anywhere
    from five minutes to a couple of hours.
'Showers today, followed by rain; rain tomorrow, followed by showers'
    Washingtonians often make fun of how forecasters try differ-
    ent ways of saying 'it's going to rain' because they have to say it
    so often.

Meanwhile, on the opposite end of the meteorological spectrum, Arizona provides us with:

dry heat, desert heat
    the not-so-serious claim that Arizona temperatures (often ex-
    ceeding 38°C/100°F) are bearable because of low humidity
snow bird
    the semi-permanent Arizona resident, primarily from 'back east'
    or places like Chicago or Minnesota, who has a second home
    in Phoenix where he or she lives for three to six months. Snow
    birds take flight to the desert to avoid the cold of snowy cities.
    The term is usually used derogatorily.

AMERICAN SOCIETY

AROUND THE HOUSE

apartment, duplex

the equivalent of a flat. A studio is a single-room apartment or a space where the living and sleeping spaces converge. A duplex is two separate residences that share a common wall.

bathroom

the room for both toilet and bathtub. Americans say they're 'in the bathroom' when they are accomplishing any of the various functions and ablutions associated with toilets and tubs. Other, more regional and marked terms are 'hopper' and though 'bathroom' will suffice. A more oblique reference is 'the facilities.' If you ask for 'the toilet,' you may be excused if you have a British accent.

closets

most homes come with built-in closets – and having adequate closet space is a focus for renters and home-owners alike. Occasionally someone will buy an armoire or wardrobe to add to existing closet space. You're likely to find armoires in the living room these days, functioning as elegant repositories for VCR's and TV's.

coffee table book

term for large, hardback books with pictures, often about art, history or photography

curtain rods

curtain rails

comforter

the more popular term for duvet, doona or continental quilt

dumpster

the large, wheeled garbage bin that sits in the back yard or near the garage. It's where you dump the contents of the wastebasket for weekly pickup by the 'garbage men' or 'trash collectors' (or, to be jocular, the 'sanitary engineers').

living room

many homes have a living room (the term for lounge) – often most used when 'company' comes – as well as a 'family room', the place the household congregates for talking and watching TV. The less formal room is also known as a 'rec room' or, if it is more elaborate, a 'media room'.

AMERICAN SOCIETY

AMERICAN SOCIETY

quilt

a particular kind of blanket or comforter, with stitched pieces of fabric. Quilts evoke a core American ethos as well as a native or folk style of décor. Handmade quilts in several folk traditions – Amish and African-American in particular – are handed down through the generations and treasured. You'll see them on walls and in museums as much as on beds. The 'quilting bee' was a popular event for girls and women in times past, for both sewing and socialising. Many quilt patterns were developed on the American frontier. In recent times quilting projects have been conducted on a national scale; best known is the AIDS quilt, each square of which commemorates a loved one who died of AIDS. It's as large as many city blocks.

shared bath

the unusual hotel or lodging situation without a bathroom in the room. Most Americans have no reference for the term 'en suite.' If the bathroom is down the hall and shared, it's referred to as 'shared bath' or 'European-style' accommodation.

yard

most homes come with a yard – back and front. A 'garden' is a plot for growing vegetables; it is ambiguous whether it means that flowers are included. A 'flower garden' makes that clear.

BEWARE THE EUPHEMISM

Since the desire for politeness often means very indirect and euphemistic speech, it's good to know what side of the Atlantic you're on. You can use it to work in your favour either way. One British woman ditched an American date who kept asking to use her 'facilities', learning later – after protesting they were closed – that he merely wanted to use her 'bathroom', using the most polite term he could think of.

DRIVING

Despite various urban mass-transit systems, like the New York subway, the Washington Metro, Chicago's El trains or San Francisco's BART (Bay Area Rapid Transit), the USA is a car culture. For the traveller, knowing that a freeway or interstate is also an expressway, highway, parkway or thruway can avoid confusion. A turnpike (tollway or toll road) means you'll pay tolls, although toll booths will appear on the other roadways too. The strip of land that divides highway lanes is known as a boulevard strip, median strip, neutral ground, grass strip, centre divider or parking strip. The side of the road is the 'shoulder'.

A parking lot is a flat slab of asphalt, dotted with rows of parking meters. If a special structure has been built for parking, it's called a carpark, parking structure, parking garage, parking ramp or parking deck. 'Meter maid' is an old-fashioned term for city employees who cruise the streets in cute little scooter-like vehicles, looking for parking violations. Pay the meter – don't get a ticket!

In some major cities a car that has blatently violated a parking code will not merely get a ticket but will get 'the boot'. The boot is a yellow steel wheel brace that makes it impossible to drive the car – until the hefty fine is paid. To deter thieves, drivers will use 'the Club' – a device that clamps and locks around the steering wheel.

In Southern California locals will refer to freeways by the name, not the number, as in the Santa Monica Freeway or 'the 5' for Interstate 5 (in Northern California, it's known as 'I-5'). In the Boston area, drivers refer to the highways or roads by number, for example, '95'. Exceptions are The Expressway (93) and The Pike (90).

If you need roadside assistance, call AAA (known as Triple A, 3-A, the American Automobile Association, or the auto club) for a tow or a tow truck.

If you're tired of driving, grab some rest or road food at a rest stop, rest area, oasis, service area or wayside.

DIRT-DIGGING

If you go off-road in a four-wheel-drive vehicle, it's called either 'off-roading' (the universal term) or 'dirt-digging'.

On icy roads in the winter you can hold onto the back bumper of a car and slide down the road – it's called 'hooky-bobbing' in Idaho.

Driving Vernacular

America is the great driving nation. Americans invented the first mass-produced automobile, and made auto driving an integral part of the national culture. Here are some terms drivers use:

Blue Book
   guide that lists the value of a used car: 'The Blue Book says this '67 Chevy is worth $550 at best.'
carpool lane, diamond lane
   the lane on some freeways, usually farthest to the left, which is reserved for cars carrying two or more people at certain times of the day. The idea was to encourage carpooling, which most people still don't do. When traffic is slow, cars in these lanes have more room to race past.

cream puff
    used car in excellent condition
doing donuts
    doing 360s – spinning the car – in a parking lot; often done in
    snow or mud for greater effect
fender bender
    a minor traffic accident
flip a bitch
    make a U-turn; also 'flip a U-eeee'
high rider
    a vehicle structurally adjusted to ride very high off the ground,
lemon
    a used car in bad shape
Louie
    a left turn
low rider
    automobile that's been modified to be more powerful and
    whose chassis is adjusted to ride very low to the ground. It has
    a long history in the USA.
picking the cherry
    running a red light
riding the turtles
    riding the disk-shaped road dividers to stay awake
road kill
    animals hit by road traffic
Roscoe
    right turn
rush hour
    peak commuting times in morning and evening; often every
    day of the week in California, New York and the Washington,
    DC area
(riding) shotgun
    the front passenger seat
squeezing the lemon
    speeding up to make it through a yellow light
tailgater
    a driver who follows too close to your back bumper; also the
    name for a party held in the parking lot of a sporting event

PUBLIC TRANSPORT

Greyhound is the major bus line; Amtrak is the major train service. You buy round-trip or one-way tickets. You'll have to make a reservation for three-day weekends (national holidays include a Monday), which are traditionally busy.

The Thanksgiving holiday (fourth Thursday in November) is the busiest time to fly. To save time at the airport, avail yourself of 'curbside check-in'. Airlines often have representatives to check in your bags the minute you get dropped off at the curb outside the terminal. Many airports direct you to 'ground transportation' – taxis and shuttle buses that will take you to your destination.

Most major cities have mass-transit systems to deal with daily commuters. Cities which cater to tourists, such as Washington, DC or San Francisco, have systems that are crowded, especially on the weekends.

Each system has its own quirks and rules – and personality, especially when you ask for help. The responses in general mirror the communicative norms of the area. For example, the New York subway personnel give brusque replies and expect quickly formed questions. The Washington, DC Metro workers react less brusquely.

SURVIVIN' DRIVIN' IN LA

Driving in LA can be intimidating, so here is some advice from a transplant who learned her way around:
- Be aggressive – drivers will let you cut in if you crowd them. In general, though, people are very considerate about taking their turn and letting others merge.
- Don't honk – People do not do this in California. It can invite road rage. Be patient.
- Learn the surface streets – sometimes they are faster and more direct than the freeways.
- It's usually OK to run yellow lights, but not to run red ones, with the exception of left-hand turners.

GENERAL GEOGRAPHY

When American folk icon Woodie Guthrie wrote his Depression-era epic, 'This Land is Your Land', the lyrics expressing the breadth and range of a country that extended 3000 miles 'from California to the New York island (Manhattan)' didn't even mention Hawaii and Alaska. They both became states in 1959. There are 50 states in the union. Outlying Alaskans refer to the 'lower 48' and islander Hawaiians refer to the 'mainland' or the continental US.

People usually are referring to the 50 states and the District of Columbia (Washington, DC) when they refer to the USA, generally excluding the territories and possessions (American Samoa, Federated States of Micronesia, Guam, Marshall Islands, Northern Mariana Islands, Palau, Puerto Rico and the Virgin Islands).

The country gets divided up in various ways, depending on whether you're a meteorologist, the census bureau, a linguist or dialectologist. Here are some terms you're likely to hear:

Deep South
   Alabama, Georgia, Louisiana, Mississippi, South Carolina
East Coast
   the eastern coastal states, especially the urban corridor from Boston to Washington, DC
Eastern Seaboard
   another term for the East Coast
Great Lakes
   bodies of water in the north and on the Canadian border: Lake Superior, Lake Michigan, Lake Huron, Lake Ontario, Lake Erie
Great Plains
   the prairie lands encompassed by the Missouri River to the east, the Rockies to the West, North Dakota to the north, and Texas to the south
Gulf Coast
   the region along the Gulf of Mexico

Middle Atlantic, Mid-Atlantic
New Jersey, New York, Pennsylvania and usually Delaware and Maryland

Midwest
a variable definition that includes the North Central states

Mountain states
Arizona, New Mexico, Nevada, Colorado, Idaho, Montana, Wyoming, Utah

New England
Connecticut, Maine, Massachusetts, New Hampshire, Rhode Island, Vermont

North Central
East North Central includes Indiana, Illinois, Michigan, Ohio and Wisconsin. West North Central includes Iowa, Kansas, Minnesota, Missouri, Nebraska, North Dakota and South Dakota.

Northeast
includes New England and the Middle Atlantic states

Northeast Corridor
the route between Washington, DC through New York City, to Boston

South
East South Central (Alabama, Kentucky, Mississippi, Tennessee), South Atlantic (Delaware, Florida, Georgia, Maryland, North Carolina, South Carolina, Virginia, West Virginia), West South Central (Arkansas, Louisiana, Oklahoma, Texas)

Upper Midwest
includes Minnesota, Wisconsin, Michigan

Pacific Northwest
Washington State and Oregon

Southwest
Arizona, New Mexico, Texas

West Coast
especially California, also Oregon and Washington

Regions are also given names for their agricultural, economic or social characteristics:

Bible Belt

informal term for Southern and central Midwestern states where fundamentalist religious beliefs dominate

Borscht Belt

the largely Jewish vacation resort area of the Catskill Mountains of southeastern New York where many stand-up comedians have honed their skills (eg, Danny Kaye, Jerry Lewis and Mel Brooks)

Corn Belt

Midwestern region where corn is grown, including Iowa, Nebraska and Kansas

Cotton Belt

region in South and Southwest where cotton is grown

Florida Keys

chain of islands off the southern tip of Florida

Rust Belt

the aging industrial areas of the East and Midwest, including Indiana and Ohio

Old South

the South before the Civil War (1861–65)

Old West

term used for the western frontier during the pioneer migration

Sun Belt

Southern and Western states including Florida, the Gulf states and California

Silicon Valley

the San Jose, California hub of computer innovation and production

STATE TO STATE

PLACENAMES & NICKNAMES

If it won't play in Peoria – that's Peoria, Illinois – that means the idea won't float in mainstream USA. This is not to say that Peoria is Podunk (the term for isolated, backwater towns or regions), it's just a reference to all of Middle America.

At opposite ends of the spectrum you have the culturally elite Brahmins (as in the upper-crust Boston Brahmins) and the souls who hang out in seedy places like the Bowery (New York), the Tenderloin (San Francisco, but originally in New York City), Skid Row (which started in pioneer Seattle and now applies to any such place) and or the Combat Zone (Boston).

Nicknames for places abound. A word of caution: don't say Frisco to a San Franciscan; it will definitely mark you as an outsider, and a hick at that. Another tip: the nation's capital is referred to as Washington, Washington, DC, The District, or just DC (the DC standing for District of Colombia). The state in the Pacific Northwest is known as Washington State. Miami is known by a few names: gateway to the Americas; Capital of the Caribbean; and Babel-by-the-Bay.

Beantown
    Boston
Beer City
    Milwaukee
The Big Apple
    New York City
The Big D
    Dallas
The Big Easy
    New Orleans
City of Brotherly Love, Philly
    Philadelphia
The District, DC
    Washington, DC (use The District to differentiate from Washington-area suburbs)
Emerald City
    Seattle

Fog City
  San Francisco
LA, Lala-Land, SoCal (Southern California)
  Los Angeles
Mile-High City
  Denver
Motown, Motor City
  Detroit
Twin Cities
  Minneapolis, St Paul
Vegas
  Las Vegas
The Windy City, The City of Big Shoulders
  Chicago

STATE TO STATE

STATE OR DISTRICT?

Washington, DC is in a unique political position – it is not a state, it's a district, and thus does not have the same political voice in the legislature that other states do. Proponents of 'home rule' finally got to put that message across in a pithy licence-plate slogan:
  'Taxation without Representation.' This was the slogan of the early colonists against their British rulers, one that every schoolchild is familiar with.

Each state has a slogan which appears on car licence plates. These are not to be confused with other state identifiers such as the state flower or the state animal, or unofficial state species like the mosquito (which Minnesota and other states lay claim to). State animals are often adopted as the team name of the major state university. Hence, the Wisconsin state animal – the badger – has spawned the nickname 'the Badger state' and has given rise to the University of Wisconsin's mascot, Bucky Badger.

STATE TO STATE

Some licence-plate slogans include:

Alabama	*Heart of Dixie*
Alaska	*The Last Frontier*
Arizona	*The Grand Canyon State*
Connecticut	*The Constitution State*
Delaware	*The First State*
Hawaii	*The Aloha State*
Idaho	*Famous Potatoes*
Illinois	*Land of Lincoln*
Kentucky	*Bluegrass State*
Michigan	*Great Lakes*
Minnesota	*10,000 Lakes*
Missouri	*Show-Me State*
Nevada	*The Silver State*
New Hampshire	*Live Free or Die*
New Jersey	*Garden State*
New Mexico	*Land of Enchantment*
North Dakota	*Peace Garden State*
Rhode Island	*Ocean State*
Tennessee	*Volunteer State*
Texas	*Lone Star State*
Vermont	*Green Mountain State*
West Virginia	*Wild, Wonderful*
Wisconsin	*America's Dairyland*

Many state names come from the native peoples who lived there or from the first settlers and explorers to the region. For example, Connecticut (don't pronounce the middle 'c'), Massachusetts, and Michigan are Algonquian words.

PISSING PEOPLE OFF

A relatively safe way to indicate an insult without invoking a racial slur is to hurl state-related invective (or its variant: city/town-related taunts). Oregonians have no love for Californians. Iowans and Minnesotans make fun of each other. Coloradans hate Texans. And everyone seems to pick on New Jersey, the favorite whipping boy of comedians, professional or amateur ('You're from Jersey? What exit?'). (See also Insults & Put-Downs in Speaking American.)

- Heard throughout the Northwest is the anti-development, anti-Californian phrase 'Don't Californicate us'.

- East Coast people can insult others by insinuating they're from West Virginia.

- In Maryland it's customary to insult someone's highway driving by calling them a 'Pennsylvania driver'.

LOOKING FOR LOVE

One way to see the USA is to look for 'love' – or 'Bliss' (ID) or 'Paradise' (CA) – in all the right places. An atlas will help you locate:

Darling, AZ, MN, PA
Eros, LA, AR
Flingsville, KY
Joy, AL, IL, KY, NY, OK, UT
Kissimee, FL, PA
Love, AZ, IL, KY, VA, TX
Loveland, WA, CO, IA, NY, OH, OK, TN, WA
Loving, GA, KY, NM, OK
Romance, WI, MO, AR, WV
Romeo, CO, FL, IL, MS, TN, MI
Sweet Lips, TN
Valentine, AZ, AR, IN, LA, NE, SC, TX, NJ, MT

STATE TO STATE

- Heads up, Pennsylvanians. It's very easy to inflame a Baltimorian – especially an Orioles fan – by singing the praises of the New York Yankees.

- Some East Coast motorists go crazy when they are stuck behind slow-moving cars with Florida plates, assuming that they are 'old-timers' (one of the many retirees in Florida – in Florida, as in Arizona, the expression is 'snow bird').

- Staten Islanders vehemently blame New Jersey for the stench from various dumps.

- A term Wisconsinites have for Illinois drivers is FIBs (fucking Illinois bastards). People in southern Wisconsin are referring to bad driving, whereas people up north use it as a term of resentment as well.

- Locals of the South Jersey shore near Atlantic City refer to beachgoers from Philadelphia as 'shoobies'. This stems from an old tale that people from Philly used to drive 'down the shore' and bring their lunches to the beach in a shoebox. Nowadays, it's a negative term used to make fun of anyone who doesn't look like they grew up at the beach (bad tan lines, wearing socks and shoes to the beach, etc).

- In Nebraska, 'outstate' used to be the term for anyone who wasn't from the (relatively) more densely populated southeastern corner of the state, but it's fallen into some disuse.

- Meanwhile, in southeastern South Dakota, 'sand lizard' refers to someone who lives in Nebraska and is (somehow) inferior.

EATING & DRINKING

You don't just eat, you can nosh, nibble, graze, snack, chow down or eat like a horse (in which case an all-you-can-eat or buffet arrangement is advised). When it comes to food in the USA, you will not be lacking choice. At any sandwich shop you'll have an array of breads, some you may have never heard of (sourdough, focaccia, torpedo and croissant are favourite choices). If it's salad you're ordering, your server will give you a list of names for dressings (like raspberry-pomegranate vinaigrette or tangerine-mint) or the more common house, blue and Thousand Island. A salad, by the way, implies something leafy and green, with a variety of extras like croutons, bacon bits, kidney beans, or carrots and cucumbers. It is usually served before the main course (the entree).

Fancy foods may be the province of urban areas or university towns, but this is changing. In the heartland, your options are fewer but equally delectable and include chicken-fried steak, biscuits and (white) gravy, hush puppies and a slice of pie. (Pie is another food item that lends itself to infinite variety.) Some restaurants will serve food 'family style' – in dishes to share, not in separate portions.

The optional first course is called an appetiser. On the table will be flatware, silverware (whether it's silver or not) or utensils. Most places will automatically serve you iced water – you have to specify 'no ice'. If the place is big enough, a 'busser' will bus your table (take away the used plates and utensils). You can ask him or her to wrap up your left-overs (a 'doggie bag') to take away with you.

When you're done with your meal and have finished your coffee and dessert, ask for the check (bill). You may split the check. Tips of 15% to 20% are in order in all but self-serve instances. You'll find your waiters, in general, to be attentive.

Restaurants are not the only places to eat. You can also frequent the following:

cafe
you'll find Italian coffee concoctions like cappuccino, mocha and latte and a few desserts or light meal items

coffee shop
much like a diner, to be differentiated from a cafe

deli
sandwiches and mayonnaise-based salads, and often Jewish food

diner
popular on the East Coast, serving standard American fare liked burgers and grilled cheese sandwiches

fast-food outlets
hamburgers and fried chicken are popular here

food court
a multi-option open area in a mall

greasy spoon
an inexpensive establishment serving lots of fried food dishes; somtimes considered somewhat unsanitary

supper club
name for restaurants in certain parts of the country, especially the Upper Midest, serving American-style steak, chops, poultry and seafood. Relish trays (a selection of free hors d'oeuvres) are common here.

Breakfast & Lunch

'Breakfast is the most important meal of the day', goes the saying. In the USA breakfast food is usually light and includes toast, cereals, pancakes, waffles. Omelettes and sausages are popular too, and potatoes are a favourite accompaniment to a breakfast out. There are hash browns (made with grated potatoes and one of the most popular breakfast foods) and potato patties (made with mashed potatoes), but perhaps the most popular are coarsely chopped fried potatoes known variously as home fries, pan fries,

American fries and American fried potatoes. Grits (made of ground corn or hominy, a maize-based food) are the breakfast starch of choice in the South (where you eat black-eyed peas on New Year's morning).

If you want something light, order a continental breakfast (coffee with a roll, croissant or muffin). A leisurely late-morning or early-afternoon repast, especially on weekends, is known as brunch. The midday meal can be referred to as lunch, luncheon or even dinner. Snacks are known as lunch or a little lunch in the North. If you're working you'll take a coffee break, break or go for coffee.

Dinner

Someone who calls lunch 'dinner' will invariably refer to dinner (the evening meal) as 'supper'.

You may attend a 'potluck', at which each guest brings a dish and you're left with a myriad of unanticipated options. Many bars have late-afternoon 'happy hours', with inexpensive drinks and various free or very cheap items to eat.

If it's late, try a diner. One useful aspect to the diner is the wide selection of food, with meals served at all times of day and night. You can usually get breakfast after a late movie or a late night out. Many donut places are open 24 hours to serve a similar clientele.

FOOD & DRINK

ONCE-OVER-EASY

Eggs come poached, soft (runny), hard-boiled, scambled, fried: 'once-over-easy' (flipped over once while cooking without breaking the yolk), 'sunny-side-up' (cooked without flipping) or 'fried hard' (no runniness). A picnic or church-supper staple is the deviled egg: the yolk of a hard-boiled egg is mixed with mayonnaise and dolloped back into the cooked white.

DINER SLANG

Diners are a unique American institution, serving comfort food to weary travellers in small boxcar-style booths. You will find diners all over the country, but especially in the Northeast. Here are some terms you'll need to know to navigate your way through the fascinating diner landscape:

Adam and Eve on a raft
  two link sausages on a pancake
bloodhounds in the hay
  hot dogs and sauerkraut
Canary Island
  vanilla soda with chocolate ice cream
a splash of red noise
  tomato soup
chewed fine with breath
  hamburger with onion
Chicago
  pineapple
CJ Boston
  cream cheese and jelly
complete chicken dinner
  two hard-boiled eggs
Dagwood special
  banana split
dusty miller
  chocolate sundae sprinkled with powdered malt
hold the mayo
  in other words 'no mayonnaise'; 'hold the...' can be applied to anything you don't want with your meal
hummingbird
  talkative soda fountain man
lacey up with spla
  hot chocolate with whipped cream

love box
  booth
magoo
  custard pie
mother and child reunion
  fried chicken and fried eggs
pitch till you win
  eat all you can
radio sandwich
  tuna fish sandwich
shivering hay
  strawberry Jell-O
sleigh ride special
  vanilla pudding
wrinkled dough and ole black joe
  waffles with coffee

– courtesy John Clarke

FOOD & DRINK

TYPICAL AMERICAN FOODS

The quintessential American foods have to be the hamburger and the hot dog. Many millions are eaten in every corner of the USA every year, and every self-respecting diner across the land will feature a 'heart attack on a bun'. This is a cheeseburger deluxe – a burger on a sesame-seed bun with meat and cheese, a leaf of lettuce, a slice of tomato, a pickle and maybe a slice of onion, slathered with mayo or a 'special sauce'. It should be washed down with a Coke.

Bread is not an essential part of American meals. It may be served, but often the bread serving is substituted with potatoes or corn, depending on the meal and the region you're in.

Bakery goods are a speciality in many parts of the country. Be on the lookout for crullers, longjohns (frosted, oblong, deep-fried pastry, also known as Chicagos), fritters and bismarcks (filled longjohns). The names will change from region to region.

Certain staples will vary by region, too. For example, in the South cornbread is not sweet, nor is it a type of cake. It is yellow bread made with corn meal and tastes a little like corn. Biscuits may or may not be fluffy. They are also a type of bread, eaten with any and all meals, not just with breakfast, as in some other parts of the USA.

'No ice!' is the phrase you may find useful if you don't like your drinks cold. In the USA, drinks are generally served with lots of ice, and without it only if requested.

Peanut butter-and-jelly sandwiches (PBJ) are very popular snacks and lunchbox foods, especially for school children.

FOOD GLORIOUS FOOD!

In the South, mayonnaise is the condiment of choice instead of ketchup. When you ask for tea in Raleigh, NC, or anywhere in the South, you'll get sweetened ice tea. When you ask for tea in New York, you'll get hot tea. Wherever you are, it will never come with milk.

Barbecue is an art and a religion in most of the South. It varies by region. For example, pork in the Carolinas and beef in Texas; dry versus moist; vinegar or without.

New Yorkers easily understand the phrase, 'Everyone was eating deli'. They're referring to delicious, Jewish-style food like corned beef. If you say 'I'm going to the Korean', it means you're going to the vegetable stand, most of which are run by Korean owners.

Comfort foods are foods we grew up with that we turn to as adults when times are tough and we need a reminder of something homey and nurturing. These are usually soft, somewhat bland, or sweet foods: macaroni and cheese, toast and chipped beef, rice, oatmeal, chicken noodle soup, donuts, peanut butter-and-jelly sandwiches, pot roast and potatoes.

American desserts and sweet foods run the gamut and fill the bill at breakfast, lunch or dinner. In particular, pumpkin pie, pecan pie, muffins, donuts, brownies and chocolate chip cookies. Pies are particularly interesting to examine by region: Shoofly Pie, Key Lime Pie, Rhubarb Pie, Grasshopper Pie (with crème de menthe, not insects), Sweet Potato Pie.

Here are some typical foodstuffs:

chicken-fried steak
　　low-grade cut of steak breaded (crumbed) and fried, covered with white gravy

hamburgers
　　called hamburg or hamburg steak in parts of the East

hush puppies
　　a southern sidedish: a concoction of cornmeal, onion and egg, shaped into balls and deep-fried

peanuts
　　also known as goobers or goober pea

popcorn
　　served at ball games and movies

potato salad
　　hot potato salad, or German potato salad in the middle of the country; served especially at picnics

yams, sweet potatoes
　　they're different, but sometimes referred to interchangeably; often served at Thanksgiving and Christmas

FOOD & DRINK

Different regions of the country offer a different assortment of foods. Here are some examples:

The West

bear claw
   a paw-shaped almond pastry
Denver omelette
   green peppers, tomatoes and cheese in an omelette
frijoles
   spicy, cooked beans; pronounced free-HOLE-ays
jerky
   spiced, dried beef
sourdough bread
   in which fermented dough is the leavening agent – a legacy of the Gold Rush
Mexican food
   enchiladas, burritos, tacos, etc.

The Delta South

gumbo
   okra stew
jambalaya
   rice and meat stew
muffaletta
   savoury, spiced and oily sandwich; a New Orleans speciality
pralines
   pecan and brown sugar candy

FOOD & DRINK

Wisconsin & Other German-Settled Areas

bratwurst
  a juicy, German-style sausage

braunschweiger
  liverwurst, liver sausage sandwich

potato pancakes
  usually another potato option with dinner

New England

Boston brown bread
  a steamed, molasses-based bread

chowder
  clam chowder (clam stew with vegetables)

dropped egg
  poached egg

grinder
  elsewhere known as a poor boy (or po'boy), sub sandwich, submarine

tonic
  soda pop

FOOD & DRINK

FOOD AT GATHERINGS

Food at county fairs is distinctive. Much of it is deep-fried. Some of it is on a stick (hot dogs). Ice cream, hot dogs and hamburgers form the basis of fair food. Cotton candy (candyfloss, spun sugar) is absolutely iconic. It all can be eaten while walking. Church suppers bring out the hot dishes ('hot dish' is a term for casserole-type food) and salads (Jell-O salad – various canned fruits and maybe marshmallows in gelatin dessert – is a prominent one).

FOOD & DRINK

IF YOU'RE IN ...

Ohio: try a buckeye. It's a peanut butter and chocolate dessert shaped to look like a buckeye, which is the seed that comes from the state tree.

Nebraska: try a runza, a meat-filled pastry.

Boston: eat the locally produced ice cream.

Cleveland: just do it and sample the pickled pig's feet; it's Eastern European 'soul food'.

Minnesota at Christmas time: find some lutefisk (white fish).

New York: eat a bagel; you may not find a good one elsewhere.

New England: eat the 'chowdah' (often advertised under this spelling) and lobster roll (in Maine, some McDonald's serve lobster rolls).

A West Coast city: gorge on the fish tacos.

At someone's Midwestern home: say yes to the smokies (miniature sausages) with your eggs. Or have the porkies (the nonsmoked variety).

Baltimore: order a crab cake.

California: know your Mexican food. A taco is crunchy, a burrito is soft, enchiladas are soft and have sauce on them (green or red, *verde* or *colorado*), a taquito is rolled and stuffed with meat and fried like a taco, flautas are big taquitos and a quesadilla is two tortillas with melted cheese and other goodies in the middle.

Texas: compare the Tex-Mex versions of Mexican food – and go for the chili.

North Carolina: help yourself to ham hock stew and collard greens.

The South: have some Frito pie (a concoction with chili, beans and Fritos corn chips).

FOREIGN INFUSIONS

Like English, which freely borrows from other languages, typical American foods have been influenced by ingredients from other cuisines. For most of the last century, faster and more frequent travel and refrigerated transportation options have brought about an increasing variety to the American diet. Cilantro (coriander) and soy sauce, for instance, were not introduced into the mainstream American diet until after WWII.

Garlic, the stinking rose, inspires a lot of nicknames. It was known as 'Bronx vanilla' and 'Italian perfume' back in the first half of the 20th century.

Immigrant cultures have also influenced American ways of eating. For example, meat- and vegetable-filled 'pasties' (not pastry) are found in places where Cornish miners settled more than a century ago, like Ishpeming or Iron Mountain, Michigan, and Nevada City, California. Basque restaurants are located in Northern California and Nevada. More widespread are Italian and Jewish foods, although they are considered best when found and consumed at their immigrant epicenters on the East Coast (the New York deli is a delicious repository of both kinds). Jewish delis are the premier places for bagels with a schmear (a portion) of cream cheese, lox (smoked salmon) and knishes (potato pastries usually eaten with mustard). Italian delis serve up mozzarella (cheese), prosciutto (cured ham), manicotti (pasta), and parmigiano reggiano. Delis are where you'll find garlic knots, ices (Italian ice drinks) and hero (submarine) sandwiches.

FOOD & DRINK

COFFEE ANYONE?

Coffee drinks are not just the province of Seattle, although Seattle is ground zero for cafe culture. If you're in Northern California try Peet's coffee (which the judge for OJ Simpson's trial, Judge Lance Ito, had flown in for the duration). In Southern California, most locals favour Coffee Bean. In New England get a coffee fribble or coffee frap (this is where Starbucks gets 'frappuccino').

Specialty foods that relate to specific immigrant settlement are found only in certain parts of the country. If the immigrant trail was Polish, it will lead to pierogi (filled dumplings). If it was Russian, it will lead to borscht (beet soup). If it was Greek, it will lead to spanakopita (spinach and egg pastry). If it was Slovakian, it will lead to kolachi (a sweet dessert roll).

Japanese sushi has some local versions which have spread nationwide: Philadelphia rolls (cream cheese and salmon), DC rolls (with crab) and California rolls (with crab and avocado) which have spread throughout the world.

Besides changing perspectives on ingredients, the foreign infusions to the American food scene are also constituted by restaurants that present the stand-alone cuisines: Chinese, Italian, Mexican, Thai, Ethiopian, German, Japanese, Indian, etc. Recent immigrants have brought Salvadoran, Burmese, Puerto Rican, Cuban and many Latin and Asian cuisines. Middle Eastern food – humus, pita, falafel, dolmas (stuffed grape leaves), and baklava – is increasingly popular and is often a standard at parties and receptions.

Ethiopian or Eritrean restaurants, in which you use the bread (injera) as a scoop for a variety of cooked vegetables and meats, are increasingly popular in cities along both coasts.

Tapas restaurants are also gaining in visibility, especially attractive to groups because of their versatility: lunch, dinner, appetiser or bar food. Tapas is a dish that consists of little pieces of food served in separate dishes and eaten with a fork or toothpick. They are placed around the table or on the bar and you are expected to pick up different pieces from all the different dishes.

One of the most popular television shows on American public television is the Japanese import, *Iron Chefs*, which pits cooking giants against chefly challengers in an exciting contest of culinary strength and creativity.

HERE'S A TIP

Many first-time visitors to the USA will be surprised to see that the 'wait staff' in restaurants are expected to be given a tip that is 15% to 20% of the actual bill (before tax). This practice is more than just a way of showing appreciation for the service received. In fact, the wait staff are sometimes paid as little as US$2 per hour by their employers who assume that they will make their real wages in tips. The tip is generally not included in the price of the meal, but may at times be stated on the menu or the bill as such. However, in most fast-food, self-service, cafeteria-style restaurants, no-one will be serving at the table so a tip or gratuity is not expected.

Bartenders, taxi drivers, hotel staff, food deliverers and beauty salon employees also receive tips. The following guidelines may be useful in figuring out how much to tip. Keep in mind that they vary by region:

Bartenders – 10% to 15%
Hotel staff: Porters – $1 a bag in ordinary hotels, $2 a bag in first class places; maids – $2–5 per day; Concierge – $5–10 depending on services rendered; coat-check clerks – $1
Taxi drivers – 10% to 20%, more if you ask them to wait for you
Food delivery – 10% to 20%
Hair salons: Shampooists – $1–$3; Colorists and Stylists – 20% of their service fee

FOOD & DRINK

DRINKS & DRINKING

To the outside world the USA is not known for the quality of its beers, which Australians sometimes refer to as lawnmower beers (something you drink when mowing the lawn). However, popular microbreweries (also known as brewpubs or pubs) are changing this impression with their unique 'designer beers', available in pints and half-pints. In your ordinary bar or tavern, you ask for a draft or a bottle. Tap (or draft) beers are usually better than bottle beers, so asking 'What's on tap?' is wise. Ordering by the pitcher is popular and economical, especially with groups of revellers after sporting events or a long working day.

Soft drinks are called pop, soda, soda pop, carbonated beverage and Coke (in some areas a generic term).

If you're invited to an event with a cash bar or no-host bar, you pay for the drinks. If someone invites you to a kegger, plan on enjoying a big rowdy party with beer in kegs (colleges and universities are famous for such parties). The alcohol-drinking and buying age in all states is 21.

A Shirley Temple is a non-alcoholic drink you get at a bar, often given to children.

★ ★ ODE TO SOUTHERN COOKING ★ ★

Sweet tea, lemonade, grits, mashed potatoes, sweet potatoes, chicken fried steak, peach cobbler, sweet onion and tomatoes, fried chicken, yams, greens, sausage gravy and eggs, and biscuits. The best grits are served in Polk County, Florida. There are restaurants where the women sit out back and peel potatoes and snap greens, and the tea is served in little jars and the meals cost between US$2.50 and $4. In the Gulf and along the coast seafood becomes a Southern thing. New Orleans has shrimp, crawfish (crayfish) étouffée, blackened and cajun spices. Basically Southern food is spicy, buttery and fried, or sweet and sugary. Except the biscuits – they must be fluffy. Baking a bad biscuit in the South is worse than setting the flag on fire.

– Mary-Denise Tabar

Java Jive

Coffee literacy in the US is no longer the birthright of residents in university towns or Euro-style enclaves anymore – Starbucks and its spawn changed all that.

Gone are those days as well as the time when a 'cuppa joe' meant brewed and boiled Maxwell House ('good to the last drop') in a white Buffalo China coffee cup poured by a waitress named Alice at a roadside diner.

Now you might want a skinny triple latte (a milky brew made with skim milk) or a double cap unleaded (a strongish cappuccino made with decaf coffee). The details and spellings will vary according to the franchise, affiliation to Italy, and section of the country – and you will be able to get your gourmet coffee fix from hinterland to heartland to rangeland to truck stop to urban jungle – but here are some of the basics:

espresso	hot pressurised water forced through freshly ground coffee beans
caffè latte	espresso with steamed milk (aka 'latte')
cappuccino	espresso with one-third steamed milk and one-third milk foam (aka 'cap')
macchiato	shot of espresso marked with hot or cold milk
mocha	caffè latte with chocolate (aka 'caffè mocha')
americano	espresso mixed with hot water
single	one shot of espresso
double	two shots of espresso
triple	three shots of espresso
quadruple	four shots of espresso
skinny	non fat or skim milk
unleaded	decaffeinated

FOOD & DRINK

FOOD & DRINK

GOOD PIZZA IN NY

- Ask a New Yorker for a recommendation.
- The place is ideally near a subway stop or movie theatre.
- The place should specialise in pizza (not burgers or breakfast); maybe also serve calzone and Italian gelati.
- The guys behind the counter should look Italian.
- The name of the place should include an Italian name.

Often criticised for their less-than-ideal health habits, Americans more than make up for their lack of athletic ability with their fanaticism over sports and sports stars. Loyal through three main seasons of sports, most fans' year begins with baseball's opening day in early April. Perhaps the most American of all sports, baseball evokes picturesque images of fathers and sons scribbling on scorecards, food vendors hawking peanuts and hot dogs, and lucky fans catching long fly balls. The 'lazy days of summer' and the 162-game season finally come to a close in mid-October with the World Series.

BASEBALL

Known as 'America's Pastime' or the 'Grand Old Game', baseball is enjoyed by fans across the USA throughout the summer and into the fall (autumn), when the season ends with the best-of-seven World Series, also called the 'Fall Classic'. If they're not attending games at ball parks, fans will be watching them on TV, listening to them on the radio or reading about their team's performance in the morning paper.

Baseball is a game of statistics and a real fan will know their favourite players' BA (batting average), RBIs (runs batted in), SBs (stolen bases) and, of course, HRs (home runs), and for pitchers, ERAs (earned run averages). It is also a game of traditions, where wooden bats and leather balls and mitts have changed little over the history of the game, where players chew tobacco and have names like Mickey, Tug and The Babe.

What's Happening?

Baseball is played on a diamond, which is named for the shape created by the four bases – first, second, third and home plate. A distance of 90 feet (about 27 metres) separates each base. In the centre of the diamond is the pitcher's mound, where the pitcher throws towards the batter standing astride the home plate.

The teams take turns trying to advance their teammates around the bases by hitting the ball past their opponent's fielders with a wooden bat. If a batter swings at a ball but misses, the home plate umpire decides whether the batter should have been able to hit it (in which case it's a strike) or whether the pitcher threw a ball that wasn't close enough for the batter to hit (in which case it's called a ball). Three strikes and you're out! Four balls and you walk (to first base). When a runner advances from first base all the way to home plate, the team is awarded a run. If a batter is able to hit the ball over the fence it's called a home run. The defensive team must catch a hit ball or tag a base runner before he reaches a base to get an out.

SPORTS

GRAND SLAM

The baseball season starts in the summer. It ends with the World Series championship, played in late October.

The World Series is comprised of a possible seven games and is won by the team which can beat the other team four times. Games alternate between two competing teams' stadiums (which is why it was called the Subway Series when the New York Mets and the New York Yankees squared off in 2000).

The New York Yankees are probably the most famous professional baseball team. They have also won the most World Series games of any team in professional baseball.

- **The positions:** Each team has nine players – pitcher, catcher, first, second and third base, shortstop, center, right and left field.
- **Best-known venues:** Wrigley Field (Chicago), Fenway Park (Boston), Yankee Stadium (New York) and Tiger Stadium (Detroit)
- **Baseball notables:** Babe Ruth, Mickey Mantle, Lou Gehrig, Ty Cobb, Yogi Berra, Hank Aaron, Pete Rose, Willie Mayes, Cal Ripkin, Mark McGuire
- **Notable teams:** Los Angeles Dodgers, New York Yankees, Chicago Cubs, Boston Red Sox, Detroit Tigers
- **Major annual event:** World Series
- **Players:** The poetic name for players is 'the boys of summer'.

Baseball Terms

Slang terms for hitting a homerun are: homer, four-bagger, dip, monster mash, dinger, street shot, blast, dong, shot, her (from the abbreviation HR).

bases loaded
　　a player on each base, upping the potential for scoring runs
double play
　　two out in one play
fly ball
　　a ball that is hit high into the air
grand slam
　　a home run with bases loaded (four runs)
hit for the cycle
　　one player who hits a single, double, triple and HR in the same game
the hot corner
　　third base (which gets lots of action)
no-hitter
　　a game in which the pitcher allows to runs to be made as a result of hits. A 'hit' is when a batter safely reaches base as a result of both him or her hitting the ball into fair play and no errors being made by the defense.

rookie
>a player in their first season

shut out
>a game in which the defensive team allows no runs to be scored

Texas leaguer
>a looping fly ball just over (out of) the infielder's reach that falls in front of outfielders

triple play
>three out in one play

THE BUSH LEAGUES

When something or someone is 'bush', it means poor quality or poor attitude. The connotation is decidedly negative. The term comes from the now-extinct Bush Leagues, a system that was known for its poor management, poor field, poor food, bad uniforms, bad equipment and limited budget. Outside of the baseball world, it's common to refer to someone who isn't capable – who isn't ready to play – as being Bush League.

SPORTS

FOOTBALL

What's (arguably) more American than baseball, mom and apple pie? Football! The game is embedded in the national psyche, occupying many a fan when the season starts in the early fall (autumn). Professional football games normally take place on Sunday afternoons, but can also be seen on Monday nights, Sunday nights or Thursday nights.

Monday Night Football is so firmly on the national schedule that many non-football, non-broadcast activities are organised around it. It has helped lead to the rise of 'football widows', generally women who don't share their partners' passion for the game and are left to their own devices most Monday nights during football season.

The championship of American professional football is called the Super Bowl. Played in a different city each year, it has become much more than just a game. The Super Bowl is normally the single most-watched event of the year and is played in late January.

College football is as popular as pro football. The end of the college season features several bowl games, scheduled to help determine who wins the National Championship. New Year's Day bowl games include the Rose Bowl, Cotton Bowl and Orange Bowl. The Rose Parade in Pasadena, Southern California, is a famous accompaniment and is aired on national TV. College football nearly always is played on Saturdays.

What's Happening?

American-style football consists of a team of 11 well-padded and helmeted men trying to get an oblong-shaped football from one end of a 100-yard field (about 91 metres) to the other, while 11 other men, similarly garbed, try to stop them by pounding whoever has the ball into whatever piece of ground is nearby. Players carry, kick or throw the ball in the direction of their goal and get four attempts (downs) to advance 10 yards, and get another four downs each time they succeed. If they do not succeed they turn the ball over to the opposing team.

- **The positions:** There are 11 players on each team. The offense includes the quarterback (leader), linemen, receivers and running backs; the defense includes linemen, linebackers, safeties.
- **Football notables:** Joe Montana, Vince Lombardi (coach), Jim Brown, Joe Namath, Johnny Unitas, OJ Simpson
- **Major annual event:** Super Bowl

SPORTS

Football Terms

the cookie, the pigskin
> the football

flea-flicker
> a trick play in which the quarter back throws a lateral pass to another player, who then throws a lateral pass back to the quarterback and then a forward pass to a receiver down field

gun
> to throw a ball hard: 'He gunned that pass.'

Hail Mary
> a long pass, usually thrown from the opposite end of the field in desperate circumstances when a team needs a touchdown to win in the last few seconds of the game

a house
> a very large player

hustle
> to run quickly, the ability to run quickly: 'He's hustling.'; 'He's got hustle.'

FANS & CHANTS

Sports stars are treated like gods in America and fans worship their stars with unabashed enthusiasm. The actual sport in question really makes no difference to serious sports fans as long as they can wear their hero's jersey, paint their faces the colours of their favourite teams and scream encouragement and obscenities in the general direction of the playing field.

Sometimes the sideshows are more entertaining than the main event though, as faithful fans lead their seatmates in raucous chants, cheers and jeers. Some cheers cross over all sports and seasons, like 'DE-fense, DE-fense' and the 'Hey' song. Most teams, however, have their own fight songs that the bands and cheerleaders recite over and over again until the fans catch on.

on the numbers
> a well-thrown pass

the wave
> a crowd activity which circles the stadium where rows of fans
> consecutively stand up with their arms raised and yell

the zone
> mental state in which a player performs exceptionally well and
> feels like time slows down

BASKETBALL

Old men, sports stars and rock'n'rollers all claim to play golf, but
the ruling game in the streets, parks and driveways of the USA
remains 'b-ball'. Even the recently popular soccer will not make a
dent any time soon. Basketball has overtaken all other sports as
the most beloved participatory American sport because it elicits
the greatest emotion, talk and player involvement.

The professional basketball championships are held in the spring
after a season which begins in the winter. The championship consists of a best-of-seven game series wherein the first team to win
three games is the champion team.

What's Happening?

Two teams run back and forth on a court, attempting to shoot
the ball into a 10-foot-high hoop and net and prevent their
opponents from doing the same. Basketball is played by two
five-member teams who move the round ball from one end of
the court to the other by bouncing (dribbling) it and passing it
to teammates. If a player with the ball takes more than two
steps before bouncing the ball, a penalty (called travelling) is
called and the ball is awarded to the other team.

- **The positions:** Each team has five players – one center, two
  forwards, two guards.
- **Best-known venue:** Boston Garden (1995 was its last season)
- **Basketball notables:** Michael Jordan, Wilt Chamberlain, Magic
  Johnson, Shaquille O'Neal, Larry Byrd, Dennis Rodman
- **Major annual event:** 'The Finals', the Championship Series

SPORTS

Basketball Terms

In the last few years, as the game has loosened up and a wide assortment of men and women have come to play, there has evolved a fascinating style of speech to accompany basketball. If you want to play serious American 'hoops', it pays to know your 'hops' from your 'stops' and a 'run' from a 'game'.

airball
    shot that completely misses the basket, hitting 'nothing but air'
bucket
    a basket, a score. From the origins of the game, when basket-balls were literally tossed into buckets.
cherry picking
    a player that discreetly hangs back around his basket waiting for a long pass and an easy bucket
D
    defence
game
    refers to one's particular style of play. In some circles how one's 'game' looks is as important as how one plays.
garbage
    ugly looking shots that go into the basket
handles
    ability to dribble: 'That guy's got handles.'
hoops
    the game of basketball
hops
    excellent jumping ability
make it, take it
    you make a basket, you keep the ball. Used in half-court games of two to ten players.
the rock
    popular term for a basketball: 'Gimme the rock.'

run

to play a game: 'Can I run with you guys?'

stop

when you keep the opposing team from scoring during a critical point in the game: 'Make a stop.'

trash, shit

irreverent contentious speech designed to unnerve the opposing team (eg, 'You ain't got no moves.'); aka 'shit'. Can also refer to an ugly style of play or a cheap basket. Talking trash is often as essential to a good game of ball as dribbling or defence.

zone

a style of defence where players guard a particular zone of the court rather than a particular player. Also refers to those magical moments when a player is hitting every shot and making every play.

ICE HOCKEY

The game is played on an oblong rink, 200 feet by 85 feet. A goal net is moored at each end; this goal will come off its moorings if collided with. A red line (the centre line) divides the rink in half, and two blue lines divide the rink roughly into thirds. The central zone is called the neutral zone, and the end zones are the offensive or defensive zones.

Players have an L-shaped stick with which to hit the puck (a thick, frozen, vulcanised rubber disk) into the goal. Players must wear helmets, gloves, a jersey with their name and number on it, a thigh-length padded girdle, high leggings and, of course, skates. The goalie has special equipment, including shin pads, a face mask, large gloves and a wider stick blade.

Fights are a frequent and expected part of the game. They often appear staged, to please fans and to intimidate the other team. Players are regularly hurt quite badly, breaking limbs, dislocating joints, straining and pulling muscles and tendons. In the past few years, concern regarding concussions has come to the fore in media reports.

The positions: Each team has many players, but only six can be on the ice at any time. There is a goalie, a right and left defenceman, a left and right forward or wing, and a centre player.

Famous players: Besides icons Wayne Gretzky and Gordie Hall, there are the notable goalies Patrick Roy and Ken Dryden, defencemen Doug Harvey and Bobby Orr, centre Mario Lemieux, and forwards Bobby Hull, Gordie Howe and Maurice 'The Rocket' Richard.

Ice Hockey Terms

finesse players

players who are known for more than just brawn. Hockey great Wayne Gretzky, famous for scoring and skating, is a notable example.

Tim Horton's

a huge national Canadian donut chain, named after the famous Toronto player who died in a car crash in 1974

Zamboni

the large machine that smooths the ice. Spectators often watch the vehicle hypnotically circling the rink between periods.

WANNA BUY A HOCKEY PLAYER?

Hockey has always been seen by Canadians as a Canadian sport, and second perhaps only to snowy winters as a feature of national identity. It is on a par with the way Americans view baseball or American football, or Britons view cricket or rugby.

US hockey teams are overwhelmingly populated by Canadian players. While the professional sport of hockey is decidedly American, untelevised hockey is firmly Canadian. Street hockey rivals basketball or baseball as summer pastimes in Canada. Any self-respecting Canadian knows that Americans buy hockey teams and players, market hockey and watch hockey on TV, but Canadians *play* hockey.

AUTO RACING

The most popular form of auto racing in the USA is stock car racing. Despite the name, the cars in the NASCAR (National Association for Stock Car Automobile Racing) Winston Cup series share nothing in common with their production-car namesakes other than their basic silhouettes. But given their heft and the blare of their big V8 engines, these cars are about as American as you can get. The biggest race of the year is the Daytona 500 in Florida.

While stock car racing is decidedly all-American, the second most popular racing series in the USA is much more international. The open-wheel race cars in the CART (Championship Auto Racing Teams) series are all built in England, powered by high-tech engines from Japan and Europe and driven by mostly foreign drivers such as Dario Franchitti and Helio Castroneves.

The majority of CART races are held on road courses, so drivers can turn left and right equally well. But they also take place on oval superspeedways where speeds can average over 220 miles (354km) per hour.

The most hallowed ground of American racing is the Indianapolis Motor Speedway, a 2.5-mile oval track in Indiana. The Indy 500, held since 1911, is now contested by the open-wheel cars of the IRL (Indy Racing League). Known as 'the Brickyard' because of its former surface, Indianapolis also hosts the Brickyard 400 stock car race and the US Grand Prix Formula One race.

Auto Racing Terms

burnout

    drag racing technique of spinning tyres while the car is stationary, to heat them up in order to get more traction before a race

SPORTS

SPORTS

dirt track racing
> production and purpose-built cars raced in short heats on quarter- and half-mile unpaved oval circuits; the spiritual centre of American motorsports

drafting
> technique used primarily in stock car racing whereby one car follows another very closely for aerodynamic benefit, either to save fuel or gain speed

drag racing
> beginning from a standstill, two vehicles attempt to cover a quarter-mile distance in the shortest elapsed time (ET)

dragster
> a car built solely for drag racing; top fuel dragsters have as much as 7,000 horsepower and cover the quarter mile in less than five seconds at over 300 miles (480km) per hour

funny car
> a dragster covered with a special body to make it look (vaguely) like a production car

loose
> when a car's tail slides easily; oversteer

midget
> small version of a sprint car

sprint car
> open-wheel, open-cockpit, single-seat race car designed for dirt tracks or short paved ovals

slam the door
> prevent a competitor from passing you by blocking them in a corner

slingshot
> passing a car directly in front of you after using drafting to gain momentum

tight
> when a car's front tyres lack grip; understeer

– courtesy Eric Gustafson

HUNTING

In a country that guarantees the right to keep and bear arms in its constitution, it is no surprise to find people who really like their guns. The gun-control debates exist alongside the continually popular sport of hunting.

In some parts of the US, particularly in rural areas, hunting is an integral part of the culture, whereas elsewhere, it's a 'weekend warrior' activity engaged in when the season rolls around. Depending on the season, you can be 'armed for bear' (fully equipped) while hunting deer, duck, or even bison. Firearms aren't the only method. Many people prefer bow hunting. Hunting regulations vary widely by location – a gun shop or sporting equipment store is the source for local rules.

A large part of the hunting experience is bonding with your hunting partners, either in a 'blind', (a camouflaged area where you wait for your targets), a 'pop-up tent trailer' (one of many ways to camp), or while walking with your pack mule out of a gulley. If you're asked to join a 'snipe hunt', don't expect a full freezer afterwards. A snipe is an imaginary creature and a snipe hunt is a joke that those in-the-know pull on greenhorns (novices).

SPORTS

Types of Hunting

dog hunting
> one or more dogs chases, or 'flushes', the game out of its cover to give the hunter an opportunity to shoot

stalk hunting
> the camouflaged hunter moves slowly and quietly through an area, attempting to detect game before being detected. Frequently used when hunting deer and some small game

stand hunting
> the hunter is concealed, for example, in a shooting house (ground level) or a tree stand (elevated), in an area believed to contain game, then waits for the game to appear

trapping

some states allow trapping of animals such as varieties of bob-cats, skunks, coyotes, foxes, minks, muscrats, nutria, opos-sum, otter or raccoon. In some instances these must be 'tagged'.

varmint or predator hunting

calls may be used to emulate the sound of a small rodent in trouble in order to lure animals such as coyotes or bobcats within shooting range. Some states pay bounties for the kill-ing of these animals, or may have organised events in which hunters compete to kill the largest number.

LACROSSE

Not many people know that Lacrosse was actually in-vented by Native Americans. The term 'lacrosse' comes from early French settlers and is a term used to describe any game played with a curved stick and a ball.

Almost exclusively played by men, lacrosse was a stickball game which used a netted racket to pick the ball up from the ground, throw it, catch it and hurl it into a goal. The ball is not allowed to be touched with the hands.

According to early documents on the game, it was played throughout the eastern half of what is now the USA, but seems to have been most concentrated around the Great Lakes. There were variations on the equipment used depending upon the tribe and/or area. For instance, among the Cherokee and Choctaw, two sticks are used (one in each hand).

Lacrosse was not just a form of recreation for the Native Americans. It also served to release aggres-sion, settle disputes over land, train young men for war, to please the Creator and even to provide a cure for any problems within the tribe. It was often sur-rounded by ceremony and victory was considered to be controlled supernaturally.

SPORTS

★ ★ ★ ULTIMATE FRISBEE ★ ★ ★

Thinking of joining those Frisbee players you see in the park? Strap on your cleats, grab a disc and a bottle of sports drink, but leave the dog at home. Likely these players are competing in the sport of Ultimate Frisbee – a game played between two seven-person teams on a field roughly the size of an American football field.

Ultimate Frisbee is played competitively at the high school, college and club level in the USA. It's a sport where men and women often play together, either in official co-ed leagues or unofficially on teams that just need good players. The official organisation for the US is the Ultimate Players Association and worldwide it is World Flying Disc Federation.

Players on the same team complete passes in any direction, including the 'dump' which is a backward pass. To score, players must complete a pass within the opposing team's endzone. Any interception or drop of the disc results in a change of possession and the other team then 'hucks', 'blades' or 'scoobers' the disc down the field in the opposite direction in their attempt to score.

You may hear some familiar sports terms like 'doubleteam', 'pick' and 'foul', but only Ultimate players will be heard calling a 'spirit foul' for unspirited play or yelling for their teammate to 'goho' (go horizontal).

In order to really fit in when you walk over to those Frisbee-throwers in the park:

- Call it a disc, not a Frisbee.
- Don't ask to bring your dog.
- Yell 'Nice bid!' or 'Two hands!' when a player lays out but misses the disc.
- If you throw a 'swilly' pass way up in the air that's hard for your teammate to read, advise them loudly to 'Get a library card' (ie, read the disc).
- Never acknowledge the hecklers on the sideline.

– **courtesy Mindy McWilliams**

SPORTS

URBAN SPORTS

They seem a mismatched pair of words – urban sports. Sports are, after all, played for the most part on fields or large spaces – something the urban setting doesn't have much of. The urban setting, for all its cluttered streets, fieldless squares and multi-storey views, offers a unique environment in which some new and different activities can take place.

Runners rejoice; there is no healthier way to explore a neighbour-hood or two by pacing what some urban runners have come to call 'the dog poop loop', a term of affection and homage to little brown packages of peril that lie in wait to strike the unwary jogger sharing the pavement with dog-walkers.

Tennis is also experiencing a renaissance of sorts in its efforts to diversify its fans and players. The late and great Arthur Ashe urbanised the game back in the 1950s and '60s when he boldly took up the game in his native, then-still-segregated Richmond, Virginia. Today there is a monument dedicated to him at the public courts where he learned the game he would ultimately come to master. Many city parks tucked away in small blocks have public courts.

The possibilities are endless. Besides music (see the Music chapter on page 105), there are comedy clubs, pool halls, poetry slams (competitive and rowdy poetry readings), bowling, miniature golf and theme and amusement parks. Bookstores are also hang-out places – especially now that many have cafes attached to them.

SHOPPING

The cliches of the USA seem to apply when it comes to shopping, especially when you consider the proliferation of outlet malls or large warehouse stores where everything is big, big, big (the popular television cartoon show, *The Simpsons*, described them as places 'where shopping is a baffling ordeal').

For groceries, you have your choice of grocery store, delicatessen, specialty store or foodmart or minimart. Despite the many large warehouse establishments like Costco, Trader Joe's and Wal-Mart, you can still find small places like corner stores, often called 'mom-and-pop' stores or general stores.

Thrifting (bargain hunting in thrift stores such as Goodwill) and antiquing (looking for antiques) are popular weekend activities. Many communities publish guides to antique and thrift stores and certain towns or places within a city are known for happy hunting in these areas. For something slightly less predictable, browse around a rummage sale or garage sale (known in some parts of the country as a jumble sale) for secondhand items or attend a larger flea market (also known as a flea mart or swap meet). Some community organisations sponsor white-elephant sales (cast-off kitsch heaven) for unwanted items.

PAPER OR PLASTIC

'Paper or plastic?' is a phrase that is not only ubiquitous, but is one that people like to use in contexts other than the trip to the grocery store, as a pseudo-diagnostic that just may say something profound or lead to a humorous revelation – about your personality. It's along the lines of reading tea leaves or asking the question that TV interviewer Barbara Walters made famous: If you were a tree, what kind of tree would you be?' (Presidential candidates on comedy talk shows often get questions like that.)

The Mall

Of course, the mall is what suburbanites use for a town centre these days. Before there were suburbs, there were cities and towns, which were very centralised, as were their shopping districts. Now a majority of the American population lives in vast expansive suburbs and old centralised shopping districts are dead. However, some major cities have refurbished these areas to make them very fun places to visit (for example, Baltimore's Harbor Place, New York's South Street Seaport, San Francisco's Ghirardelli Square).

MALL OF AMERICA

America is well known for its abundance of shopping malls, but none compares to the sheer size of the Mall of America just outside Minneapolis, Minnesota. Four floors and the size of seven baseball stadiums, the famous mall boasts 50 restaurants and more than 500 shops. Popular stores like the Gap even have two locations, one at either end of the mall.

Some visitors do not make the trip to shop at all. There are plenty of diversions like the mini amusement park (complete with roller coaster), a Lego Imagination city, a miniature golf course and megaplex movie theatres.

Shopping malls are not just for shopping. They are places where suburban youths hang out, meet their friends, learn about the opposite sex and have their first after-school jobs. Mall parking lots are often the site of weekend farmers' markets or Christmas tree sellers (in season).

Malls are often enclosed in a huge building, usually two or three storeys high, and surrounded by acres of asphalt parking lot. Usually, the roofed malls have a large, open central atrium with trees and fountains to simulate a pleasant outdoor environment. Since malls are private property, security officers are able to throw out anyone they don't like, and malls are thus usually pretty free of crime.

ENTERTAINMENT

The Bigger the Better

Warehouse stores seem to be a manifestation of a cultural ethos: Americans like things large. In the last decade or two large chain stores have swallowed up smaller competitors and have realised that they can save on the double cost of warehouse and retail space by warehousing goods right in the store, or by selling goods out of the warehouse. Extra large shopping carts are now made to hold the bulk quantities in which items are now often sold. But don't expect to find everything you need – what warehouse stores offer is not variety, but quantity. A few require you to purchase a yearly membership for a moderate fee. Warehouse stores include Costco, Smart & Final, Iris, Fry's Electronics, Home Depot and, of course, WalMart. Office supply stores are also prominent – Staples, Office Depot, Office Max. The movement has even extended to books, with Barnes & Noble and Borders Books & Music doing for literature exactly what Starbucks has done for coffee.

THE MOVIES

The elegant, old-time movie theatre has been replaced, in most instances, by utilitarian multiplexes, some with more than 20 screens. Popcorn comes salted; your only option is to hold the fake butter. The movie rating system is G (general audiences), PG (parental guidance suggested), PG-13 (some material not suitable for children under 13), R (restricted; no one under 17 allowed without parent or guardian), NC-17 (no one under 17 allowed) and X. This rating has been replaced by NC-17; current reference is to porn movies. (See also Movies in the Visual Media chapter p149.)

★ ★ ★ ★ INDEPENDENT FILMS ★ ★ ★ ★

In the 1970s, it was all the rage to start a garage band. In the 1980s, the 'in' thing was to write computer programs. (Some high school kids – especially those in the Santa Clara Valley – would sell computer programs to companies and make money for college.) In the 1990s, the rage was to make an independent movie.

There are innumerable independent movies being made now, right across the country. New film festivals are springing up each year in every state. When Steven Soderberg won the top prize at the Sundance Film Festival in 1989 for *Sex, Lies and Videotape* (which went on to earn millions of dollars at the box office), Sundance emerged as the premiere independent film festival in the United States. Then in 1997, *The English Patient* won a sack of Oscars; the movie came not from one of the major studios but from the independent production company of Saul Zaentz. This gave the term 'independent film' its cachet (and overlooked the fact that the movie had numerous big-name Hollywood stars).

The way independent films gain attention is via film festivals. The most prestigious are Sundance, Toronto and Telluride. Competition for acceptance is fierce. New technologies in low-cost digital video have placed the means of production in the hands of more people than ever before, and these festivals receive thousands of submissions for only a few slots on the program.

The centre of the independent film world is really New York, although Los Angeles has its share as well. There is a great deal of debate about what exactly makes an independent film – does it have to do with the source of financing or is it also about attitude, edge and other content-related elements? One thing is for sure, the market is beginning to strain under the weight of the super-low-budget, technically rough movies with absolutely no known faces in them. The heady days of the early 1990s may be giving way to the economic realities of the new millennium.

– courtesy Greg Tennant

ENTERTAINMENT

MUSIC & CLUBS

With so many sounds and styles to choose from in the USA, music fans have a hard time picking just one bar or club that caters to their musical preferences. Most major cities are famous for certain types of music (New Orleans for jazz, Chicago for blues, New York for techno/underground, LA for hip-hop), but almost every town in America offers a variety of venues for listening and dancing to live music.

Live Music Venues

The most popular destination is the neighbourhood bar that features local bands. Stroll down any main street and look for bar signs touting upcoming live performances. Most cities and college towns also offer free weeklies (weekly magazines) with performance listings.

If you are in a metropolitan area there are undoubtedly more clubs featuring live music than you can visit in one trip. Most of these concert venues are partial to certain music styles, so consult a city paper if you are looking for pop or rock or heavy metal.

Dance Clubs

If live music is not your thing but you're looking for room to dance, consult the club listings in local magazines. Disc jockeys (DJs) run the show, playing anything from 1970s disco to new-age techno, depending on the club and the night of the week. Most clubs now advertise '70s nights, '80s night and house nights.

You may also hear about raves as alternatives to commercial dance clubs. While clubs are established businesses, raves are warehouse parties that change location and music style every weekend. City weeklies offer updated listings on these parties, but there are generally no signs or directions. Word-of-mouth is the best way to get the latest scoop on the next big rave. Because they are not established places of business, raves are generally for ages 18 and over and are often criticised in the press for promoting alcohol and drug use.

Comedy Clubs

Always a popular tourist destination, comedy clubs offer a more relaxed evening out if you're not in the mood to fight the crowds at a music or dance club. Drinking is usually a central part of any comedy club and some clubs require a two-drink minimum for a show (thinking you'll laugh more if you drink more). Unless a big name is headlining, most clubs feature two or three stand-up comedians each night. And it is fairly common knowledge that audience members seated in the front are more likely to be picked on by the performer. So retreat to the back of the room if you'd rather laugh at your companions than be the target of the comedy routine.

PUPPET & POETRY SLAMS

In the 1980s a poet from Chicago named Marc Smith started poetry competition nights at a local bar where several members from the audience would be asked to score the poems. Smith's idea spread to other places around the country and it was soon defined as a poetry slam. At poetry slams, the audience is still an integral part of the experience, and audience members are encouraged to express their approval or disdain as poetry is being read.

Puppet slams – opportunities for puppeteers to perform live in front of an audience – are performances modelled on poetry slams. As another variation on a club act, puppet slams (as well as community puppet theatre) are cropping up all over the country and attract professionals as well as amateurs.

ENTERTAINMENT

Music & Club Terms

bouncer

large security personnel stationed at the entrance to charge cover and maintain order

cover

fee charged at the door for entering a club

DJ

disk jockey; sometimes famous DJs are featured at dance clubs

gig

a band performance

ladies night

some bars do not charge women a cover as incentive for more men to pay the entry fee

rave

informal party usually located in a warehouse or empty building

stand-up

comedy performances are also known as stand-up performances

THEME & AMUSEMENT PARKS

Despite the fact that theme parks were invented in Europe, it was the opening of Disneyland in Anaheim, California, nearly 50 years ago that marked the birth of the modern theme park in the USA and around the world. There are now about 40 large-scale and 55 moderate-scale parks throughout the US.

Theme parks tend to have a family appeal, an environment with live shows and parades where a lot of performers and musicians also perform for free. And long but well-organised lines. Traditionally theme parks housed several themes (Disneyland, for instance, has Tomorrowland, Frontierland, Main Street, etc). Recently, however, the trend is toward the mono-theme: theme parks have started to develop around a single idea, like aquatic and children's parks. Some theme parks are connected to retail shopping areas, like Mall of America in Minneapolis.

ENTERTAINMENT

The Disneyland-type theme park with multiple attractions has been the most popular. A single (somewhat expensive) ticket lets you into the park and lets you try everything. Nearly every middle-class American has been to at least one of the most popular theme parks in the US.

A fully fledged theme park doesn't stop with the costumes or decor; it also makes sure the language reflects the 'world' that's being created. You'll not likely hear the words 'cool' or 'duuuude' out of the mouths of Magic Kingdom employees in Frontierland, for instance. Even the familiar characters behave just like you'd expect, with language helping to convey a great deal of their personalities (Goofy says 'Gawrsh!' a lot).

Ride names reflect both the theme and the potential for fun: Gadget's Go Coaster (Disneyland); Wild Mouse, Lightning Racer (Hershey Park); Taxi Jam; Top Gun; Flying Super Saturator (Paramount's Carowinds); Medusa; Road Runner Railway; Blackbeard's Lost Treasure Train (Six Flags Great Adventure); Woody Woodpecker's Nuthouse Coaster (Universal Studios, Florida).

TV TRADITIONS

Watching the Macy's Thanksgiving Parade on that day and the Rose Bowl Parade on New Year's Day is an enduring holiday memory for many Americans.

Macy's parade, which takes place in New York City, was started in 1920 by employees who wanted to celebrate the day in a European way. The parade is well known for its huge helium-filled balloons. It's been televised since 1950.

The **Rose Bowl** (one of the college bowl games) and Tournament of Roses Parade, which takes place in Pasadena, California, is more than a century old, celebrating flowers, music and sports. The Rose Parade float frames are built of steel and chicken wire – but the amazing thing is that everything else on the float must be flowers – or leaves, seeds or bark.

ENTERTAINMENT

FESTIVALS & PARADES

Festivals and parades take place in every single community in the USA, big or small. It's a great way to mingle with locals, listen to what's on their minds and figure out what makes an area unique. It could be pumpkins, honeybees, Fourth of July, potatoes, garlic, the county fair, strawberries, crawfish, chili, art, history – often something to do with food, industry, holidays, independence or a local custom. Often it is a fundraiser for a community endeavour.

Summer is the best time for parades, though you'll encounter them at any time of the year. Cinco de Mayo is celebrated by Mexican and Chicano communities on May 5 to mark Mexico's victory over the French at the Battle of Puebla; Syttende Mai (May 17) is Norwegian independence day, celebrated by Norwegian-American communities; Irish-Americans might celebrate Samhain (pronounced 'SA-win'). The pagan holiday known as Halloween has inspired many parades of costumed revellers – Washington, DC's somewhat gay-centric Dupont Circle, for one, is known for its annual 'drag races'.

St Patrick's Day has spawned a number of famous big-city parades (and smaller-town carousing and partying). Most notable among them is Chicago's, the largest Irish parade in the USA, held the Sunday before March 17. Be prepared for green beer and a green-tinged river.

New Orleans becomes even more colourful and exotic during Mardi Gras, the day before Ash Wednesday (before Easter), with its many krewe-sponsored parades and festivities. (A krewe is a group whose members organise the balls, parades and other festivities of Carnival. The word is a deliberately fanciful spelling of 'crew'.) Parade watchers compete eagerly for the trinkets that get thrown from the passing floats.

Also held throughout the country each year are Pride parades for lesbian, gay, bisexual and transgender people. The biggest of these takes place in San Francisco and attracts a crowd of hundreds of thousands. Pride parades are extremely colourful events where participants often dress in outrageous costumes to celebrate the unity, creativity, visibility, diversity and dignity of gay and lesbian people. These parades also aim to educate the general public about gay and lesbian issues and to decrease prejudice and bias.

Food festivals are very popular throughout the country. The Gilroy (California) Garlic Festival, held the last full weekend in July, is considered by some to be the best. It's a huge draw, full of food, wine, arts and crafts and everything garlic (including garlic ice cream). Miss Gilroy Garlic is chosen on the basis of her interview, talent and 'garlic speech'.

JUNETEENTH & KWANZAA

Juneteenth – African-American Emancipation Day, June 19 – is a celebration that first marked the end of slavery (Galveston, Texas, started the celebration in 1865) and now commemorates African-American freedom and achievement. The Juneteenth celebration varies by community, sometimes lasting for up to a month, and features guest speakers, family reunions and picnics.

Kwanzaa (pronounced 'quan-sa') is a seven-day holiday (26 December to 1 January) based on African festivals which encourage people to reflect on their African roots and their American lives. Kwanzaa, which means 'the first fruits', was started by Dr Maulana Karenga in 1966.

ENTERTAINMENT

GAMBLING
Casino Gambling

In casino gambling, those who wager do so against the 'banker' or the 'house' which may limit the amount of bets to assure the casino's ability to pay off. Frequently they are open 24 hours a day, seven days a week. Casino games popular in the USA include blackjack, poker, crap shooting, slot and video poker machines, bingo and, to a lesser extent than elsewhere, roulette. Slot machines are often called 'one-armed bandits'.

You can play the slots for as little as a nickel (five cents). Casinos often also offer simulcast horse betting. Since the casinos have carefully calculated the odds to ensure that it rarely loses money, they can afford to draw gamblers with extravagant or discounted accommodations.

For many years Las Vegas and a few other sites in Nevada operated the only legal casinos in the USA, although it has taken root in Atlantic City, New Jersey in the last 25 years. In recent years, riverboats have also become homes for legal casinos.

PROFITS FOR FUNDS

Indian reservations have also become sites for casinos. They operate under the auspices of the National Indian Gaming Commission and the Indian Gaming Regulatory Improvements Act and are not subject to state anti-gambling laws. Though the concept has been controversial, casino profits provide funds for often impoverished tribes. Roughly half of the states in the USA have tribal-state compacts, or agreements – roughly 200 out of the 558 federally recognised tribes are engaged in approximately 350 tribal gaming operations.

ENTERTAINMENT

Racetrack Gambling

There are both greyhound and horse racing tracks in the USA. Legal racetrack gambling is of the 'pari-mutuel' variety. A pari-mutuel is a common betting pool in which those who win share the pool with the track management; there is no betting 'against the house', all bets are against other gamblers. As bets are placed, they are mechanically recorded and the approximate odds on each horse or dog in the race are displayed almost immediately.

There is typically a separate pool for each type of wager. Types of wagers include:

place
    bet is on which entrant will either win first or second place
show
    first, second or third place getters
win
    bet is on which horse or dog will win the race

There are also special pools for:

daily double
    wagerer has placed a bet on the winners of the first two races
perfecta
    wagerer has placed a bet on the win and place winners, in the winning order, in one race
quinella
    wagerer has placed a bet on the win and place winners in one race, but not in order
trifecta
    bet is on win, place and show winners of one race, in order

ENTERTAINMENT

Other Wagering

'Parlay' wagering involving betting on two or more outcomes as a bundle. If you win your payoff is bigger than it would have been on a wager placed separately on each outcome.

A 'round robin wager' is a series of parlay wagers. 'Teaser wagers' allow you to bet, for example, that your team will win by a selected number of points.

The bookmaker's job is to determine odds then receive and pay off bets on the outcome of various contests or competitions. There are few legal bookmaking operations in the USA, and those are located primarily in Nevada, New York and New Jersey. Legal bookmakers take bets on horses racing and professional sports.

American music is made by its American context. Picture the drum-and-fife duos of the American Revolution, country fiddlers at hoedowns, harmonicas on the trails of the West, buglers of the Civil War, spirituals in the cotton fields, chants in the churches, brass bands of Fourth of July parades and ice cream socials.

Across the United States you will hear music as diverse as its people, with origins and influences from across the globe. From the Afro-Cuban rhythms that dominate the airwaves of Miami to the distorted guitar-driven rock originating from Seattle, music is a cornerstone of the vast number of different cultures in the USA, providing a forum for celebration, resistance and the demonstration of cultural identity. A trek across the country means hearing this vast range of styles, from Latin to country, hardcore rock to rap, and R&B to folk. Even a simple trip across your radio dial will reveal the quilt-like fabric of American music and society.

The top-selling artists of the day generally come from five different genres of music: rock'n'roll, rap, rhythm and blues, country and pop. Within these five most popular forms of American music, there is a wide variety of distinct sub-genres and fusions. However, these forms only begin to scratch the surface of the range of music that exists within the United States. Musical forms such as zydeco, ska, bluegrass and techno have all carved out significant niches in the expanse of American culture.

THE BLUES

The Blues began in the American South, as African Americans lamented their economic and social conditions in the post-Civil War era. These conditions were wretched. Slavery was over but segregation, Jim Crow laws (which legalised segregation laws between blacks and whites) and an unjust criminal justice and electoral system left the African-American community in a position that was very similar to slavery and indentured servitude.

Victims of rampant and brutal racial injustice, African Americans had to make the choice of labouring long days on the plantations as they had during slavery, or heading north to new cities that offered work during the peak of the American Industrial Era.

Drawing from African musical traditions and gospels, the early blues sounded much like the old field songs slaves had sung to each other before the Civil War, consisting of slow solemn calls about the hardships of working in the fields and the pain of life as an African American in the South. The first celebrated blues artists like Blind Lemon Jefferson took these rhythms and calls and moulded them into a unique style that became known distinctly as the blues.

The South became the home of the blues as it became an established art form at the beginning of the 20th century. People like Robert Johnson and Charley Patton, icons in the early blues days, began cementing 'delta' blues into the history of American music by recording the blues just as the music industry in the United States was establishing itself.

As African Americans began moving north to find work during what is known as the Great Migration, so too did the blues, establishing Chicago, Illinois as its second home. As the blues moved north, two things happened. The tempo of the songs tended to increase and the electric guitar, a new instrument in the 1940s, began to take the foreground, driving the wailing sounds of the blues home in a more powerful way than ever. T-Bone Walker, heavily influenced by jazz, was one of greatest of the city-blues electric guitarists. With this movement, the blues became firmly rooted in the American music scene. It has since inspired musicians throughout the globe and dramatically impacted on the evolution of American music. Blues is still an incredibly powerful force in music, as living legends like BB King continue to carry the torch of America's first musical genre.

MUSIC

JAZZ

Jazz is perhaps the most important musical form developed in the United States. African-American musicians began developing it early in the 20th century, originally as a melding of blues forms with European harmony. It has become a complex art music involving both composition and improvisation. It is an eclectic music which has taken on influences as diverse as ragtime, marching bands, Cuban and Brazilian music, classical music, modern funk rhythms, and Broadway show tunes.

There are two features of jazz that give the music its character. The first is the improvisational aspect. Both in ensemble playing and as soloists, the musicians rely very little on written music. While a piece typically begins with a written theme on a chord progression, the musicians then improvise other melodies on the same chord progression to create their solos and accompaniment. The development of individual styles is highly valued. The second feature is the rhythmic feel. The 'swing' feel that is the hallmark of most jazz is unique to this style, and has entranced generations of listeners and musicians.

DUKE & JAZZ

Jazz great Duke Ellington was born and raised in Washington, DC in the early decades of the 20th century in the thriving African-American middle class community that existed during the years of racial segregation. Like many other talented musicians, Ellington left Washington to make his career elsewhere, notably in New York's Harlem in the 1920s and '30s.

Touring with his big band, Ellington often returned to DC, frequenting the recently restored Lincoln Theater, now a featured attraction in the revitalised U Street corridor of the city. Ellington's contributions to American music have likewise been revitalised, with scholars and critics revisiting his talent and pronouncing it prodigiously good.

In less than a hundred years, jazz has moved through a number of styles as it spread out from New Orleans, where the Dixieland style began. This style was based on ensemble improvisation, simple chords, and a two-beat feel. In the '30s and '40s the swing style predominated, with a smoother 4/4 feel. Big bands were very popular at this time, particularly for dancing.

The advent of the bebop style after World War II moved jazz away from popular music, as this style was very fast and complex. From that point the music began to branch out in many different directions: the cool school, Latin jazz, European jazz, fusion, third-stream, and free improvisation all have had their adherents.

In whatever style, at its best the music remains a vehicle for personal expression within a framework of ensemble playing. The excitement of a jazz concert comes from its spontaneity, the teamwork involved, the emotional expressiveness of the players, as well as their technical ability. When it all comes together, many fans feel there is no better listening experience.

ROCK'N'ROLL

The 1950s were a time of great prosperity in the United States, but the social climate was increasingly conservative. The 1950s was not a time to stand out and be different; it was a time that placed great emphasis on hard work, money and the traditional American family.

The automobile and the television spread rapidly throughout the American suburbs, and TV shows like *Ozzie and Harriet* and *Leave It to Beaver* defined a generation rooted in conservative family values and hidden from social turmoil. At the same time, however, the inner cities of the United States and many of America's youth were not feeling the effects of, nor were they interested in, this conservative American prosperity. To the youth who did not fight in the World Wars and did not dream of a nice house with white picket fences, the conformity of the times was disillusioning. Searching for a forum for resistance, a new musical form drawing heavily upon the faster forms of the blues emerged – it was called rock'n'roll.

Rock'n'roll offered an easily accessible style that featured electric guitars playing quick-paced, two-stringed chords with easy-to-follow and easy-to-dance-to beats in 4/4 time. This music was viewed by the authorities as violent and antisocial. Early rockers like Bill Haley, Elvis Presley and Chuck Berry were censored and considered to be a threat to societal stability.

Bill Haley, who began his career with the label of a country and western singer, is often credited with being the first of the popular rock'n'roll stars, recording albums from 1952 to 1955 that would clearly define the rock'n'roll of the 1950s, with classic hits that are still heard today like 'Rock Around the Clock'.

In 1956 perhaps the biggest icon in the history of American music exploded onto the music scene by belting out soulful rock music, shaking his hips and scaring parents around the nation. 'The King', Elvis Presley, emitted a powerful and sexual energy that bolted rock music directly into the forefront of American culture. His songs and his dance moves captivated the younger generation of the late 1950s and drove fans into a frenzied state of musical elation, pounding yet another spike into the gap between young and old, through which throngs of early rock pioneers like Little Richard, Chuck Berry and Jerry Lee Lewis drove into stardom and controversy.

ROCK'N'ROLL

The term 'rock'n'roll' was first used around 1951 by DJ Alan Freedman, a keen exponent of the new, raucous, rebellious music of the fifties. Although stories vary, he probably took the term from the 1948 song, 'We're Gonna Rock, We're Gonna Roll' by Wild Bill Moore. Freedman tried unsuccessfully to copyright the term.

MUSIC

A CHANGIN' TIMES

As the prosperity of the 1950s waned and the more turbulent era of the 1960s emerged, music provided the ideal forum for protest. As the civil rights movement grew domestically, and the Vietnam War grew abroad, the 'good times' of the fifties were replaced by social and political division within the United States. Patriotism died along with the thousands of young soldiers abroad and at home who were fighting losing battles for and against their government.

During this time rock'n'roll changed along with the political and social climate, incorporating elements from a wider variety of musical traditions, from British pop to traditional folk music. Rock songs shifted messages as well, moving from the more riotous, upbeat celebrations of youthful rebellion to the darker, more political protestations that have become married to the culture of the late 1960s.

LONG LIVE THE KING!

Elvis Presley may have met his maker decades ago but his spirit lives on in his fans. Elvis conventions, memorabilia and – best of all – impersonation contests add texture to the cultural landscape. The grocery store tabloids rarely let a week go by without some big scoop about his ghost, or his corporeal self, or his offspring, or his transmissions from the great beyond. He does fall from the sky from time to time: The Flying Elvises skydiving team performs around the country.

On the other side of the cultural tracks, scholars themselves are fascinated by the legend and his continuing resonance and produce a great deal of academic work trying to figure out how The King achieved this.

Folk and rock blended together in artists like Bob Dylan, whose understated songs spoke of the darker side of politics, with hope for better times for all peoples. This was the era of the 'hippie', a generation disillusioned by politics, the Vietnam War and social inequality, who frequently turned to non-violent forms of protest and recreational drugs for salvation from America. Through this movement, music was the primary channel for their message of non-violent reconciliation and peace.

This era culminated in one of the most important moments in American music history, Woodstock, a three-day concert to celebrate peace that was attended by the biggest names in rock and folk as well as thousands of fans. This was the quintessential moment in music at the time, and marked the musical end to two decades that saw tremendous change in the landscape of American music.

One of the best-known Woodstock musicians is Wavy Gravy, dubbed the 'clown prince' of the counterculture by Ken (*Electric Kool-Aid Acid Test*) Kesey. His fame continues: the national Ben and Jerry's ice cream company has paid homage by naming an ice cream flavour after him. Meanwhile, at home in Berkeley, California, Wavy lives at the now-historic collective known as The Hog Farm and runs a successful camp for underprivileged kids, Camp Winnarainbow.

NEW FORMS OF THE 1970s

As the sun set on the musical revelations of the 1960s, the airwaves in America began to change. Musical styles that had been more regionally centred began to populate the radio more and more, and several new forms emerged as hybrids of multiple styles.

The style that had been around the longest in America and evolved the most was soul. Soul music, a key to the origins of most American music, remained an incredibly popular form of music in the African-American communities of the South. Throughout the first half of the 20th century its most commonly heard manifestation was in gospel music, a religious, highly harmonised version of the traditional soul music of the 19th century.

MUSIC

During the late 1960s soul music underwent a major transformation, primarily brought about by the 'Hardest Working Man in Show Business', the Godfather of Soul himself, James Brown. James Brown was a widely energetic performer who breathed new life into soul by combining it with new instrumentation and arrangements. Brown took soul from the American South into living rooms across the country.

In the 1970s soul began to decline in popularity and a derivative style emerged to help define the period – funk. Funk music combined soul with the movements of jazz and rock'n'roll to produce a powerful, yet danceable music full of more robust rhythms and beats than had been heard in America.

In the second half of the 1970s elements of funk music were taken to create another new musical style, disco, which used synthesised music and slightly altered dance beats to not only create a sound but to define the culture at that time.

The Punk Explosion

Yet another major musical form with lasting impact evolved in the 1970s. Punk rock emerged at a time when both rock'n'roll and popular music was increasingly stylised and synthesised – it represented a major shift from ornamentation to raw, stripped down musical rebellion against all things material and garish. Drawing upon some of the basic principles of rock'n'roll, such as 4/4 time and simple guitar-bass-drums instrumentation, punk rock cast style away and revelled in extremely simple and discordant guitar riffs with angry lyrics that aimed to break down the establishments of music, politics and society.

Punk rock actually has its roots in the early 1970s with The Stooges, The Velvet Underground and, later, the Ramones. Since Punk, rock'n'roll and harder styles of rock music have constantly played off each other, creating new but similar sounding styles: from heavy metal, which rose from the underground clubs of New York and Los Angeles to major radio popularity in the 1980s, to glam rock which celebrated rebellious behaviour while revelling in the excess that punk rock originally protested. Glam rock really originated in the UK with artists such as David Bowie and Marc Bolan, but just as famous were US glam artists Lou Reed, Alice Cooper and the New York Dolls.

MUSIC

EVOLVING TRADITIONS (1980s & '90s)

Just as soul music formed the roots of funk, funk and disco music formed the roots of one of the most widely heard musical styles in America today, Rap, which would partially define the music of the 1980s and '90s. Rap music evolved from the inner cities of the United States. Rap artists took disco music and looped it, making its main melodies repeat, and added more interesting and identifiable drum beats. Over that music artists would rap, a vocal style characterised by more talkative, less sung lyrics. Rap music became a central part of much of African-American culture during the 1980s. It served as a space for social protest against the poor conditions of the inner city and against the racial and class barriers that placed many blacks in extremely difficult social situations.

A more extreme form of rap music emerged in the late 1980s as a form of protest. This was 'gangster rap', which specifically highlighted the difficulties of growing up in the inner city and often called out to many African Americans to rebel against these conditions, both violently and non-violently. Rap music, often criticised for its violent, misogynistic lyrics, is still an incredibly popular style of music that is prevalent throughout the country.

Grunge Music

Grunge is yet another form which dominated the airwaves in the early 1990s by vanquishing excess and returning to more simple, stripped down musical textures. Also known as the Seattle Sound, hardcore marked a return to the punk rock tradition of angst-full vocals with highly dissonant guitars in the second half of the 1990s. The band Nirvana were probably the most well-known exponents of the grunge style of music. The term grunge encompasses not only a music style but one of dress and attitude.

Techno & Raves

If you're not concerned with lyrics and have no desire to slow dance with a significant other, Techno/House/club music relies on a loud, pulsing beat to get the crowds moving. Many mainstream clubs advertise Techno music on the weekends, and more hardcore fans seek out raves (usually held in warehouses or unmarked buildings) to get their Techno fix. Rather than famous radio artists, popular DJs are featured at clubs to spin House music. Kid Rock made his name early on in New York clubs, and Boy George is resurfacing now as a club DJ in England and America. Teenagers and college students are typically the biggest fans of the drum and bass-heavy sound, as there is also a club culture associated with the music. Trendy clothes, piercings, hair styles and accessories (like candy pacifiers and glowsticks) make their debut at clubs and raves, and the music is associated with this sort of young, energised spirit.

Techno music comes in different forms, some of which include: Acid Techno (high pitched), Jungle Techno (heavy African beat underneath), Ambient Techno (slower beat and more musical creativity), and House music (popular on the radio).

SOCIALLY CONSCIOUS ROCK

Inspired by the anti-corporate rock sentiments of punk rock in the 1970s, the Washington, DC music scene produced a brand of music known as harDCore (with capitals as noted) in the 1980s.

An important part of this local scene, the band Minor Threat, later went on to national and international fame. Some members went on to form Fugazi. This group was – and is – well known for maintaining strong ties to the city, even as they have become internationally renowned in the world of independent rock music. They play several free shows a year in DC to benefit local progressive social service agencies and social justice causes.

MIXING & MATCHING

One truth about American music is that it is difficult to put songs and artists into clearly defined genres. Drawing from such a broad range of cultures and traditions, American music has at times blended many different musical styles to blur these borders in profound ways. Throughout the years, artists like Elvis Presley have borrowed from different genres like the blues and country to create new styles unique to themselves. Never before has the blurring of these lines been so prevalent as it is today. A majority of today's most popular songs and artists cannot be clearly labeled as rap, pop or hip hop.

One emergent style of music that symbolises this trend is the rock and rap combination. In 1985 the popular rap group Run DMC released the *Kings of Rock* album, featuring rap music over heavy metal guitar music. They followed up on that album in 1986 with the song 'Walk This Way,' which they performed with a popular hard rock band from the 1970s, Aerosmith. This was the first major effort at combining rock and rap and vaulted rap music into popularity outside of the inner cities.

Today the rock and rap combination can be found throughout popular music as rap stars like Sean 'Puffy' Combs and House of Pain continue to incorporate heavy distorted guitar riffs into their music, and rock bands such as Kid Rock, Limp Bizkit and Korn employ rap-style vocals and turntables similar to those used in hip hop music.

Another related trend in today's music is that of the crossover. In America, artists are said to have 'crossed over' when they are popular in one distinct genre of music and then become popular in another. Today this is seen quite frequently. One common source for crossover acts comes from country music. Artists like Faith Hill began their careers as country singers, but are now also extremely popular on the pop charts.

Another fertile ground for crossing over in today's music comes from styles that originated outside of the United States. 1999, for instance, was classified as the year of the 'Latin invasion' by many in the American music industry, as a large number of artists such as Ricky Martin, Enrique Iglesies and Jennifer Lopez made music with elements of different Latin styles and became incredibly successful in the United States and around the world.

MUSIC

MUSIC

The modern trends of mixing and matching represent the core elements of American music. As with most things American, the music is a mixture of many different styles that have originated from the myriad roots of the American peoples. Not yet fully integrated, but not exactly distinct and segregated, American music is a mirror for American life and culture, reflecting and embedding its cultures in a way unlike any other art form.

SAINT SELENA

For Texans, Tejano music fans and Latin-Americans throughout the USA, the vocally talented Selena is as much of an idol and an icon as Elvis or Marilyn. By age 23, when she was shot to death by a disgruntled employee, Texas-born Selena (Quintanilla Perez) was beloved as the Queen of Tejano music, had a Grammy and was responsible for a thriving beauty and clothing boutique chain in Texas.

Since her death in 1995 her fame has grown through tributes, movies, books and documentaries. Her grave at Seaside Cemetery in her native Corpus Christi draws thousands each week – one of many Selena pilgrimage sites in that town. Her life reflects the complexities, contradictions, accommodations and rich opportunities that living on the border – any border – produces.

A native speaker of English, she learned Spanish to extend her audience reach (earning some raised eyebrows for her Texas accent as well as sky-high ratings in the Spanish charts). She preferred the Anglicised pronunciation of her name: Suh-LEE-nuh, not Say-LAY-nuh. Her fans are both English and Spanish speakers. She put her own stamp on Tejano (tay-HA-no) – the music of the Texas-Mexico border and itself a blend of polka, pop, Tex-Mex rhythms and mariachi – and is credited for being true to her roots, her Americanness and herself.

MUSIC

COUNTRY

The image of country is working class, Southern, rural, as American as NASCAR and free-market capitalism (so runs the tale). But like pie-in-the-sky economics, American country music isn't simply American anymore. Heck, it never was, not really. Many songs of early Appalachian country were transported Scottish and Irish ballads from the 18th century and before; songs reborn in the folk revival of the 1950s and '60s (think 'Tom Dooley' and 'Knoxville Girl').

Depending upon your source, old-time country stole its banjo either from African-American slaves or from the white Minstrel Show performers of the early and mid-19th century, who borrowed from and parodied black performers. Country's musical roots reside in the blues, gospel and pop, and its voice has likewise varied over the years, pulling in strands of other popular music genres for good (the jump of swing) and bad (the lull of pop orchestration).

Beyond its international debts, country has exported its product across national borders and won converts and spurred artistic imports all over hill and dale. Canada sent down country legend Hank Snow, radio sweetheart Anne Murray, and video pin-up Shania Twain. Ageless warbler Slim Whitman crossed the Atlantic in the 1950s to become bigger in the UK than he ever was Stateside. In Australia Slim Dusty followed the path of Woody Guthrie to forge a country music that's more outback than Ayers Rock. Japanese bluegrass fiddler Shoji Tabuchi overcame the essential conservatism of country fans to become the most expensive ticket in Branson, MO, the country music mall of America.

In America the audience of country music is no longer just the Southern rural working class. For one, the new South doesn't fit that profile. Increasingly its population is urban and suburban, much of it transplanted from the North, reversing the process of labour movements after WWII. Although its lyrics evoke the rural South, country music travels well past those borders. With 20% of the national radio market, country has become the nation's dominant radio format, a designation it earned in the 1990s, on the coat-tails of Garth Brooks, a popular favourite.

MUSIC

Like most popular music, country sings mostly about love gained and lost (lots of it lost, a running moan across all country music styles, white blues, honky tonk and radio country).

In the 1940s the country music industry centred in Nashville, thanks largely to Roy Acuff and Hank Williams, who made the city the mecca for songwriters it is today (although Austin and Los Angeles remain regional hubs of a more Western sound). From those Nashville songwriters come the nearly self-parodic titles that define country to outsiders: 'I'll Hold You in My Heart (Till I Can Hold You in My Arms)', 'Pick Me Up On Your Way Down', 'The Last Word In Lonesome is Me', 'Heaven's Just a Sin Away', 'Friends in Low Places'.

Country music has been commercial from the start, but the commercial pressures that have pushed country music performers have too often sent it towards a pop sound and eroded its core of deep feeling, basic instrumentation and raw vocalisation. Eddy Arnold went from a wandering cowboy in the 1940s to a country Perry Como by the 1960s, a path soon trod by Ray Price, whose song 1970 song, 'For the Good Times', is worlds away from his shuffling 1956 hit, 'Crazy Arms'.

Patsy Cline's vocals remained heartfelt throughout her career but she didn't enjoy great commercial success until her musical backing became more night club than honky tonk and she moved from bar girl to chanteuse. Dolly Parton had already conquered country in the mid-1970s when she set her sights on the big world of pop, moving two doors down to a mainstream sound that featured drum kits and synthesisers, leaving her stellar songwriting ('Jolene', 'Coat of Many Colors') behind, and making enough money along the way to open Dollywood, her own Appalachian 'Disneyworld' in Pigeon Forge, Tennessee.

There's a lot to be said for Tony Bennett, Frank Sinatra, Bing Crosby and the smooth singers that made *Your Hit Parade* the listening post of middle-of-the-road America. Tin Pan Alley created some of the finest music of the 20th century, and crooners from

Gene Austin to Harry Connick Jr, have rendered them with elegance and style. But crooners aren't country anymore than rockers are. As Dale Watson has put it, 'Rock and roll back in the '70s are country hits today'. For all the greater commercial success that cross-over sound has given country, modern country production values like tinkling pianos, crashing cymbals, backing synthesisers and rocking lead guitars don't redefine country so much as push it into other camps. That cross-over appeal allows Faith Hill and LeAnn Rimes to make both the Billboard country and Adult Contemporary top ten.

GRAND OLE OPRY

The Grand Ole Opry got its start in Nashville, Tennessee in 1925 and has been a beacon for country performers ever since. Once a more-or-less regional gig offering another weekend entertainment option, over the years it has become a steadfast tourist attraction, especially since 1974 when the Opry moved itself to Opryland.

Popular as he once was, Hank Williams Sr himself might not make it on mainstream country radio today. Fifty years after his death, Williams remains the standard bearer for the deep country that endures in artists like Dale Watson. In part, Williams' status arises from the hard-living, self-destructive tendencies that had him dead at 29, the embodiment of Faron Young's 'Live Fast, Love Hard, Die Young'. But more than his biography, Hank Williams represents the apex of real country music because he was a direct, emotional singer and its best songwriter. Williams understood the appeal of the country song: not just three chords and truth, but a vocal delivery that crawled around the corners of a spare lyric and rendered it with an intensity and twang that carried the dust of an Alabama dirt road.

The best country music knows the lyrical and musical conventions of the genre, pushes its boundaries, discovers the personal and distinct in the general and familiar, turns a phrase in ways not silly (Bobby Bare's 'Dropkick Me, Jesus') but scary, sad, smart and true (DeMent's 'You've Done Nothing Wrong'). The best country music echoes and distorts our own pains and pleasures, lets us whoop it up, mourn sudden betrayal, or just cry quiet, cathartic tears. And who among us doesn't need that?

COMMUNITY BANDS

Many small communities throughout the USA have community bands – made up of citizens whose clarinets or trumpets would otherwise gather dust – which perform throughout the summer at free concerts in public bandstands, riverside parks, gazebos or parades (Flag Day in June, Fourth of July in July, Labor Day in September). The marches of American 'March King' John Philip Sousa are a familiar staple.

CAJUN

Cajun music essentially is the equivalent of country or folk music but from a tiny area in South Central Louisiana, particularly around Lafayette and the surrounding areas in which French Acadians (Cajuns) settled a couple of hundred years ago from Canada. It comes out of an impoverished, Anglo environment, similar to bluegrass and, unlike blues, which is strictly an African-American tradition. The lyrics in Cajun music, not surprisingly, are often French.

Cajun music uses some less traditional instruments, such as accordion and washboard which is played with spoons. People from Southern Louisiana like Cajun music for the most part because it gives them an original musical tradition to identify with and of which to be proud. One of the most prominent uses of the Cajun music style by a huge, mainstream popular artist was by Paul Simon on his mid-1980s album *Graceland*. Clifton Chenier, a famous Cajun accordion player, performed on that album and is mentioned in one of the song's lyrics.

MUSIC

FOLK MUSIC

Believe it or not, the conservative, wonkish Washington, DC is home to many traditions encompassed by the umbrella term 'folk music' – and it is one place where it is easy to hear folk performers without getting lost in the mountains. Proximity to the bluegrass and traditional string band music of the Appalachian mountain region has produced a strong local following for these musical forms, both among audiences and performers.

The Irish, Scottish and other Celtic music which, combined with African-American influences, were the foundation of bluegrass and traditional mountain music are well represented locally. Many coffee houses and clubs feature music in these traditions, along with many forms of singer-songwriter performance. The Birchmere club in nearby Alexandria, Virginia is a prime venue for all manner of folk, blues and traditional music performance, including many national and international touring artists.

ART MUSIC

Besides the vernacular musical forms, American music has nurtured a classical tradition. The late Aaron Copland is at the top of the list of 20th-century renowned composers, followed by his near-contemporary Charles Ives. Copland's symphonic work incorporates vernacular and folk themes in a recognisable way, whereas Ives conveys Americana in a less obvious manner – sort of the difference between artist Grant Wood, known for the dour, pitchfork-holding couple in *American Gothic*, and Jackson Pollock, whose splatter paintings of the middle decades of the 20th century covered new ground in American art.

More recent composers have continued with both innovation and reflection on contemporary themes, among them the late Frank Zappa, minimalist Philip Glass and the prolific Augusta Read Thomas.

MUSIC

One of the great cultural resources in Washington, DC is the annual Festival of American Folklife sponsored by the Smithsonian Institution and The National Park Service. It takes place in late June and early July each year on the mall between the federal buildings and Smithsonian museums. The festival features music, food, crafts, history and culture from a wide range of US and international traditions.

FAMOUS FESTIVALS

Santa Fe Opera (NM)
opera 'out of the box' and (partially) under New Mexico skies

Tanglewood
site in Lenox, MA holding a range of famous festivals and concerts and the summer home of the Boston Symphony Orchestra

Aspen Music Festival (CO)
set in the Colorado Rockies, it runs concurrently with a famous music school during the summer months

Monterey Jazz Festival (CA)
long-running and important summer jazz festival on California's central coast

New Orleans Jazz Festival (LA)
held for one week every spring, this festival focuses on jazz, blues and pop and features parades, exhibitions and music workshops

Newport (RI)
site of the equally venerable JVC Jazz Festival

Ravinia (Ravinia, IL)
summer home of the Chicago Symphony Orchestra and international summer festival of performing arts

SLANG & JARGON

Creativity in language comes in many forms, from the 'high' forms of poetry, verbal games and performance to the equally creative, but less valued vernacular forms: advertising slogans and product names and slang.

Slang has a social function – to differentiate groups, to mark insider from outsider. It is often ephemeral, but some terms persist over time and over generations ('cool' and 'hot'; 'hella' in California). Slang is usually found in more casual, less formal contexts, among friends or close associates. Just as most people dress up in good clothes for church or synagogue, fancy restaurants or awards ceremonies, most people easily shift into a more slang-free manner of speaking required for more formal occasions or distant interactions.

The lines are somewhat blurry but slang is referred to as jargon when it becomes part of the convention and practice of a profession. It still differentiates insider from outsider, but its function is to also help get the job done; jargon encodes shared knowledge and eliminates the need for constant re-explanations. It saves time. Journalists talk about grafs and ledes (paragraphs, first grafs of a story), school administrators about FTEs and classified personnel (full-time equivalent students and secretaries), cops about perps and collars (bad guys), doctors about procedures (operations) and sailors about popping the chute (deploying the spinnaker).

The examples listed here are slang usages (and a little bit of jargon) that have persisted over time and will likely be around for some time to come although, because it's slang, there are no guarantees on that.

SLANG & JARGON

GREETINGS

hey bitch!

to mark connection and friendship, this phrase is only used among close women friends. Depending on who's talking to whom, it can be insulting.

que pasa?

the Spanish equivalent, as used by white teens and college students among friends and peers of 'what's happening?'; very friendly and casual and often paired with other markers of solidarity like 'dude': 'Hey dude. Que pasa?'

whassup? waazup?

this African-American vernacular English greeting has been adopted by advertising and is now an oft-heard greeting among younger people of all backgrounds

yo, hey, hey there, howdy

informal greetings that can also be used among strangers

QUE PASA?

Many Spanish terms have been adopted into mainstream English:

hola	hello
que pasa?	what's happening?; wazzup?
gracias	thank you
adios	goodbye

RESPONSES

as if!

    a sarcastic response, contradicting or negating the other person's comment: 'He said he heard I was from the Valley. As if!'

duh! cha! sha!

    duh is a classic retort, used when someone says something obvious and unnecessary: 'If I hadn't run the red light, I wouldn't have gotten that ticket.' 'Duh.' It can be said with level or falling intonation, or the vowel can be lengthened and the pitch varied ('duuuuhhhhh'). A variant in California is 'Cha!', similar to the response 'Sha!' from the movie *Wayne's World.*

no shit, Sherlock

    another 'that-was-obvious' response

thank you for sharing

    a sarcastic response uttered when the listener didn't really want to hear what the speaker had to say, often because the information shared was too graphic or personal – about either party: 'Your hair looks awful.'; 'Thank you for sharing.'; 'I thought the oatmeal looked like vomit.'; 'Thank you for sharing.'

W

    'Whatever', expressed with the fingers forming the letter W or as the shorthand letter in email

whatever, whuh

    a response that is used frequently to indicate 'it doesn't make any difference', 'I don't want to pursue this topic', 'Up to you – your turn to reply' or 'I really don't have a meaningful comment on that'. It can be interjected at almost any point, even as a conversational filler like 'um' or 'uh'. The shortened form is 'whuh'. Given the reported similarities between the 2000 presidential candidates on many issues, a metropolitan newspaper had this front page headline after one of the pre-election debates: 'Gore. Bush. Whatever.'

SLANG & JARGON

OTHER TERMS

24/7

24 hours a day, 7 days a week, all the time, continually, constantly. Once used only among teens, it's now used to refer to full coverage for Internet commerce

all over, stoked

really excited about something: 'I'm all over that party tonight, dude.'

awesome

great, wonderful, cool, totally cool, spectacular. Used as an adjective ('that was an awesome thing you did', 'that's awesome coffee', 'you are awesome') or an exclamation. Often lengthened in speech: 'Awwwwesome!'

check it out

listen up, I have something to say

chill

take it easy, calm down

chill pill

to indicate a need to calm down: 'You need a chill pill.' (medication not literally suggested)

chill'n

massively hip, hanging out

crap out

quit, got tired: 'He crapped out on me.'

dis

to show disrespect to someone, either by actions or words: 'Carol dissed us by not coming to our party.'

DJ, deejay

disk jockey – someone on radio or at parties who sets up the recorded music for the occasion; a special position in hip hop

dropping bass

when people who have installed speakers in their cars turn up the bass very loud as they drive around the streets

eye candy, arm candy
> generally a woman, someone who looks good or makes some-one (a male who is accompanying her) look good, and thus it suggests a superficial appreciation or relationship – often to raise social status. A model is arm candy.

flake
> forget to do something: 'We had dinner plans but she flaked on me.'

honkin'
> very windy (sailing slang); can also mean 'big' as in 'Her tattoo was honkin.'

my bad
> my error or my mistake

pig out
> to feast on food

skank
> raunchy girl

sucks
> this word – which marks something unfavourable – still causes shivers among older speakers as a taboo word you wouldn't use in polite company, but for people under 40 it's popular. 'It sucks' or 'He sucks' is a common reply to, or comment on, any unfavourable or undesirable situation or person.

trophy wife
> a spouse who is often younger than her husband and meets a standard of beauty and attractiveness

veg, veg out
> to sit around and do nothing

whack
> to kill

what's the deal?
> what's going on?; tell me about the situation

wigger
> a white person who acts or appears to want to be black, used among teens. Generally very derogatory.

SLANG & JARGON

SURF SPEAK

So much of skate speak, snowboard speak, slacker speak and general California speak comes from Southern California surfer speak. And a lot of surfer speak goes beyond the act of surfing and is used in general conversation. Here's a small sample;

ankle slappers
  tiny waves that aren't worth surfing

burly
  very cold outside

closed out
  describes a wave face that is breaking all at once; also means unsurfable: 'It's closed out today.'

the green room
  inside the tube of a wave

grommet
  disciple of a soul surfer, surfing novice ('gremlin') or surf groupie ('dismo')

grunts
  food: 'Let's grab some grunts.'

gun, big gun
  surfboard; big guns are usually longboards

hair ball
  a big wave that is surfable: also 'grinder'

hard core
  tough, dedicated, committed

insane
  totally great: 'Look at those insane waves.'

locals only
  the prevailing attitude in many surf sports – surfers often don't like outsiders coming in to crowd the waves

nip factor
  how cold it is outside

quiver
  your collection of surfboards

raw
  excellent: 'Hey, you've got some raw moves, man.'

SLANG & JARGON

shred
  to surf very well
skegging
  a lot of fun
soul surfer
  a surfer who surfs for the feel not the look: 'Those who understand cannot explain, those who explain do not understand.'

RANDOM IN LA

One of the biggest linguistic differences newcomers notice about LA is the use of the ubiquitous word 'random'.
A versatile word, 'random' can be used in every part of
speech in Southern California. Meaning varying degrees
of unlikeliness, unexpectedness, randomness, it is easy
to pick up and use. When there is nothing else to say,
interject with 'Random' and it is almost always appropriate. You hear the phrase everywhere.

- as a noun, 'a random' is usually an unwelcome person or a bunch of strangers: 'We went out with a bunch
  of randoms.' or 'The bar was filled with a bunch of
  randoms from UCLA.' Used in a dismissive way.
- as an adjective it is used similarly: 'The guy from
  UCLA was so random.'; 'I totally went off on a random tangent when I was talking to her.'
- as a verb it is a little more restricted, usually only
  used when talking about oneself: 'I totally
  randomed the get-together' can either mean 'I
  crashed a party' or it can mean 'my presence
  made things awkward', ie, 'I intruded in a group
  of good friends.'
- as an adverb it means unexpectedly or strangely:
  'We randomly went out in Westwood tonight.'
- most often used as an exclamation: 'Random!' It
  can apply to anything out of the ordinary or odd.
  'Random! I can't believe you just said/did that!'

stoked

intense feeling about something awesome you did

styling

surfing really well; aka 'killing it'

walled up

when the entire wave breaks at the same time. One can't ride walls without getting 'worked'.

worked

crushed by a wave

Wilma

a dumb babe

zipper

a fast-breaking wave

SKATE TALK

aggro

intense

bail

prematurely exit the trick, crash

cobb'n

southern word for 'raging'

flip tricker

someone who flips the board. A flip tricker does 'shifties' (which are shifts on the board in the air) and 'slappies' (doing a trick on a curb or an object).

fully

complete, solid, true or 'I'm serious'

Kodak courage

an extra dose of courage; the tendency to go beyond one's usual physical limits when being filmed or photographed (also used in other action sports such as snowboarding and extreme skiing)

making lines

performing as many tricks in a row as possible. This pertains more to skiing and snowboarding.

manual
> rolling on only one set of wheels, either front or back

rager
> a great skater, aka 'ripper'

ride
> skate

sick
> awesome: 'That was a sick move.' Used also in surfing, skiing and snowboarding.

SLANG & JARGON

MADE IN CALIFORNIA

such the X
> this phrase is used by people in place of 'a' and indicates something superlative: 'I am such the rock star for getting an A on my midterm.'

rock star
> this term gets thrown around like people would use 'hero' everywhere else in the United States. As the term has become more common it is also used as a compliment, to mean a cool person. But in that context you say it about people you know well, not someone you have just met: 'You are such the rock star.'

aggro
> aggravated or annoyed, often used with 'all': 'He had a bad day so he was all aggro when he got home.'

misto
> missing, often a substitute for MIA (missing in action) which is in common usage. Used when someone who is usually around is not: 'Rachel has been misto lately because of her deadlines.'

rad, dope
> excellent, great

GAY TALK

Gay culture is marked by language usage – slang, jargon, terms and neologisms – as well as ways of talking (pronunciation, manner of complimenting and putting down, tone of voice, ways to signal disagreement or connection) that characterise the community and create cohesion. 'Queer' is a term that is still used pejoratively, but has been reappropriated by gays as a word of self-reference.

While cities and neighbourhoods have become comfortable places for gays to live in the USA, homophobia is still rampant in many parts of the country, leading to tragedies like the murder of college student Matthew Shepard, whose death highlights the very kind of pervasive hate some Americans still foster for gay people as he was murdered for no reason, save his sexual orientation.

bear
  self-affirming description of a large and hairy gay or bisexual man
butch
  a masculine man or woman, usually signified by a short hair-cut as well as dress, carriage and attitude
clone
  a type of gay male known for wearing the same basic 'uniform' day in and day out. 'Castro Clone' is a frequently used term referring to the homogeneous look of the men who cruise Castro Street in San Francisco.
the closet
  metaphorical closed-in place that people 'come out of' when they announce to their friends and family that they are gay. Such an announcement is called 'coming out', which echoes the language of society debutante balls.
come out (of the closet)
  to reveal and be open about your sexuality to the world around you
dish
  the latest gossip, or a 'hot guy' in drag queen parlance

dyke
>   similar to 'fag' for men, a sometimes pejorative term used for lesbians and bisexual women that has been reclaimed by many homosexual women to describe themselves

fag
>   a pejorative term used by heterosexuals for a gay person, but now reappropriated by gay people as a political statement. Don't try using it unless you are a bonafide member of the club!

fag hag
>   straight woman who hangs out with gay and bisexual men, and whose love interests are often, frustratingly, gay men

femme
>   a feminine woman or man; often juxtaposed with 'butch', though less so now than in the mid to late 20th century

gaydar
>   the well-honed ability to know when there are homosexuals in the house

gender identity
>   a term for how male or female one feels, regardless of the sex one was born into

girlfriend
>   a term for women who are lovers; also a gay male term of endearment, which started out as a black straight female term

GLBT

an umbrella term for people who aren't straight. It stands for Gay, Lesbian, Bisexual and Transgender.

in transition

the process by which a transgender person physically and psychologicall changes from one gender to the other; changed can include taking hormones, surgery, and altering dress, name and pronouns

Nellie

a term used by gay people to describe overly prissy and bitchy gay men

outing, to out

announcing that someone else is gay, when that person didn't want the news to become public. Seen as an act of aggression. Allegedly coined by *Time* magazine, but made famous by the work of ACT-UP (AIDS Coalition to Unleash Power) and the writings of Michelangelo Signorile.

PWAs

People With AIDS

queen

can be a generic term gay men use to refer to themselves, but it is usually used to describe an effeminate, melodramatic person; somewhat pejorative

transgender

an umbrella term for people whose gender is not rigidly and biologically defined; can include cross-dressers, people in transition, butch women and transsexuals

trolls

a pejorative term for older gay men

TV

transvestite, drag

twink

a young, often inexperienced, gay or bisexual man

A number of notable places, people, events and symbols have become well known in America's gay community and indeed around the world:

Castro District
> a neighbourhood in central San Francisco with a large gay community; for some, ground zero for the gay universe

Female FYI
> a lesbian humour magazine with a fun, irreverent, sex-positive slant

pink triangle
> a symbol of pride for gay and bisexual men, which originated in the Holocaust when gay men in concentration camps were forced to wear a pink triangle to mark themselves as gay.

rainbow flag
> a gay pride symbol, this is a flag of different colors in horizontal bands that represents the diversity within the GLBT community

Stonewall
> the name of a club in New York where, in 1969, dozens of gay men, lesbians and drag queens fought back to defend themselves against a routine police raid of gay bars. This gave rise to the US gay pride movement and increased visibility and acceptance of GLBT people. 'Remember Stonewall' is a term that evokes the tragedy of the ongoing raids and rallies people to work for further gay rights.

BUSINESS & CORPORATE WORLD

In the USA, language in the business world is a fast-moving target. What becomes acceptable business terminology tends to ricochet from one management fad-of-the-month to another, driven by hype in the business press, the latest management self-help books by corporate consultants, technological change and New! Improved! business models. 'Harnessing the power of the Internet' is the most recent rage, so the purveyors of business language are talking about networking, internetworking and all manner of e-business, e-strategy, e-learning and e-marketing. Now that the dot-com boom has gone bust, even these high-tech terms will cycle in and out of favour. This selection of terms and phrases provides a starting point.

B2B
> business to business; a profit model seen as more lucrative than B2C (business to consumer) or C2C (consumer to consumer)

bleeding edge
> newer than cutting edge technologies; may not be tested as thoroughly

blue chip
> dependable stock of an established corporation that can be relied upon to maintain a high purchase price per share

cubicle farm
> term for an office in which employees use cubicles as workspaces – pretty much the majority of offices in the USA

the Dow
> short for Dow Jones Industrial Average (DJIA), an index of 40 blue-chip stocks used to gauge the overall health of the US stock market (and therefore its economy)

drop the ball
> slacking on one's responsibilities

given the pink slip
> fired (or made redundant)

head hunter
> person who hires top talent away from a competitor or an employment agency for management personnel

SLANG & JARGON

in the black
    posting a profit
in the red
    posting a loss
junk bonds
    high risk, potentially high yield bonds
McJob
    a term first noted by Canadian author Douglas Coupland in
    his book *Generation X*; ostensibly used by overeducated slacker
    youth to describe the endless stream of low-pay, low-brain,
    no-future jobs available to them
white knight
    a company that saves another from a hostile takeover by be-
    nevolent investment

MONDO EXPANDO

blunt
    an emptied cigar that is then re-rolled with a large
    quantity of marijuana. A very good demonstration
    of this can be seen in the film *Kids*.
dank
    very high quality
expando
    marijuana
riding the white horse
    on cocaine
rolling
    being on X (Ecstasy)
shwag
    lower quality weed that is loose and not in the form
    of buds – very popular for rolling blunts

TRUCKER SLANG

Truckers became cultural icons in the 1980s, no doubt in part due to the popularity of the movie *Smokey and the Bandit*, as well as the proliferation of CB (citizens band) radios and the popularity of CB handles, or nicknames, not dissimilar to email names – for example, freshpeach@nowhere.com.

The trucking industry is organised by one of the nation's most powerful labour unions, the International Brotherhood of Teamsters (IBT).

Besides being woven into the country's economic and political fabric, trucker culture is part of popular culture too. The open road, restless movement, geographic autonomy – and real blue-collar connection to people and landscape – are part of the romantic appeal. Truckers have been immortalised in song, film, comedy routine and academic tome.

As well as their mythic appeal, truckers have a language all of their own, developed as a kind of CB shorthand.

alligator
    a bad piece of tyre in the road
bad shoe
    flat tyre
bear in the air
    CB lingo for cops in aeroplanes checking for speeders
boogie
    top gear
Boy Scouts
    state police
breaker
    another CB user wants to break into the channel
bug out
    a CB user is leaving the channel
bumper sticker
    a car that is following too closely
Christmas tree
    truck with lots of lights around it

SLANG & JARGON

SLANG & JARGON

county mounty
  highway patrol
feed the bears
  get a ticket
lot lizard
  (truck stop) prostitute
new shoe
  new tyre
ole smoky
  cop
rig
  truck
road dog
  hitchhiker or street person
tarp your load
  put a condom on; trucker graffiti found on truck stop condom machines
tonka toy
  big truck
window wash
  a rainstorm

In addition to the slang, there are unofficial '10-codes'. For example, 'What's your twenty?' or 10-20, is 'Where are you?' or 'What's your location?'. 10-34 means 'Trouble at this station, help needed'. Perhaps the most familiar in the US is 10-4 which means 'OK, message received.'

PENTAGON

The Pentagon in Arlington, Virginia, across the river from Washington, DC is the headquarters of the United States Department of Defense and its nerve centre for command and control. The building houses 23,000 military and civilian employees and about 3000 non-defence support personnel. It also hosts a unique, longstanding culture with its own ways of talking and jargon. Occasionally the jargon will make it to the outside and civilians will be able to read about 'weapons of mass destruction' and their consequence, 'collateral damage'.

Perhaps the most significant phrase to enter the popular and political culture from the military in the 1990s was 'Don't ask, don't tell'. This is the policy by which gays in the military are allowed a certain measure of tolerance – the military are not to ask and the individuals are not to tell.

The US Coast Guard is part of the Department of Transportation during peace time, but during war it becomes part of the Department of the Navy. There are also reserve forces for each of the forces, including the Coast Guard as well as an Army National Guard, an Air National Guard and about half a million individuals. These reserve forces represent about half of the total uniformed force of the USA, according to the DoD (Department of Defense) Web site.

The Pentagon – named for its five-sided shape – was completed in 1943 to consolidate the 17 buildings occupied by the War Department. It is designed for efficiency; despite 17.5 miles (28km) of corridor, the average walk between any two points in the building is only seven minutes.

Some phrases, words and acronyms used regularly are:

ate up
    messed up
Bird Colonel
    distinguishes him from a Lieutenant Colonel
blue top
    Pentagon press release

SLANG & JARGON

BOHICA
Bend Over, Here It Comes Again (when things are just not working out the way you thought they should)

cannon cocker
artilleryman

fly boys
the Air Force

full bird
slang for a full colonel in the Army or Marine Corps

ground pounders
any ground force

grunts
the Army

gunney
slang term for Gunnery Sergeant in Field Artillery Battery

jar heads, leathernecks
the Marine Corps

LHA
Luxury Hotel Afloat (Marine term for a Navy ship)

marching jodie
song or verse to help marching soldiers keep cadence

milicrat
military bureaucrat

old man
any commander

queen
infantryman; used because the Infantry is known as the Queen of Battle

rocket jockeys
Air Force pilots

Roger that
I agree, I understand

smoke
slang term for Chief of Firing Battery in the Field Artillery

SNAFU
Situation Normal, All Fouled Up ('fouled' is the polite word for 'fucked')

squid
Army's name for a Navy personnel

swabbies
the Navy

top
slang term for First Sergeant (Senior Sergeant in a Company or Battery)

Uncle Sugar
Federal Government

WETSU
We Eat This Stuff Up ('stuff' is the polite word for 'shit')

Wilco
Will Comply

zoomies
Air Force pilots

'Hooah' means 'I hear you', 'I understand you', 'good job', 'excellent', etc. It is probably the most understood slang in the Army – most other branches have the same or similar sounds.

SLANG & JARGON

PSYCHOBABBLE

'Psychobabble' was actually a term that arose during the latter part of the 20th century in response to a variety of popularised, or pop, versions of psychology. The term is typically used as a put-down of a set of ideas, a way to trivialise both the person espousing the ideas and the ideas themselves, particularly when a person not formally trained in psychology uses its terminology in conversation with others also not formally trained in psychology. The term psychobabble is rarely used in educated, polite or sophisticated circles. It is not politically correct and can be considered offensive.

Psychology in the United States, no less than elsewhere, has diverged widely from the writings of Freud. Different schools or types of psychology are used to respond to different needs. Often their boundaries blur across body-spirit-mind and are likely to include consideration of intuition, dreams, hypnotherapy, breath- and bodywork, energy movement and channelling, 12-Step or Recovery programs based on traditions established by Alcoholics Anonymous, and self-expression through art, drama or other means.

Currently you may encounter forms of psychology which draw from new technologies. It is possible to find, for example, online counsellors – presumably licenced and available in real-time. There is also an evolving field called cyberpsychology which explores how people react to and behave within the psychological dimen- sions of environments created by computers and online networks.

Terms that have entered the popular lexicon:

actualize
  to manifest one's infinite potential
adult child
  one whose childhood experiences have left them with limited resources for dealing with adult situations; used in Recovery/ 12-step circles
affirmations
  phrases read or said to oneself to induce or enhance courage, resilience, self-esteem and strength

baggage

> unresolved emotional concerns from past relationships that affect the way one behaves in the present

boundaries

> the place where you stop and I begin; often delineated when someone gathers the courage to say no

channelling

> acting as a conduit for energy other than one's own

consciousness, mindfulness, presence

> paying attention to what you're doing and to the moment at hand

higher self

> your in-tune, in-touch, spiritually together self

I hear you

> an indication that you've been really listening, perhaps at an emotional level, to your conversational partner

I need my space

> room to think, breathe; also used to create distance in a relationship when one lacks the words necessary for rejecting another

inner child

> a part of one's self which lacks adequate resources for dealing with adult situations because of past trauma; in recovery circles, one can re-parent oneself, often under the tutelage of a person more experienced in recovery, called a sponsor

issues

> deep psychological difficulties: 'It appears you have issues with your father.'

male bonding

> a movement that encourages men to expose their emotions to one another and to find authentically masculine approaches to doing so

past-life regression

> in this practice, based on concepts of reincarnation, one is led to re-experience the many past lives of the soul

process

> the way you 'do' life or work out your issues

SLANG & JARGON

recovery
> a process of healing from an addiction and learning alternate coping strategies

safe space, safe place
> a place that allows you the safety to heal from past emotional wounds so that you can process, then let go of, your baggage or issues

shrink, head shrinker
> psychiatrist

survivor
> one who has recovered from past victimisation

'Thank you for sharing'
sometimes used sarcastically, but in serious groups, an expression of gratitude and recognition that someone risked extreme emotional vulnerability to share

toxic
> unhealthy: 'This is an emotionally toxic relationship.'

MOVIES

Movies are made and movies are watched. Then they're critiqued and, you know what they say, 'everyone's a critic'. Even movie critics have spawned a catchphrase or two, like 'Two thumbs up!' (Its variant: 'Two thumbs up! Way up!'). This phrase from Chicago film critics Roger Ebert and the late Gene Siskel, known for their weekly televised movie reviews, means full approbation and approval. The phrase has been taken outside the realm of film. It can also be used to refer to something excellent in general, as in response to a great meal, for instance.

Movie stages are called sound stages – and the sound stages are something of a metaphor for Hollywood, the heart of the film industry itself. They are large, plain and hangar-like on the outside, but inside are filled with fanciful recreations of just about any place in the world, or in other worlds.

In LA you hear about entertainment like you'd hear about politics in DC, or the tech industry in San Jose, or chili in Texas. Here are some basics to follow the conversation:

Industry Speak

above the line
  costs incurred before filming even begins – it's the creative people whose salaries can fluctuate a great deal, including the main actors and director. Below the line is technical crew, whose salaries are fairly standard.

close-up
  a shot from the head up

coverage
  a synopsis and critique written about a script, often by interns or junior agents. A document used by bigwigs as a reference or guideline for whom to sign and what scripts to buy.

DGA
  Directors Guild of America

gross
  the amount of money a movie earns in ticket sales before the proceeds are divided up by the various participants: the studio, theatres and so forth

honey wagon
> a trailer with actors' dressing rooms in it. You see them on the streets of LA and New York all the time; it's one of the signs that filming is going on somewhere nearby.

the industry
> the entertainment industry; very few will call it 'the Biz', and those that do are probably wannabes

in the can
> a film that has completed photography; not yet released and possibly not finished

juicer
> electrician on a movie set; lesser used term is 'sparker'

leaving word
> this term is known in several media industries; it means leave a message

the majors
> the top film studios: Universal, Paramount, Disney, Sony, Warner Brothers, MGM/UA and 20th Century Fox

numbers
> a production's performance at the box office, ie, how many tickets sold. Alternately, a TV show's performance in the Nielsen Ratings, a measure of how many households watched a given program.

Q
> celebrity's recognisability quotient

rip-o-matic
> a video of storyboards used to entice production companies into investing in your project. Alternately, editing together of pre-existing movie footage to show one's editing style.

SAG
> Screen Actors Guild

skin flick
> pornographic movie

specs
> you'll hear this word a lot when you're out. It means a script for a TV show or genre that is not sold or produced. It is often used to get agents or to shop for writing jobs. A lot of people in LA are working on specs.

sound bite
    short pithy quote from a subject
stinger
    extension cord
the trades
    daily entertainment-industry trade publications, eg, *Variety*,
    Hollywood Reporter
a treatment
    this is a brief idea for a script that outlines plot and characters,
    and sometimes refers to budgets
walk away
    another way to say, 'That's good, leave it, perfect, stop!'. Used
    on movie sets.

Movie Ratings

The officially stated purpose for movie ratings, developed by the
Motion Picture Association of America, is to inform parents or
guardians about the content and character of American movies.
Always the subject of debate, they often come under heavy fire
from politicians who believe that movie companies market adult-
oriented products to young people.

There is also a great deal of controversy over what gets labelled
R and what's rated with either of the PG ratings, as well as the
difference between what warrants an R versus an NC-17.

With American movies it is well known that it takes a great
deal of violence to move up a notch on the ratings scale but only
a little bit of sexual content to achieve the same effect.

G
    General audiences. Technically this means anyone and every-
    one can come, but it really means the movie is for kids.
PG
    Parental Guidance suggested. This still means anyone can come,
    but parents are advised that some material may not be suitable
    for younger children.
PG-13
    Parents strongly cautioned. This still means that anyone can
    come, but PG-13 warns that the movie may be inappropriate
    for slightly older children, up to the age of 13.

R

Restricted. Children under the age of 17 must be accompanied by a parent or an adult guardian. This is one of the least-understood movie ratings, especially by politicians who think it means the corruption of morals. It still means that anyone can come.

NC-17

No one under 17 admitted.

KLINGON

If you find yourself travelling through the galaxy you may find a few words of Klingon very useful, whether or not your companions are Kirk or Spock. Klingon was invented by Washington (via Berkeley) linguist Marc Okrand for the *Star Trek* series and films. As a linguist, Okrand was able to create not just a few words to make the Klingons sound foreign, but to give it the status of a fully formed language, complete with its own distinctive grammar, vocabulary and orthography – rules, words and spelling. (Later *Star Trek* movies and books that feature Klingons use other alphabets as well, attributed to Michael Okuda.) According to one of the many Web sites on the language, Hamlet has been translated into Klingon, and the bible is next, 'not from English, but from the original Hebrew'. Useful Klingon words and phrases are:

Yes.	HIja' or HISLaH
No.	ghobe'
Yes/OK/I'll do it.	lu' or luq
What's happening?	qaStaH nuq?
Well done!	MajQa'
Where is the bathroom?	nuqDaq 'oH puchpa' 'e'
Huh?	nuqjatlh?
Happy birthday!	qoSlIj DatIvjaj
(to more than one person:)	qoSraj botIvjaj

VISUAL MEDIA

What's a Grip? A Gaffer?

Grips carry stuff. That's the basis of their name. They also assemble, set up and rig stuff. Together with the electricians (who handle specifically lights and power cords), they are the set crew.

A gaffer is the chief electrician. The term comes from the early days of shooting on stages, when the crew used a gaffing hook to reach up and adjust the lights on the overhead lighting rigs. The name stuck even though gaffing hooks are not used any more.

key grip
    chief of the grip squad
best boy grips
    second in command to the grip. (Think of Mr Spock as Captain Kirk's best boy.)
gaffer
    chief of the electrician squad
best boy
    second in command to the gaffer, the electric first mate

AND THAT'S THE WAY IT IS

With each new TV season comes another chance for a new buzz word, catchphrase or slang form to enjoy a brief life span and either fall into obscurity or live on in the collective lexicon. People of a certain age have reported being influenced by the TV show *Friends*. Most noticeable is mimicking the chararacter Chandler's characteristic intonation: 'Could you BE any more annoying? Could I HAVE any more work to do?'. The increasing use of the word 'so' – 'That is SO over' – corresponds approximately to the release of the movie *Clueless*.

Retired CBS news anchor Walter Cronkite, the 'most trusted man in America' in his day, ended each broadcast with a phrase that anyone over 30 remembers: 'And that's the way it is'.

VISUAL MEDIA

TELEVISION

Like the weather, one safe topic of conversation is TV. Ask some-one his or her favourite television program and you'll not lack for chatter. It's even better if you have seen the show yourself, and start up a volley of 'remember when Frasier did X' or 'wasn't that awful when Monica did Y'. TV's a safe conversational bet even when the person hates TV – ask why. You're guaranteed to hear strong words backed by even stronger beliefs.

So widespread is American television that the topic will be an easy one for any visitor to sustain. Many programs have long-running histories; the impact of American TV in other places is so great that many networks and shows now have versions made for specific re-gional markets across the globe. Music Television (MTV) is one such example, with versions now in Latin America, Asia and Europe.

Americans watch a lot of television but they customarily don't think of themselves as doing so. Despite the self-generated image of a healthy, nature-loving population of amateur athletes, most people in the United States are more likely to be found spending their leisure hours in front of a television than on a bicycle or nature trail. It has spawned the term 'couch potato'.

To watch television is to observe a particular set of views of American society, some idealised and some perhaps shocking. In truth the lives of most Americans are neither as wealthy, nor as violent as depicted on TV. Television doesn't reflect what Ameri-can life is really like so much as it shows a set of fantasies of what Americans believe about other Americans.

Part of the fun of watching television is to enjoy forming a morally superior response to it. Sometimes the fun is in the shared experience. Some shows, such as the now-defunct *Melrose Place*, have such a following that in many major cities they're broadcast at local bars; patrons come to watch – and respond loudly for the benefit of their peers.

TV Advertising

Television advertising reflects a number of points about American culture. For instance, television is not particularly sophisticated about the use of nudity and sexuality in advertising (Americans are notoriously puritanical about the body, meaning that they are endlessly fascinated with it). So important are ads to American television that a kind of 'TV holiday' has grown up around them. Each January during the Superbowl – the biggest football game and sporting event of the year – American corporations make a point of showcasing their newest ads. Many people watch the Superbowl just to see the splashy and expensive commercials that will dominate the airwaves for the coming six months.

FRANKLY MY DEAR

- 'Yyyeah, baybee!' [yeah baby]; 'Oh, behayve!' [oh behave] (*Austin Powers*)
- 'Ahl be bahk.' [I'll be back] (Schwarzenegger's signature sign-off from the *Terminator* movies)
- 'Llllllewser!' [loser] (Jim Carrey, whose physical moves are often mimicked)
- What-everrrrrr.' [whatever] This means 'You bore me, I don't care, I'm tired of you', and so forth. (*Clueless*)
- 'Go ahead, make my day.' (Clint Eastwood, *Sudden Impact*)
- 'I love the smell of napalm in the morning.' (*Apocalypse Now*)
- 'Doh!' (Homer Simpson, *The Simpsons*)
- 'Is that your final answer?' (Regis Philbin, *Who Wants to Be a Millionaire?*)
- 'Frankly, my dear, I don't give a damn.' (Clarke Gable, *Gone with the Wind*)
- 'Play it again, Sam.' (conventional misquotation from *Casablanca*)
- 'Blame Canada.' (*South Park*)
- 'Rosebud!' (*Citizen Kane*)

Some TV slogans are so well known that they have entered the American vernacular:

Finger-lickin' good.
    KFC
I like the Sprite in you
    Sprite soft drink
It's Grrrrrrrrrreat!
    Kellogg's Frosted Flakes
I've fallen, and I can't get up.
    ad for medic alert system company
Just Do It
    Nike
Takes a licking and keeps on ticking.
    Timex watches
Whassup?
    Budweiser beer
(See also Advertising & Brand Names in the Influences from US Culture chapter.)

'NOT!'

The semi-antiquated movie *Wayne's World* created an immensely popular usage of the word 'Not!' to negate the sentence immediately preceding it. How amusing to say: 'Your dress looks really awful on you. Not!' Turns out this negation device predates *Wayne's World*. Way. *Great Gatsby* author F. Scott Fitzgerald is reported to have used it, among other notable American writers.

'Election 2000: We Will Remember.' This and other similar bumper stickers will no doubt adorn the motor vehicles of America for some time to come. Here are some essential terms to fill in the gaps when discussing the latest presidential election or antics:

AMERICAN POLITICAL PRIMER

bicameral
> the structure of the US Congress. Literally, it means Congress is composed of two legislative chambers or branches. It is the structure of 49 state legislatures, as well. The Nebraska Legislature is unicameral.

cabinet
> the group of advisors a president appoints to help administer laws and federal programs. Most cabinet members head departments of the Federal Government and are referred to as Secretary of that department.

electoral college
> the venue for winning the presidency. Candidates compete for electors in a winner-take-all election in each of the 50 states. Electors are proportional to a state's population. Each state has the same number of electors as it has members in the House of Representatives and Senate.

impeachment
> method for removing a president from office by bringing the chief executive to trial before the US Senate. The House votes whether to impeach the president, and the Senate votes on whether to remove the president from office. A president may be impeached for 'high crimes and misdemeanors'.

justices
> judges who serve in the federal judiciary. Justices are appointed by the President and approved by the Senate. Nine justices serve on the Supreme Court.

lobbyist

a person engaged by an interest group to influence legislation

majority leader

title given to the leader of the political party who holds the majority of seats in the Senate and in the House of Representatives. The majority leader is elected by members of that political party.

member of congress

technically, any of the 435 members of the House of Representatives or 100 members of the United States Senate. In practice, however, members of the House of Representatives are generally referred to as Congressmen, while members of the Senate are referred to as Senators.

minority leader

title given to the leader of the political party who holds the minority of seats in the Senate and in the House of Representatives. The minority leader is elected by members of that political party.

president

the chief executive of the Federal Government. The President is elected every four years and is limited by the Constitution to two consecutive terms. His chief powers and duties include: proposing legislation to Congress, vetoing legislation passed by Congress, signing legislation into law, and administering law with the help of a cabinet of advisors. The President also delivers an annual State of the Union address to Congress.

POLITICS

senatorial approval
> the process by which the Senate approves treaties (known as ratification) and presidential appointments to the executive (cabinet) and judicial (court) branches of government

senior senator
> the senator from a particular state who has been in office the longest

separation of powers
> the Constitutional delegation of authority to three separate branches of government. Specifically, Congress makes the laws, the President enforces the laws and the Supreme Court interprets discrepancies in the law.

speaker of the house
> presiding officer of the US House of Representatives. The Speaker is elected by the members of the House generally in a party-line vote at the beginning of each Congressional session.

split decision
> a Supreme Court ruling made with some justices voting for the ruling and others voting against it

POLITICAL JARGON

background
> a condition agreed on by a reporter and a source that confirms a fact the reporter suspects but does not allow any type of attribution: 'Staff members tried privately to convince the Senator to resign.'

not for attribution
> a condition agreed on by a reporter and a source that allows information to be used without attributing it to the person by name: 'A source familiar with the investigation.'

off the record
> a condition agreed on by a reporter and a source that allows information to be used without any traceable attribution and only if a reporter can verify it with at least one other source: 'Sources say …'

pencils

> slang term used by press secretaries to refer to print reporters. It refers to the tool they carry and use at a press event. It commonly is used to point print reporters to the seats they occupy during a press event: 'Pencils over there.'

photo op

> an appearance by a politician or government official where television and print photographers are allowed to take pictures, but no questions are asked

pool reporter

> a reporter who is allowed to travel with a politician or government official during specific times when a large press contingent is not feasible. The reporter acts as a surrogate and shares information about the event with other reporters.

press availability

> an appearance by a politician or government official where journalists are allowed to ask questions on topics the journalists decide

press conference

> a formal event called by a politician or government official to announce something

press corps

> the collective body of reporters assigned to cover government and politics in Washington, DC and the 50 state capitals

sticks

> slang term used by press secretaries to refer to television reporters. It refers to the tool they carry (a tripod) and use at a press event. It commonly is used to point cameras to the space they occupy during a press event: 'Sticks over there.'

talking heads

> originally, slang for television anchors who read the news. It has been extended to include guests and political surrogates who appear on political talk shows to give opinions on the news.

POLITICS

POLITICAL CAMPAIGNS

Democrat

one of the two major political parties, organised in 1828 as the result of a split in the Democratic-Republican Party. It is generally considered the more liberal party.

DNC (and DTripleC)

the Democratic National Committee is the official governing body of the Democratic Party. The Democratic Congressional Campaign Committee is a special committee run by Congressional Democrats to raise money and campaign for Democratic Congressional candidates. The DNC and DTripleC raise millions of dollars and provide staff support for national campaigns.

flack

a mid-level campaign spokesperson, such as a deputy press secretary

GOTV (Get Out the Vote)

common rallying cry the campaign field operation makes to mobilise likely voters during the absentee voting period and on election day

hired gun

a consultant with a speciality hired to a campaign for a specific purpose. Generally well paid.

message

a broad theme that states in one or two sentences what a political campaign is about. Issues are couched and presented to voters in that context.

Republican

one of the two major political parties, organised in 1854 to oppose slavery. It is generally considered the more conservative party.

POLITICS

RNC (and RTripleC)

the Republican National Committee is the official governing body of the Republican Party. The Republican Congressional Campaign Committee is a special committee run by Congressional Republicans to raise money and campaign for Republican Congressional Candidates. Like its Democratic counterpart, the RNC and RTripleC raise millions of dollars and provide staff support for national campaigns.

slogan

a snappy phrase that embodies the campaign message: 'Building a Bridge to the 21st Century.'

soft money

money raised by political parties that, by law, can be spent only on party building activities and issue-based advertising. Federal law limits the amount of money a person can contribute to a specific candidate but there is no limit to the amount of money a person can give to a political party. In recent elections some candidates have helped raise soft money that critics say was spent by the parties on activities that benefit their specific candidacies.

spin

the positive slant a campaign offers on an issue, breaking news or a campaign development

spin doctor

hired gun representing politicians and business, whose job is to provide a favourable 'spin' to any news that affects the client. Used to deflect criticism or redefine negative news in a positive light.

two-party system

the unofficial configuration of the American political system. For the entire 20th century two parties – Republicans and Democrats – traded control of the presidency and Congress. Third parties occasionally emerged during presidential elections (1912, 1948, 1980, 1992 and 2000), but none contended seriously for votes in the electoral college.

POLITICS

TIMELESS TERMS

Chippaquiddick
> Massachusetts town near a bridge where Senator Ted Kennedy was involved in an automobile accident that took the life of a young woman passenger in his car. The scandal that followed damaged his chances for the presidency. In the ensuing decade, the name has accrued a metaphorical significance akin to Napolean's Waterloo and is used to refer to tragic incidents that a politician is responsible for that might effectively derail his or her career plans.

Deep Throat
> the still-unidentified source that provided information to the Washington Post during the Watergate investigation. Also the name of a famous porn movie released a few years earlier. Outside of Washington it's become a generic reference for any unnamed source, as in 'Who's your Deep Throat?'.

FLOTUS (Flow-tus)
> the nickname Secret Service, campaign staff and reporters use for the First Lady. It stands for First Lady of the United States.

POTUS (Poh-tus)
> the nickname Secret Service, campaign staff and reporters use for the President. It stands for President of the United States.

the Gipper
> nostalgic nickname president and former actor Ronald Reagan gave himself while campaigning during the 1980s. Reagan would draw cheers from loyalists at campaign rallies when he would challenge Republicans to go out and 'win one more for the Gipper'. In the 1940 classic *Knute Rockne All American*, Reagan played a Notre Dame football player George Gipp, who on his deathbed asks team mates to 'win one for the Gipper'.

the Silver Fox
> pet name President George H.W. Bush used for First Lady Barbara Bush

stagflation
> term used during the late 1970s to describe the puzzle of economic stagnation and high inflation

POLITICS

Watergate

Washington, DC housing and shopping complex – the site of the famous break-in orchestrated by the Nixon White House in the 1970s. Media are so attached to its significance that, 30 years later, virtually any news story that has a hint of scandal draws a tag of (you-name-it)GATE. Contra-gate and Monica-gate are recent examples.

Whitewater

a failed real estate development in Arkansas that was the genesis for an investigation into Hillary and Bill Clinton's financial dealings as the first family of Arkansas. The Clintons eventually were cleared of wrongdoing in the matter.

WIN button

'Whip Inflation Now' buttons (badges) that President Ford encouraged people to wear during the economic downturn in his administration

TEXAS TALK

If someone says something's 'the size of Texas', they mean it's really big. The big state is full of big talk. The Lone Star State has even coined its own term for its own brand of political lore: Texana.

Nicknames have long been part of Texas political culture. When George W Bush ran for governor of Texas in 1994, skeptics dubbed him Shrub (little Bush). Six years later he stepped onto the national stage as a presidential contender with a newer, simpler moniker: 'W'. Rallies were peppered with 'Dubya' ('w' said with a Southern drawl) supporters holding locked thumbs and extended index fingers upward for a handmade replica of the letter.

Bush's predecessor, Ann Richards, was once dubbed the Big Hair by a prominent capital TV reporter struck by the height of her style. That hair, her quick wit and grandmotherly charm catapulted Richards to national prominence in 1988 when she proclaimed that Bush's father was 'born with a silver foot in his mouth'.

POLITICS

Texas Senator Phil Gramm flirted briefly with a presidential bid in 1996. When his campaign failed to draw support from his senatorial colleagues, the explanation was Grammstanding, a term senators had coined for Gramm's habit of taking credit for the work of others.

PROMISES PROMISES

LBJ. Lyndon Baines Johnson, elected 1964 on the slogan 'All the way with LBJ'. He told Americans he was against sending American boys to Asia to fight a war Asian boys should be fighting.

Tricky Dick. Richard Nixon, elected 1968 and 1972 by supporters he termed 'the silent majority'. He told Americans he had nothing to do with the events of the Watergate break-in.

Great Communicator. Ronald Reagan, elected 1980 and 1984 with images of 'morning in America'. He told Americans he didn't know anything about trading arms for hostages in the Iran-Contra affair.

Wimp Factor. George HW Bush, elected 1988 despite questions about his ability to stand up to Congress. He told Americans to 'read his lips' that he would stand firmly behind his pledge of 'no new taxes'.

Slick Willy. Bill Clinton, elected 1992 and 1996 as 'the man from Hope (Arkansas)', promising the most ethical administration in history. Impeached for charges related to perjury, after he told Americans he did not have sexual relations with Monica Lewinsky.

Dubya. George W Bush, elected 2000 in one of the lowest turnouts in modern times. He promised that his administration would end 'a season of cynicism'.

POLITICS

Texas House Speaker Gib Lewis so often mixed metaphors and mangled his grammar that he was credited for creating a language of his own: Gibberish. The daily news conference Lewis held on adjournment of the House came to be known as Gibgab.

The 10 best and worst legislators are ceremoniously named after each session by *Texas Monthly* magazine. A few years back some legislators had done so little during the session that the magazine said it was impossible to distinguish them from their chairs and created a third category: best, worst and furniture. One member served so long and made the list so many times, he was moved to a special category of antique furniture.

POLITICS

COMMERCE & CULTURE

Fast food franchises such as McDonald's and global chains such as the Gap, 7-Eleven or Blockbuster have made a great deal of American culture familiar outside its bounds – and now a great deal of American culture, in turn, has appropriated popular culture from around the world. From Pokémon to pad Thai, from Ichiban anime to Ikea furniture, the global culture is influencing what Americans choose to consume.

Despite the global cross-fertilisation, there are still the American-wrought 'big ones', and they are big: Wal-Mart or Target for everything, Barnes and Noble for books, Starbucks for coffee, Home Depot for do-it-yourself, etc. Big doesn't mean more variety, as is the case with Blockbuster and Hollywood Video, two of the largest video chains in the USA. They have essentially curtailed the production of serious, adult-themed dramatic films by Hollywood filmmakers because of their refusal to carry titles rated NC-17.

ADVERTISING & BRAND NAMES

The reach of advertising and public relations is so prevalent throughout US culture that many of the jargon words and terms used within the 'persuasion industries' are in common usage:

blurb
> short article about a client in the print press; a short article or brief description

flack
> a publicist; someone who speaks on behalf of another

handholding
> reassuring a nervous client or customer

ink
> press coverage

plug
to promote

road block
saturation of the airwaves with ads for the same product to
guarantee viewer awareness and freeze out the competition

teaser
a brief, often provocative, glimpse of a product or show in
order to pique people's interest

Commonly Used Brand Names

Ace bandage
non-adhesive wrap for sprains and strains

Band-aids
adhesive strips for small cuts and scrapes

Bud
Budweiser beer – your basic, cheap, good-time party beer

Coke
either the cola beverage itself, or a regional generic reference to
a soft drink

Dumpster
big metal outdoor container for dumping garbage and refuse

FedEx
Federal Express – overnight delivery service. Also used as a verb:
'I'll FedEx that to you.'

Jacuzzi
spa, Whirlpool

Jell-O
fruit-flavoured gelatin dessert

Kitty Litter
absorbent material in a cat's litter box

Kleenex
tissue for blowing your nose, wiping off makeup, etc

Luckies
Lucky Strike cigarettes

Muzak
nerveless piped music heard in many stores

Off!
insect repellent

Scotch Tape
cellophane (sticky) tape, Sellotape

Starbucks
universal coffee place, and name of its coffee. Starbucks brought 'coffee locutions' into everyone's standard vocabulary and a yearning for lattes to every corner of the USA.

Vaseline
greasy, clear petroleum jelly for chapped lips, baby's bottoms, and rooster combs (makes 'em glisten at the county fair)

Windbreaker
lightweight windproof casual jacket

Xerox
photocopy

DOT-COMS & NEW TECHNOLOGY

Language associated with computers and related technologies has run through so many cycles of change in such a short time that this process could define the 'Internet Revolution' just by itself. Before the Internet made its inroads, it was referred to as the 'information superhighway', a term that has been supplanted by 'e-commerce'. The concept of 'virtual' is edging out the notion of 'cyberspace'. Notions of 'interactivity' are overriding 'community'.

No surprise that words associated with the Internet are in frequent flux, changing as fast as the software and hardware, making it nearly impossible to upgrade linguistically unless you're in the business. Chat rooms, IMing (instant-messaging), newsgroups and technology-assisted interactivity has made the Information Age or the Digital Age an age of new language.

The language of the Information Age is distinctive in part because it attempts to make concrete the fact that cyberspace is electrical pulses and non-tangible data. It is also distinctive because it reflects changing norms in familiar contexts, like conversation, writing and work.

As work cultures have changed in the New Economy, so have job titles; many a high-tech corporation now has a 'chief evangelist', among others. Meanwhile, spelling conventions are changing – becoming phonetic and abbreviated – in the contexts of chat rooms and instant messaging. Shortcuts are used to help typing speed catch up with the speed of normal speech: 'how r u?' 'gr8, u?', 'ok'. Contractions come without apostrophes and capitalisation is overlooked.

Some terms have lost their original cyber-contextual meanings and have filtered into the common lexicon with a more general meaning, phrases such as 'down time' for a break ('I took some down time after my exam') or 'process' for deal with or respond to ('I need some time to process that.').

★ ★ ★ ★ **OLD FOR NEW** ★ ★ ★ ★

Invention can be the mother of language. When scientists began to genetically engineer foodstuffs, someone dubbed it 'frankenfood', but the term never quite caught on. The life span of a new word depends on who invents it, who uses it and how relevant it is.

We borrow words from old technology to describe new technology. The word 'car' comes from the previous mode of transportation, the carriage. The word 'carriage' had come from 'chariot'.

And we still 'roll up' our car windows even though most are power-driven these days and simply rise with the flip of a switch instead of a crank.

Look at the Internet to see how software writers are giving us familiar terms for cyberspace functions. We 'bookmark' favourite Web sites. We store material in 'folders'. We use 'yellow pages' and 'channels'.

– **Barbara Yost**, *Arizona Republic*

Networking Lingo

applet
  small program or 'application'

barf
  to malfunction in an unexpected way; to go haywire

BLOB (Binary Large Object)
  a very large binary file

bot
  a software program that can resemble the way a person would sound or act online

box
  a computer

brain bag
  a laptop carry bag

bug
  a problem in the software

chat or IRC (Internet Relay Chat)
  synchronous online chat between two or more people

cookie
  small data file intended to identify and track you on the Internet. It is sent by a server and stored on your computer's hard drive.

crawler, robot, spider
  a bot (software program) that roams the Internet looking for information. Most search engines use this technology.

daemon
  a program that lurks in the background of a computer performing necessary functions without the user's knowledge

emoticons
  smiley faces or other graphical images created in a textual environment to show emotion, wit, sarcasm, etc

flaming, flame war
  irate nasty personal attacks posted to a newsgroup, bulletin board systems, or any electronic message area

I-anything
  Internet-ready device

Internet years/ time
  shortened/compressed sense of time

killer app
  winner software application

kludge
  a clumsy, one-off solution to a computer problem

mousetrapping
  preventing exit from a Web site

MP3
  music sound file, downloadable over the Internet

newsgroup
  one of thousands of public discussion groups on the Internet

SILICONIA

'Silicon Valley' has spawned a number of related nicknames or terms of reference elsewhere where technology production is big. Some places have competing terms, but these are the ones that appear to be winning out:

Boston	route 128 or Silicon Necklace
San Francisco	Multimedia Gulch
New York	Silicon Alley
Chicago	Silicon Prairie
Phoenix, AZ	Silicon Desert
Austin, TX	Silicon Hills
Washington, DC/ Virginia/Maryland area	Dulles Corridor

PDA
> Personal Digital Assistant (eg, the Palm Pilot)

plug-in
> piece of software usually available for free download off the Internet that enhances the capabilities of your Web browser

portal
> entry site to the Web

snail mail
> postal mail (because it's so slow)

spam, spamming
> the electronic equivalent of junk mail. Spamming is to post unwanted messages to a public forum or to many users.

threads
> a conversation or string of messages

URL
> Universal Resource Locator – the address of a Web page on the Internet

trap door
> a piece of sabotage inserted into a computer program while it is written, which allows unauthorised access in the future

wired, jacked in
> plugged into the Internet

Geek Chic

Technical terms also have a social side that moves swiftly through the high-tech culture. Here are a few sample terms from the dot-com arena:

bio-break
> a short respite usually from programming or hacking to attend to the call of nature

borgified
> being assimilated into the culture of an Internet firm

cracker
> a derogatory term invented by hackers to refer to either the criminal hacker or the less-than-savvy hacker

cube farm
   collection of cubicles arranged for the lowly programmers

cybersquat
   to register a web site address intending to sell it

cyborg
   half human, half machine living organism, originally from
   science fiction

cypherpunks/cyberpunks
   Silicon Valley inhabitants

decompress
   wind down: 'I'm still decompressing after that wild weekend.'

geek
   for years, computer programmers have had the reputation as
   geeks and nerds, giving rise to the epithet 'computer geek', a
   label they've embraced. Nowadays it's cool to be a geek.

geek chic
   styles made popular by nerds

gearhead
   someone with an obsessive interest in acquiring new bits of
   computer hardware

grok
   understand (from Robert Heinlein's science fiction novel
   Stranger in a Strange Land)

hacker
   knowledgeable computer user who can bypass secure systems

identity hacking
   giving a false identity (invented or 'stolen' from someone else)
   when using an online service

I FEEL SO :-)!

:-O	Wow!	:-D	laughing
:-)	happy	:-o	surprise
:'-(	crying	:-@	screaming
(:-(	frowning	;-)	winking

lurker

someone who reads electronic messages in a chat room but doesn't post

netiquette

network etiquette – norms for posting messages online

newbie

a newcomer to any cyber arena

power user

a user with an in-depth knowledge of their software over and above the norm

slave

a computer or disk that is controlled by another computer or disk (which is known as the 'master')

wired

plugged into the cyber scene; alternately, *Wired Magazine*, a hip, stylish, cyber rag

E-Commerce

Many tech phrases and references are shop-based and vary greatly (one tech company's 'zorch' may be another's 'tornado') and many are industry wide, ostensibly here to stay. These include:

clone

a generic sort of copy

co-opetition

the uneasy alliances formed between large computer companies who find it necessary to work together to establish mutually beneficial standards or protocols

cyberpork

government money that flows to well-connected information superhighway contractors

data mining

extracting useful information from an enormous database. Large companies have to 'mine' value from the bewildering bedrock of (seemingly) unrelated statistics and numbers.

dot-com
   a company which has a Web site address ending in '.com'
e-tail
   retail business on the Web
timebomb, logic bomb
   an instruction planted in a program which can destroy valuable
   data if some condition is not met. Typically used by disaffected
   employees and unscrupulous contractors.

Chat Room Acronyms

LOL
   laughing out loud (or lots of love)
WRT
   with respect to
BTW
   by the way
G/G
   gotta go
TTFN
   ta ta for now
IMHO
   in my humble opinion
OTTOMH
   off the top of my head
GR8
   great
PMFJI
   pardon me for jumping in
MYOB
   mind your own business: mind your own beeswax
NIMBY
   not in my back yard

3M	Minnesota Mining and Manufacturing – creator of the Post-It Note and other office products
4-H	a youth organisation sponsored by the Department of Agriculture whose members exhibit their home-economics projects and livestock at county fairs. They wear green and white uniforms.
AA	Administrative assistant; in Washington, DC the senior staff person serving a legislator
AA	Alcoholics Anonymous
AAA	American Automobile Association – the people to consult for maps and travel itineraries and for emergency roadside assistance

ABC	American Broadcasting Company – one of the major commercial TV networks
Amex	American Express
Amtrak	not many people know this means 'American travel by track'. Amtrak is the nation's federally sponsored train company.
AP	The Associated Press – source of many news stories
ASAP	as soon as possible
AT&T	known as 'the phone company' – one of many since deregulation
ATM	automated teller machine – the place to find crisp $20 bills (known in various parts of the country as Tyme machines or Cashpoints)

ATV	all-terrain vehicle – used in off-road transportation
BYOB	Bring Your Own Beer
CBS	Central Broadcasting System – one of the major commercial television networks
CEO	Chief Executive Officer – of a company, business or corporation
CIA	Central Intelligence Agency – the information-gathering arm of the government
CNN	Cable News Network – the best place for international broadcast news
Conrail	Consolidated Rail Corporation – in charge of several Northeast railroads
CST	Central Standard Time – the time zone of the middle of the country
DEA	Drug Enforcement Agency
MC	also 'emcee' – master of ceremonies
ERA	(baseball) earned run average
EST	Eastern Standard Time – the time zone of the East
FBI	Federal Bureau of Investigation – investigates federal crimes
GE	General Electric – former utility is now a major conglomerate and owner of CBS
GOP	Grand Old Party – the Republicans
HQ	headquarters
IBM	International Business Machines – known for computers and office machines
IRS	Internal Revenue Service – the tax collectors (all income taxes are due April 15)
LA	Los Angeles
LDS	Church of Jesus Christ of Latter-day Saints – the Mormons
MADD	Mothers Against Drunk Driving
MGM	Metro-Goldwyn-Mayer – an entertainment conglomerate
mph	miles per hour (rate of vehicle speed)

MST	Mountain Standard Time – the time zone of the Rockies
MTV	Music Television – video and music mix on cable TV; extremely popular with teenagers and twentysomethings
NAACP	National Association for the Advancement of Colored People
NASA	the folks who put a man on the moon (National Aeronautics and Space Administration)
NBC	National Broadcasting Corporation – one of the major commercial TV networks
NOW	National Organization for Women – strong proponents of women's rights
NRA	National Rifle Association – strong proponents of the right to bear arms

NYSE	New York Stock Exchange
PBS	Public Broadcasting System – non-commercial TV known for nature shows, British imports and Pavarotti
PC	personal computer; politically correct
PMS	premenstrual syndrome
PST	Pacific Standard Time – the time zone of the West Coast
PTA	Parent-Teacher Association – there's a version of this in every elementary school
SRO	standing room only – as at a music or theatre event or lecture

SS#	Social Security Number – required for employment and subsequent financial social security benefits upon retirement
the Met	(New York) Metropolitan Opera or the Metropolitan Museum of Art – not to be confused with the Mets ball team
UFO	unidentified flying object
WASP	white, Anglo-Saxon Protestant
zip	zip code – the five- or nine-digit code following addresses

ABBREVIATIONS
& ACRONYMS

BRITISH & AMERICAN ENGLISH

Some words just really don't have a counterpart. These include apple butter (a sweet, dark apple sauce you spread on toast as an equivalent to jam), bobby pin (a type of hair pin) or shellac (a type of wood finish). A joint is a marijuana cigarette and never a piece of meat. Pants are generally preferred to trousers, although both are in use.

AMERICAN TERM	BRITISH TERM
apartment	flat
bangs	fringe
bathing suit, swimming suit	swimming costume
bathroom or restroom	toilet, lavatory, WC
buck, clam, smacker	dollar
buddy, pal, bud	mate
business hours	opening times
call (on the telephone)	ring
candy	sweets
chips, potato chips	crisps
cigarettes	smokes, fags, coffin nails, cancer sticks
comforter	duvet, doona
cookie	biscuit
cot	campbed
crib	cot
curb	kerb
dessert	pudding

BRITISH & AMERICAN
ENGLISH

diaper	nappy
downtown	city centre, in town
drugstore	chemist
drunk	pissed
eggplant	aubergine
elevator	lift
exit (traffic direction)	way out
fanny	bottom
fart	trump
faucet	tap
fries, french fries	chips
gal	bird
garbage can, trash can	rubbish bin
garbage, trash	rubbish
gas, gasoline	petrol
get a woman pregnant	knock up
give someone a ride	give someone a lift
grand, 'K'	a thousand dollars
guy (also refers to women)	bloke
half past 12	half 12
hood (of a car)	bonnet
mail	post
mailbox	postbox
Main Street	High Street
make fun of	take the piss out of, take the mickey out of
napkin	serviette
oatmeal	porridge
pacifier, soother	child's dummy
pail	bucket
pen	biro
pissed, pissed off	angry, irritated
PMS (premenstrual syndrome)	PMT (premenstrual tension)

raincoat	waterproof, mac
sausage	banger
sick	ill, unwell
sidewalk	pavement, footpath
simple	noddy
skillet	frying pan
stroller	pram
stuff	kit
suspenders	braces
sweater	jumper

toilet paper (TP)	loo roll
trashcan or wastebasket	bin
truck	lorry
trunk (of a car)	boot
TV	telly
underwear, briefs, boxers	underpants
vacation	holiday
vacuum	hoover
vest	waistcoat
wrench	spanner
yield (traffic signal)	give way
zucchini	courgette

TIPS FOR BRITS

- If you want *hot* tea, you have to ask for it explicitly.
- Beware the hidden sugar in bread, soft drinks and low-fat desserts.
- Portion sizes are big.
- The milk tastes funny but the ice cream is great.
- A libation is a beverage – a term usually used at an 'establishment'.
- Tipping is at least 15% in restaurants – it really is.
- Don't ask to rent an estate wagon – ask for a station wagon.
- The clerk in the store will not answer to 'clark'.
- Use the Yellow Pages if you need to look up a phone number – but watch out for a difference in categories (car stuff under Auto; bed stuff under Mattress, etc).
- The major department store in a mall is known as an anchor.
- Don't use 'toilet', use 'ladies' room' or 'bathroom'.

While Americans have the reputation for talking incessantly about personal details, they will be reticent about publicly criticising someone's behaviour in any direct manner – unless they're in the throes of road rage or acting pushy in a museum line.

BRITISH & AMERICAN ENGLISH

REGIONAL
VARIATIONS

Many Americans don't consider that the dialect of their own region developed because of historical influences and the combination of indigenous, colonial and immigrant languages unique to their area. But regional differences are indeed the by-product of the settlement patterns of North America – an intermingling of the speech of London and northern England with non-English speakers.

The dialect areas of the eastern states (Northern, Mid-Atlantic and Southern) have always been fairly distinct and well documented. In the course of the European settling of the West in the mid- to late 19th century, these dialect features spread and diffused, becoming less distinctive as migration fanned out westward.

The process is called 'dialect levelling', but it's much more fun to think about wagon trains bound for the glories of the California Gold Rush starting in Pennsylvania, South Carolina or Massachusetts. Everyone has packed their buckets (or pails), their spiders (or skillets or frying pans) and have eaten their flapjacks (or pancakes or griddlecakes) and other greasy (pronounced greecy or greazzzy) breakfast fare. Along the Oregon Trail, the Mormon Trail, the Santa Fe Trail – those famous corridors to the West – folks exchanged words while fending off varmints, eating victuals and circling the wagons.

Adding to the general regional mix are social dialects which carry more or less status than others. Whether you pronounce that 'r' or not can mean something in terms of prestige, as well as characterising a region (the rest of the country knows you 'pahk the cah' in New England). In the early days of the republic, New York would look to London for what carried prestige, and followed the changing fortunes of the 'r' as they occurred in England. Dropping your 'r' used to be high status in the USA, but since WWII including the 'r' is more prestigious. (Linguist Leanne Hinton said that California educators put New York kids into speech therapy to correct their 'impediment' before the East Coast 'r' was restored in common usage.)

As far as social prestige goes, people from the South get a bad rap, as do speakers of what many call a New Jersey accent. They're viewed as dim or backwards. People with strong regional accents from Minnesota or the Upper Midwest – made famous by the movie *Fargo* – are viewed as cute and maybe a little naive. Non-native speakers also are stigmatised because of their foreign accents. There's a big business in accent reduction classes for both new-comers and old-timers, an enterprise which is built on negative evaluations of dialect.

Differences are not just in the accent. There are also vocabu-lary differences across the country and variations in how people interact socially. For example, getting to the point is valued in Texas, but not as much in Appalachia, Tennessee and environs, where reinforcing social relationships and etiquette takes priority. In Minnesota understatement is the normal way to talk; in California, effusive expressions of enthusiasm are preferred.

In the USA, where strong regional accents capture the imagin-ation, evoke strong reactions and are frequently the basis of jokes, you can bet that the other person is the one who talks funny, who has the accent. While some folks consider that the Southern drawl, the distinctive New York accents, the singsong chirps of the Up-per Midwest and the flat vowels of the West are the extent of regional difference, the *Dictionary of American Regional English* divides the country into 37 separate areas. This might intrigue the Professor Higginses among you, but the average traveller need only be aware that differences exist.

SPEAKING LIKE SHAKESPEARE

Travellers to historically isolated areas of the eastern USA frequently comment that the speech in small communities sounds just like Elizabethan English or Shakespearean English. Could it really be true that miners in small towns in the Appalachian mountains or fishermen on small islands off the East Coast have managed to preserve intact the English of the latter half of the 16th century, with all its old-fashioned features like 'thou' for you, 'doth' for does, and 'most unkindest' cuts (*Julius Caesar*, Act 3, Scene 2)?

At first glance, it looks like there's some truth to the notion. The island of Ocracoke, North Carolina, on the southeast coast of the USA, was first inhabited by English speakers in the late 17th century and has existed in relative isolation from the mainland for most of its long history. Residents of the island, especially those who can trace their ancestry a long way back, can still be heard to utter words like 'mommuck' (to harass or bother) and 'qualmish' (nauseated or queasy). These words sound completely foreign to most of today's English speakers but were in daily use in Shakespeare's day and are even found in his plays.

Ocracokers (or O'cockers, as they call themselves) also use old-fashioned verb forms like a-huntin' and a-fishin', as well as pronunciations that might have come straight out of the mouths of the Bard's loyal fans. For example, they pronounce words like 'house' and 'mouse' as something like 'hoos' and 'moose', and words like 'ride' and 'tide' as something like 'roid' and 'toid'.

But no dialect is an island, even those you find on islands, and the Ocracoke dialect (or 'brogue,' as it is often called) hasn't been completely immune to the countless changes that shaped the English language in the centuries since it first established itself in the New World, back in the day of Queen Elizabeth I. Just like their counterparts on the US mainland (not to mention their distant relatives in the British Isles), O'cockers have relinquished their 'thou' and 'ye' for plain old 'you', and given up all the 'walketh's and 'talketh's in favour of the mundane 'walks' and 'talks' we all know so well. And not only that, islanders over the course of the past 300 or so years have invented lots of words and phrases without outside influence. For example, islanders now use words like 'dingbatter' (outsider) and 'meehonkey' (a childhood game) side by side with 'mommuck' and 'qualmish', along with expressions like 'call the mail' (distribute the mail) and 'say a word' (talk a lot).

In this way the Ocracoke brogue is no different from that of any other historically isolated language variety – or any living language, for that matter. All languages and dialects change over time, even those in the most remote and hard-to-reach places.

Dialects derive their unique characters, not just from their historical roots, but from the way speakers shape their language as they use it in daily interaction, skillfully blending borrowed words or pronunciations with the tried-and-true turns of phrase that have served them well for centuries.

Ocracokers and residents of other remote East Coast communities may not speak exactly like Shakespeare, but they're certainly just as creative with the English language.

VOCABULARY

'Do you call it a pail or a bucket? Do you draw water from a faucet or from a spicket? Do you pull down the blinds, the shades, or the curtains when it gets dark? ... Do [anglers] bait the hook with an earthworm, angleworm, angle dog, fishworm, redworm, or with a night crawler or night walker? ... Where is a doughnut known as a cruller, a fried cake, a fatcake, a cookie; ... a wheatcake as a battercake, a flannel cake, a fritter, a pancake, a hotcake? Do you fry your eggs in a spider, in a skillet, or in a frying pan?'

Hans Kurath, author and director of various American dialect surveys, notably *A Word Geography of the Eastern United States*

Specific regional vocabulary in this chapter and in each chapter of this section still only covers the tip of the iceberg (see Further Reading at the end of A Short History chapter for more references). The regions of a country are only one contributing factor to the whole language picture. Age, gender, education, occupation and other social factors influence word choice and language usage.

Some terms are known to a wider audience, like the different words for a carbonated beverage or soft drink: pop, soda, soda pop, tonic, Coke. Other words don't have much currency outside their particular locale, like frappe (Boston area) and cabinet (Rhode Island) for the ice cream-and-milk mix known generally as a milkshake.

Depending on which part of the country you're in, you'll hear these variants (the ones listed first are usually the most widely used):

- couch, sofa, davenport, chesterfield
- bag, sack, paper bag, poke
- cobweb, spider web
- porch, stoop, veranda, steps, piazza
- gutters, eavestroughs, spouts, spouting (the metal or wood gutters surrounding the edge of a roof)
- dust, lint, dustballs, dust kittens, dust bunnies, lint balls (the stuff that gathers under the bed)
- my family, my folks, my relations, my kin
- a tune-up, a lube job, a grease job (service done on an automobile)
- turnpike, toll road, tollway, freeway, interstate, parkway, thruway, expressway (names for major thoroughfares and roadways, the first three listed here charge a fee)
- rest stop, rest area, oasis, service area, wayside (the place to stop for relief and refreshment while on the road)
- fire hydrant, fire plug, hydrant
- boulevard strip, median strip, neutral ground, grass strip, centre divider, parking strip (the strip dividing roadways)
- sidewalk, walk, path
- mutt, mongrel, Heinz 57, sooner, cur (a dog of mixed or unknown breed)
- rubber band, gumband, rubber binder, elastic binder, elastic band, elastic
- water cooler, drinking fountain, bubbler, cooler
- snack, bite, lunch, nosh
- bathroom, toilet, john, can, biffy, commode, throne

- condom, rubber, Trojan, jimmy-hat
- sweet roll, pastry, Danish, Danish roll
- melon, cantaloupe, muskmelon, mushmelon
- boots, rubbers, galoshes
- sneakers, tennis shoes

Common Colloquialisms

Some expressions have lost their regional moorings and are used in various pockets of the country or by various types of people (like farmers or journalists or computer programmers) no matter where they live. Other expressions have been farmed out via television or a big movie or by anyone who moves to another part of the country and are thus used, or at least understood, more widely. Here is a list of expressions you may hear. They suggest a rural, folksy or casual style and are used in urban and rural areas alike, depending on local conditions.

allowed as
    granted or acknowledged: 'He allowed as he was unhappy about the outcome.'
bigger than a Mack truck
    very big and heavy
booty call
    contact with someone for the purpose of sexual gratification

can't walk and chew gum at the same time
    awkward, uncoordinated

crick
    small stream

don't get your knickers in a knot
    don't get all riled up

doohickey, thingamajig
    anything you don't know the proper name for

fixin'
    getting ready to do something: 'I'm fixin' to cook supper.'

gimme a holler, gimme a ring, gimme a jingle
    give me a phone call

good ole boy
    a more polite term for redneck; good ole boys themselves now
    refer to themselves as such

grab (or get) a hold (or a holt)
    to get a grip, or hold, of an object or concept: 'I kept calling,
    but I never could get a holt of him.'

happy camper
    someone who's satisfied: 'She's a happy camper.'

heads up
    an alert or notice: 'Thanks for the heads up on that stock.'

now we're cooking!, Now we're cooking with gas!
    a comment on progress made on some activity

on a toot, on a bender
    getting drunk

on account of
    because of

out of the loop
    not privy to important inside information

redneck
    pejorative way of referring to a poor, white, rural Southerner
    who is regarded as ignorant, bigoted and violent

a shellacking
    a beating

slim pickin's
   not much to choose from
smackers, smackeroos
   dollars
squealing like a stuck pig
   bitching or moaning, or really yelling and hollering
well, if that don't beat all
   Isn't that something?
you don't know jack(shit)
   you don't know anything
you're my dad!
   an expression meaning someone did something really cool or nice
yup, yep, u-huh
   yes

REGIONAL VARIATIONS

WEST COAST

The West Coast includes Washington and Oregon (which make up the Pacific Northwest), but it also embodies a state of mind and style that correlates most closely with California – derisively dubbed the Land of Fruits and Nuts. And in California the divisions are between North and South, with Los Angeles and San Francisco leading the way. The struggle over water – the North has it and the South needs it – has long played out in the state's history and is perhaps a reason behind most enmity today.

The regions are linguistically diverse. They always have been, even when Native Americans were the only people in the place, and before the Spanish settlements that long predated the 1849 Gold Rush or statehood. The diversity has expanded in recent years with increased immigration from Asia and the Pacific Rim, especially in the North, and from Mexico and other Latin American countries in the South.

Socioeconomically, Hollywood and the film industry have made a mark on Southern California (SoCal or So Cool) styles of speech, while a strong, gay activist community in San Francisco and the explosion of the dot-com industries in the Silicon Valley have influenced ways of speaking and thinking in the Bay Area.

A single word neatly demarcates North from South: 'hella', an intensifier which means very or really, as in 'she's hella cool'. Southern Californians know the term, which easily identifies someone from the Bay Area, but never use it. (A variant is 'hecka', but avoid it if possible.) 'Hella's' East Coast correlate is Boston's 'wicked', which has spread to some degree throughout New England (Mainers use it). In Boston you can say something is wicked, period; in Berkeley or Moraga or surrounding areas of the Bay Area, the word cannot stand alone.

Meanwhile people from SoCal convey their general disdain for the North by commonly referring to the area as NoCal instead of NorCal. 'Grippa' is a sometimes-heard SoCal term meant to deride the NorCal 'hella'. It is used in the same way as hella, but in a condescending or sarcastic manner: 'Being from NoCal is grippa cool' – not.

GENERAL CALIFORNIA

attitude queen
  someone with a really snobbish air

The Big One
  the inevitable earthquake of the future that will level cities and
  cause the state to fall into the Pacific Ocean

burbs
  suburbs

clock
  to watch something or someone very closely: 'She's been clock-
  ing me all night.'; punch someone

couple-three
  a few

crotch rockets
  racing-style motorcycles

fierce
  all-purpose adjective of approval: 'That's fierce.'

full on
  quite; extremely

fully
  totally or completely

gated community
  an affluent subdivision surrounded by walls or fences intended
  to offer privacy and safety

going postal (or aggro, ballistic, apeshit)
  to go crazy

going Richter
  blowing one's top, getting really angry (after the Richter scale,
  which measures the strength of earthquakes)

hang a left/right, bang a left/right
  make a left turn/make a right turn

out there
  strange

Sacto
  Sacramento, state capital in the central part of the state
split the sheets
  divorce (a term used in Far Northern California, from
  Sacramento northwards)
U-ey
  a U-turn: 'You better flip a U-ey.'
uncool
  inappropriate
wiggin'
  stressing or freaking out

VALLEY GIRL ROCKS ON

'Like', 'Dude', and 'Totally' are remnants from the Valley Girl lexicon that live robustly throughout the state. *Valley Girl* was a teen flick from the early 1980s.

'Like' is used when narrating a story to put emphasis on the act being described: 'I was like shopping and I like bought a new pair of shoes today'.

'Dude' is used as a term of reference: 'Check out that dude.' It is most commonly used to express astonishment: 'Dude! I can't believe you just did that!' or 'Dude. Come on now.' Can be used twice in an utterance: 'Dude, that dude is such the rock star.' Do not use 'dudette', the once-popular feminine version, or you will look like a huge nerd.

'Totally' has retained its meaning over the years. It replaces 'very' and means 'more than very', as in 'That guy is totally hot'.

Also standard in story-telling are phrases like 'I'm all' or 'she's/he's all' or 'we're all'. These phrases are used when describing situations or narrative or relating contexts. It usually means 'I/he/we said', but it can also be used to describe gestures or attitudes as in, 'I was all, hi', 'then he was all, how are you?', 'And I was all, fine'.

LOS ANGELES AREA

Angelenos
  people who live in LA or environs

chronic
  LA gang term for marijuana

Citywalk
  at Universal Studios (also known as Universal Citywalk), a trendy place to get outdoors at night

El Toro Y
  where freeways form a Y in El Toro in southern Orange County – the 5 and the 405

Inland Empire
  the San Gabriel Valley – a vast, low-profile but heavily populated region to the east of downtown LA and Pasadena

Los Feliz
  trendy area, pronounced Los FEE-liss, which varies from the Spanish pronunciation generally followed in California

map the heavens
  to tag (or spray paint) on hard-to-reach freeway signs

marine layer
  moisture leading to haze, which out-of-towners incorrectly mistake for smog. It's created by moist air from the ocean.

NoHo
  North Hollywood

The Orange Crush
  traffic report term to describe where several major freeways come together in Orange County, very near the El Toro Y

The Orange Curtain
  cultural and political barrier separating LA proper from Orange County, behind which lies a notoriously conservative Republican bastion

over the hill
  from the West Side and Hollywood to the San Fernando Valley – and vice versa. The hills in question are the Santa Monica Mountains.

Pacoima
> a neighbourhood in the San Fernando Valley used to suggest someplace very far away – when something is way out in the Valley, too far to even think of, you use Pacoima as the reference point: 'That's like way out in Pacoima or somewhere!'

The Promenade
> the Santa Monica 3rd Street Promenade – replaced Westwood as the trendiest westside place, but now competes with Citywalk

Santa Anas
> strong, dry, usually warm winds that come over the mountains from the deserts at certain times of the year

Sig Alert
> traffic is completely stopped – invented by a traffic reporter named Sigmund

smog
> smoke plus fog

The Southland
> what TV news people call the area

surface streets
> city streets and boulevards and such, as opposed to the freeways, which are very often raised or lowered from ground level

The Swish Alps
> Silverlake and nearby Los Feliz comprise a populous gay enclave in the city

TV parking
> finding a parking spot right in front of where you want to be, a miracle that only happens on TV shows

tag, to tag
> one's graffiti signature; to apply one's graffiti signature

The 3 Bs

Brentwood, Bel Air and Beverly Hills – rich, predominantly white, star-studded enclaves

transition

when a freeway merges into another, also called connector roads

WeHo

West Hollywood

SOCAL GEOGRAPHY

Know the difference between the Valley and LA and Orange County, as people in Southern California get offended when these three areas are lumped together.

- The Valley is North; on the 405 anything north of Mullholland is the Valley. On 101 or 5 it's anything north of Hollywood/Burbank. While there are nice places, it is essentially a congested suburb. The Valley wants to secede from LA County – a notion that meets no resistance.

- LA is everything between Orange County (OC) and the Valley, possibly including Long Beach and Pasadena. It's the place where things happen: theatres, music, movie studio headquarters (most soundstages are in the Valley). It's home to people of all ethnicities and socioeconomic classes.

- OC is Orange County, home of Disneyland and Knott's Berry Farm. An hour south of downtown LA, it is like a high-end version of the Valley. Because it has a reputation for political conservatism, people from Northern California especially worry about what happens 'Behind the Orange Curtain'. It is home to some of the best beaches in SoCal and one of the best places to surf in the world – especially Newport Beach. People here consider themselves separate from LA. It has a distinct culture and is a beautiful place to visit.

C'MON BABY LIGHT MY FIRE

'Burning Man' is a 'happening' that takes place in Nevada's Black Rock Desert, drawing thousands who come in costume and constructed personas, culminating in the ceremonial burning of the 'man'. And while the fire is literal during the six-day festival, it's metaphorical for the rest of the year.

The event's goal is to create a temporary community, the spirit and fire of which the participants carry within themselves as they return to their normal, work-day worlds. The goals are lofty in this experiment in temporary community: caring for others, building community, connecting to self – and leaving the desert as clean as it was found. The methods are down-to-earth: fire, group circles and chants.

SAN FRANCISCO BAY AREA

The Avenues
> western part of San Francisco that is very residential where the streets are numbered avenues. One of its connotations is that it's far from the centre of things – if you're 'living out in the avenues', you're far away from downtown.

Barbary Coast
> legendary name for post-Gold Rush San Francisco, notorious for gambling dens and brothels

BART
> Bay Area Rapid Transit; train system linking San Francisco with the East Bay and parts of the South Bay

Bezerkeley, Berserkeley
> nickname for Berkeley which underscores the historically anarchical nature of the town, its residents and its city council

The City
> never, ever 'Cisco' or 'Frisco', seldom San Francisco, and selectively referred to as 'The City'

Critical Mass

a monthly gathering of the San Francisco bicycle tribe on busy Market Street in defiance of the prevailing car culture. Attendees are often church-like in their devotion to two-wheeled and other non-fossil-fuelled transport.

Fog Belt

area west of Twin Peaks

Forty-Niners

the name for the early settlers of San Francisco who came west in 1849 in search of gold in the nearby Sierra Nevada foothills. Now most often refers to the local professional football team, which also goes by Niners.

Gourmet Ghetto

stretch of north Shattuck Avenue in Berkeley where you'll find Chez Panisse, a well-known Mediterranean-Californian restaurant

RABBLE-ROUSING

The 1960s, for some, began and ended in the East Bay, starting with the birth of the Free Speech Movement on Sproul Plaza at UC Berkeley in 1964 and ending with Altamount, the 'second Woodstock', held at nearby Altamount Speedway in December 1969. This one turned ugly when a man was pummeled to death by Hell's Angels 'security guards' after pointing a gun at rocker Mick Jagger.

Berkeley has since retained its aura as the bastion of free speech and liberal social activity, although as time has passed and younger generations have supplanted the older, idealistic Boomers, those rabble-rousing notions are beginning to look a little quaint in some sectors. Sproul Plaza and Altamount are local terms with national resonance.

gnar-gnar
> variant on 'gnarly' and usually means something bad or gross: 'Avoid gnar-gnar things.'

gnarly
> a way of saying something is good or bad: 'That's gnarly, dude.'

The Granite Lady
> the Old Mint, 5th and Mission

The Haight
> what people now call the Haight-Ashbury neighbourhood, centre of the hippie scene and focal point for the historic Summer of Love of 1968

Haightball
> a particularly intense brand of pick-up basketball found in the Panhandle near Haight Street

harsh my mellow
> upset me; ruin my calm state

the hills and the flats
> two distinct socioeconomic and geographical areas of Berkeley and Oakland – the hills are affluent, the flats are not

Jerry's kids
> grungy, nomadic, perennially broke Deadheads that hung out on Haight Street when the Grateful Dead were in town; after the late, great guitarist Jerry Garcia

KGB
> Killer Green Bud – pot from Humboldt County via Hawaii

Kind Buds
  marijuana. The term people mutter when they walk down the
  street, quietly looking for buyers.

later
  goodbye; see you later

The Maze
  the place where all the freeways from the Bay Area meet to go
  through the toll plaza to cross the Bay Bridge west towards
  San Francisco. The multiple lanes of traffic and possibilities
  for freeway changes are very confusing.

The Mission
  San Francisco's melting pot; started as an Irish neighbourhood,
  became Latino, and in recent years has added Asians, African
  Americans and white hipsters. It's rapidly becoming gentrified.

HI-TECH VALLEY

The Silicon Valley is located in the Santa Clara Valley,
at the south end of the San Francisco Bay near the
cities of Mountain View, San Jose and Palo Alto (also
known as the peninsula or the South Bay).

The Silicon Valley of fable and legend began in
the late 1950s and early '60s. Stanford University was
a major factor, drawing William Hewlett and David
Packard. Early presences include Xerox PARC (Palo
Alto Research Center) and Fairchild Semiconductor.
Robert Noyce and Gordon Moore formed Intel in the
late 1960s, followed by Steve Jobs and Steve Wozniak
who made personal computers in their garages, and
the founding of Apple in the 1970s. The Internet in
the 1990s led to Netscape and Yahoo! and other
notable companies which have turned the Silicon
Valley into a world centre for hi-tech.

Mount Tam
> Mount Tamalpais, just over the Golden Gate Bridge in Marin and a geographical point of reference

Multimedia Gulch
> area South of Market which has become home to popular clubs and bars as well as dot-com operations

no doubt
> a conversational response cue like 'uh-huh'

The Park
> Golden Gate Park (in conversation you'll usually differentiate it from the many other small neighbourhood parks)

rad
> short for 'radical'; good

SOMA
> South of Market Street

The Stick
> the still-extant term for what once was Candlestick Park, a windy, cold, yet beautiful stadium where the 49ers play. The stadium is now officially named, thanks to corporate sponsorship, 3Com Park.

OREGON

First of all, it's pronounced 'ORyg'n', not 'oryGON'. And slough, as in the many tidal salt marshes that dot the state, is pronounced 'slew'. The Oregon Trail, which led to The Great Migration starting in 1843, was a major route to the West. The Graveyard of the Pacific is another name for the mouth of the Columbia River due to the many maritime deaths that have occurred there. If you have a chance, find a thunderegg, the state rock, break it open and you see great agate formations.

When in Oregon (and many parts of the Northwest) you're likely to encounter the following linguistic behaviours, some of which owe their provenance to immigration from the Midwestern states in the early to middle part of the 19th century:

- If answering a phone, 'Yell-O' is used (mostly Eastern Oregon).
- Instead of 'anyhow', 'anywho' is said (and written).
- When using a camera, it's taking pictures, not taking photos.
- A small running body of water is a 'creek' or a 'crick' more than a stream; it is never a 'run'.
- Small crustaceans are 'crawdads', not 'crayfish'.
- The place where the ocean meets the shore is 'the coast' more than 'the beach,' and is never 'the shore'.
- 'Going up' somewhere either means you are travelling north or you are climbing some sort of hill or mountain to get there. If you are travelling westward or to the flatland, you are not going 'up'.
- Trucks: a 'pick-up' is a little vehicle, a 'truck' is a big vehicle, a 'pick-up truck' is one of those in-between things and something that hauls freight is a 'semi'.
- 'Harvest' is a Christmas tree thing. Everything else is noted by name: 'strawberry harvest', 'green bean harvest', etc. A person doing the work will be 'picking strawberries' or 'picking beans' instead of harvesting the same.

- The state has 'valleys' and 'ravines'. There is only one 'gorge' and that's where the Columbia flows to the east of Portland.
- Coho salmon nesting grounds are known as coho condos.
- Birkenstocks, the Northwest's footwear of choice, are not to be confused with 'fake-in-stocks', the fraudulent variety.
- Hazelnuts are 'filberts' and soda is 'pop'.

NORTHWEST

ALASKAN LINGO

Alaska Native is the term for someone of indigenous, non-European ancestry; Native Alaskan refers to someone who was born in Alaska. The undeveloped areas of the state are known as the Bush, home to settlements of primarily Alaska Natives.

'Sourdough' is the somewhat jocular term of reference for someone who's lived and worked in Alaska for a considerable length of time. Facetiously defined as someone who has 'soured' on the state but doesn't have the 'dough' (money to leave).

'Pioneer' is the more formal term for sourdough or longterm resident (to contrast with newcomers, known as cheechakos, a word from the 19th-century pidgin language, Chinook Jargon).

Many words in Alaska English were borrowed from native languages, among them potlatch (gift; a giving) from Nootka, which has come to mean a commemorative celebration or gathering. One makes potlatch (holds a feast) and potlatches (gives) various foods.

Portland itself comes with several monikers. The Clearing was the original name for the one-acre site that later became Portland, known also as Stumptown and Bridgetown (11 bridges span the Willamette River). Rip City is another nickname for Portland, named in honour of the Blazers, the pro football team only rarely referred to as the Trail Blazers. Burnside is the great north/south divider of Portland and is the local equivalent of skid row. There is some perverse logic to the fact that the city's most notoriously crime-riddin thoroughfare goes by the name of Killingsworth. Portland's brand of rock'n'roll is known as Puddle-stomp. The 'ash report' was big in the '80s, when neighbouring volcanoes were smoking, thereby affecting the air quality.

WASHINGTON

Ability to pronounce Puyallup ('pew-al-up') and Sequim ('squim') is a tell-tale sign you're in the know. Also, people in the Northwest really do care that you refer to 'Sasquatch' instead of 'Bigfoot', and 'Yeti' as opposed to 'Abominable Snowman.' The mood lightens for greetings – 'Hey' is the customary one. Some of the following terms are particular to Seattle.

Alki
    the peninsula where the first white settlers arrived in 1851; known today for its thriving beach scene and tourist crowds

Aurora Ave
    Route 99, fabled 'highway to Alaska'

The Ave
    University Way in the U-District

Bucky
    to send a package by messenger. Named after Seattle-based Bucky's Courier Systems.

Calvinists
    term coined by the late Kurt Cobain for disciples of indie label pioneer and Beat Happening front man, Calvin Johnson of K Records in nearby Olympia

NORTHWEST

copycycles
> cops on bikes. This Seattle innovation produces five times the arrest rate as cops in cars.

Diaper Run
> 10.10 am ferry from Bainbridge Island filled with parents and babies on their way to Seattle

Do the Puyallup (pronounced 'pew-al-up')
> go to the State Fair in Puyallup

Fauntleroy
> Peninsula of Seattle

Geoduck (pronounced 'gooey duck')
> a West Coast clam with an edible neck. A local speciality, and mascot of Evergreen State College

graveyard shift
> expression in general use coined in Seattle when early merchants voted to remove, in the middle of the night, graves buried underneath the original cobblestone streets

Jet City
> so named because Seattle is the headquarters of Boeing, a major employer in the Puget Sound region

The Mountain
> 14,410 foot (4323 m) Mt Rainier. 'The mountain is out today' is a standard refrain.

Sasquatch
> Northwest Native American name for Bigfoot, the large hairy creature said to inhabit the Pacific Northwest

Seattle
> named after Chief Sealth who saved some white folk one winter on Alki Point. They eventually took over land that had been in the hands of various native peoples since the 6th century.

Skid Row
> expression came from skidding freshly cut logs down Yesler Street to Henry Yesler's sawmill on Elliott Bay. The hill used to be so steep they finally pushed it into the bay, forming what is now Harbor Island, the second largest artificial island in the USA.

BETWEEN THE COASTS

It's not really fair to bunch an extremely diverse range of speaking styles, accents and regional varieties into one small section, but it's enough to give you a flavour of the vast possibilities and variations that exist between the West Coast and the East Coast. There are plenty of active towns, cities and metropolitan regions but there is so much physical space in the 'Heartland' that a great deal of the variation – at least until a short time ago – is still rooted in the rural or has been developed from longstanding settlement patterns or the features of indigenous languages.

The ways of speaking in places away from the coasts are not as well known except, perhaps, along some stereotypical lines. They represent equally stylish and sophisticated modes of communication as well as offering different types of story-telling, humour, forms of address, community allegiances and cultural contexts from which unique wordplay is created.

IDAHO & UTAH

In Idaho and Utah, a great deal of the culture and linguistic character revolves around the production of potatoes and the presence of the Mormon Church (the Mormons emigrated to Utah in the late 1840s to pursue religious freedom and then into Idaho). The area is also known for skiing and the delights of the mountainous outdoors, drawing many tourists.

digger
    machinery used to harvest potatoes
fetch
    a Mormon slang word used like 'dammit'
Gentiles
    members of the Mormon faith refer to all non-Mormons, even Jews, as Gentiles
Mormon Church/LDS
    The official name of the Mormon Church is The Church of Jesus Christ of Latter-day Saints. You will hear people shorten it to the acronym saying, 'I am LDS'. It is considered more formal than 'Mormon'.

Mormon Temple
    the centre of Mormon ritual practice. Sunday religious services are held in churchhouses, but the rest of the week Mormons perform religious rituals in the Temple. Temples are usually architecturally prominent.

Saints
    members of the Mormon faith also refer to themselves as Saints

spud
    potato

The Wasatch Front
    the major urban areas located at the west base of the Wasatch mountains in Utah. Major cities on the Wasatch Front include Ogden, Bountiful, Salt Lake City, Sandy and Provo.

THE GREAT PLAINS

The Great Plains encompasses a wide swath of big sky and wide open spaces from the Texas panhandle north up into Alberta, Canada. 'Plains states' include Texas, Oklahoma, Kansas, Nebraska, the Dakotas, and the eastern portions of Colorado, Wyoming and Montana.

The prairie and the pioneer helped define these lands – culturally and linguistically. Influences in the language come from the Native Americans and the immigrant Europeans, as well as through the agrarian origins of the nation's vast rangelands and bountiful 'bread basket'. A selective sampling includes the following:

ag
> agriculture

aggies
> students who attend colleges that are known for agricultural programs; students majoring in those programs

Aksarben
> Nebraska spelled backwards. Name for the longstanding colosseum and event centre in Omaha.

beans
> soybeans, raised to feed hogs, not for making tofu

caught kind of cornered
> don't know the answer

chips (cow chips)
> dried cow or buffalo manure used for fuel

duallies
> big pick-up trucks that have two back wheels on each side

dust devil
> a 'mini-tornado' of dust that occurs on flat lands when it's hot

gully washer
> big rainstorm

in the bin
> never count your income from crops until they are 'in the bin', or 'in the elevator'

jackalope
    fictional animal that's a cross between a jackrabbit and antelope
plumb crazy
    indisputably bonkers
pool hall yield
    exaggerated crop yield. Used by farmers in casual, off-work
    conversation, for example, when they go down to the local
    bar or pool hall.
puttin' out to flower
    planting sunflower in a field
rattlers
    rattlesnakes
reckon
    figure or guess, as in 'I reckon I'll be moseying along.'
roach killers
    cowboy boots with really pointy toes
runza
    the Nebraskan take on an Eastern European meat-filled pastry.
    It is so popular in Nebraska that there are a dozen or so Runza
    Huts and Runza Drive-Ins.
shimmy
    just a little bit – as in 'scoot over just a shimmy' or
    'shimmy that way a little'
shit kickers
    cowboy boots
10-gallon hat, John B
    cowboy hat
tumbleweed
    a ball of tangled weeds and dead plants that blows around
    in the wind
Wallace's Farmer
    the major publication of the farm belt
yonder
    over there

WISCONSIN & THE UPPER MIDWEST

A native Minnesotan and linguist we know really loved the Coen Brothers' movie, *Fargo* (which took place mostly in Minnesota even though the title refers to the North Dakota town), but didn't hear 'his' accent, the one that sounded more like the rest of the country. Ya … That's how it goes … anyhey.

People from the Upper Midwest will vary, like anywhere else, the extent to which they embrace the more 'local sounds' versus the more generic sounds of Mainstream US English (MUSE). To whatever degree someone possesses an accent of the Upper Midwest, they will always pronounce their state or town names 'correctly', for example, Scansin (Wisconsin), MinneSOHta, M'wakee (Milwaukee), Prairie d'sheen (Prairie du Chien), etc.

anyhey
    placed at the end of an utterance, something equivalent to 'isn't it?'
Believe you me!
    placed at the beginning or end of an utterance for emphasis, equivalent to 'really!' or 'I mean business'
borrow
    lend: 'Borrow me some quarters for a pop.'
brat
    pronounced 'braht' – bratwurst, a popular regional sausage (with Johnsonville or Usinger brats among the favourites)
bubbler
    drinking fountain
budge
    to butt in line
by
    to – a result of influence from German: 'Let's go by Mom's.'
cheesehead, cheddarhead
    someone from Wisconsin, a term embraced by Wisconsinites (especially the ones who wear Styrofoam cheese 'heads' at Packers football games)

c'meer once
  asking someone to come along with you

Cripes!, Cripes-sake!, Criminey!
  expletive – strong stuff

Dontcha know?
  tag question at the end of an utterance

fish fry
  the term for a Friday night fish meal (when you 'go out for fish')

Geez!
  often pronounced, unintentionally, like 'cheeese'

hairs
  used by some people instead of the collective noun 'hair':
  'C'meer once! Let me see! Yah, your hairs look great that way!'

How's by you?
  a common greeting

oh, yah
  response to someone's claim (agreeing or not)

stop and go lights
  traffic lights

uff-da
  all purpose response (from the Norwegian) to something un-
  pleasant or taxing; similar to 'oy vey'

ya, sure, youbetcha
  signals agreement – used throughout the Upper Midwest

ya hey
  used at several points in a conversation: at the beginning for
  focus or affirmation, in the middle to hold the floor and comment on nothing in particular, at the end to signal emphasis or
  another's turn

youse
  used in some areas as the second-person plural form of 'you'

DA YOOPERS

The state of Michigan is broken up into two peninsulas – the Lower Peninsula and the Upper Peninsula – connected by the Mackinac Bridge. The Upper Peninsula of Michigan, referred to widely as The UP, has a distinct dialect. If you're from the UP you're a Yooper. Residents call themselves Da Yoopers (honouring the dialect rule that changes 'th' sounds to 'd'), and will often refer to the Upper Peninsula as Yooperland. The UP was settled by Northern Europeans, many of Finnish extraction.

In the Yooper dialect most sounds are pronounced differently than in the rest of the Midwest. For example, 'da' instead of 'the', vowels sound longer and rounded ('sno-o-oh' for 'snow'), and will often end a sentence with an 'eh' (eg, 'Sure is cold, eh?').

Yoopers take great pride in their region and their distinctiveness. A popular band, Da Yoopers, elevates aspects of the culture in their songs ('Yooper Talk' is a witty, musical mini-dialect lesson – poking fun at outsider interest at the same time). Thanks to the Internet, Yooper pride has reached cyber proportions, and there are surprisingly many sites and word lists to indoctrinate the distant fan. Here are a few distinct words and expressions:

apple knocker
    a person from the Lower Peninsula
choppers
    a deer skin mitten with a wool mitten insert
cudighi
    a hamburger-like sandwich with a spicier meat, mozzarella cheese and tomato sauce
Da Mitten
    another name for the Lower Peninsula of Michigan (which looks roughly like a mitten)
give 'er tarpaper
    to work feverishly
lats
    skis, usually homemade

ARKANSAS

Former President Bill Clinton hails from Arkansas (pronounced 'ar-ken-saw') and thus aspects of the dialect have been put on the world stage. The Leader of the Free World still couldn't erase some of the stigma associated with rural varieties which people love to mock – especially on the level of pronunciation.

Here are some pronunciation rules (if you will mock, at least do it right):

- The 'eye' sound in words like 'ice' or 'tyre' or 'like' or 'knife' becomes 'ah'.
- The 'or' in words like foreigner becomes 'er'.
- The unstressed syllables seem to disappear: 'belligerent' sounds like 'b'liger'nt', 'foreigner' comes out as 'ferner', and 'Mississippi' comes out as 'miss sippy'.
- Notice an extra 'r' gets inserted in certain places in a word, so 'criticise' sounds like 'crittercise,' 'idea' like 'idear'.
- The 'r' gets deleted in words like 'porch', coming out like 'poach,' or phrases like 'tore up' ('toe up').
- The 'eh' sound in words like 'hell' becomes 'ay' (hayl) and words like 'many' becomes 'ih' (minny).

The following are some terms you might hear in Arkansas:

Arkansawyer
correct appellation for someone from 'the natural state': 'Arkansan' is okay if you're a 'ferner.'

Arkie
more pejorative form of Arkansawyer, though it is sometimes embraced by Arkansawyers as a term of endearment among themselves

Bama
the state to the South, Alabama. Often used in reference to University of Alabama football team, the Crimson Tide.

bird nest on the ground
   a cushy job
a bubble off plumb
   not all there, mentally unlevel
calf slobber
   meringue on a pie
disappear like a blue-jay on Friday
   vanish
doin' alright?
   a frequent Arkansas greeting. It's akin to 'How's it going?'
enough to make a buzzard puke
   offensive or distasteful
a face so long he could eat oats out of a churn
   dejected, downcast
Fayettenam
   Fayetteville, Arkansas; home of the University of Arkansas where
   the students party so hard that surviving socially and academi-
   cally is as taxing and precarious as fighting a war
fill ya up?
   after you eat dinner in Arkansas you're likely to be asked not
   whether the food tasted good, not whether you're satisfied,
   but 'Did it fill ya up?'
got a hitch in my get along
   saddled with a minor ailment
grinning like a fox eating yellow jackets
   a smile caused by inconvenient circumstances
The Hogs
   nickname for the University of Arkansas Razorbacks, which
   Arkansawyers are positively fanatical about. As the saying goes,
   'If you ain't a Razorbacker, you ain't shit'.
hot as a June bride in a feather bed
   real hot weather
in high cotton
   in a great mood or situation

it's getting drunk outside
   a way of saying one is totally wasted
No Little Rock
   North Little Rock
seeing double and feeling single
   inebriated and incautiously carefree
that dog'll hunt
   that will work

KENTUCKY

Kentuckians may have a Southern accent but by no means do
they strictly identify with Dixie. In fact Kentucky was neutral in
the Civil War and rests above the fabled Mason-Dixon line.

Dick Miller
   all-purpose expression: 'Oh, Dick Miller!'. Equivalent of 'what
   the heck'.
George
   good
Hey Nicky
   happy greeting from one Kentuckian to another
Loouh-vull
   Louisville
monkey time
   let's roll: 'Let's go with it. It's monkey time.'
oilheads
   people who drink a lot of whiskey
run for the roses
   the Kentucky Derby
that's monkey
   don't bullshit me
Tom
   bad; opposite of 'George'

PENNSYLVANIA & THEREABOUTS

Pronunciation is a prime way to identify people from Pittsburgh or Philadelphia and any of the more rural regions of Pennsylvania, Indiana and thereabouts. Here, 'water' sounds like 'wooder' – 'wooderier' if it's more diluted. 'Coop' sounds like 'kewp' and 'creek' is pronounced 'crick'. G's are 'dropped' as in goin' or doin'. Some words are lengthened: 'downtown' becomes 'daantaan'. Other words are shortened in certain phrases, as in 'goin' up 'ere'. 'Rule, role, roll' are all pronounced identically, as are 'Mary, merry, marry', and 'coal' and 'cool'.

YOUSE WANNA SCRAPPLE?

Philadelphia's dialect is interesting in that the 'r' is pronounced here, despite its being surrounded by the 'r-less' regions of New England, New York and the coastal South. The city has its own vocabulary, too. Some words in common usage in the Philly area are:

anymore
   at the present time, currently: 'I work at the library anymore.'
baby coach
   baby carriage
hoagie
   submarine sandwich
pavement
   sidewalk
scrapple
   a local breakfast dish
square
   city block
youse, you all
   you plural

BETWEEN
THE COASTS

Both Hoosiers (people from Indiana) and Pennsylvanians favour the question form that ends in 'at': 'Where are you at?', which emphasises the question. Some Pennsylvanians use 'younse' (yinz) – particularly Pittsburghers – to indicate the second-person plural pronoun, while in Philly it's 'yous'; 'OK, I'll see younse later.'; 'What can I get younse?'

Natives also note a slower pace to life and time for telling stories, talking in a leisurely fashion, and eating Dilly bars at the local Dairy Queen (a popular place throughout the USA for soft ice cream).

City and rural life and other class distinctions find their way into the language: a 'ridgerunner' is a Western Pennsylvanian equivalent of 'redneck'; 'cake eater' is a serious insult in New Castle, PA, a term for kids in the neighbouring township because they are more well-to-do. It's also become a way to tell someone they're showing off or acting like a snob. A vacuum is a 'sweeper' and to 'red up' means to clean up.

The East Coast stretches from Maine to Washington, DC, where it begins to become the Southeast and the variation is considerable. Still, within the region there are some recognisable overlaps: 'aunt' pronounced 'auhnt', not 'ant'; 'dungarees' for jeans; 'ice box' for refrigerator; 'swim trunks' for swim suit. Even Boston's famous intensifier – 'wicked' – is fairly widespread throughout New England.

NEW YORK CITY

In New York speed is of the essence. Talk fast, and then faster. New Yorkers have a lot to say and never enough time to say it all. Hence the ubiquitous machine-gun question, thrown in at any point during someone's reply to a previous machine-gun question. When using the machine-gun question the key is to interrupt someone's reply, answer questions for them, punctuate their answer with asides to create the effect that 'we're answering this together'. It's known as a high-involvement style.

NEW YORK

'New Yorkers seem to think the best thing two people can do is talk. Silence is okay when you're watching a movie (though it might be better if punctuated by clever asides) or when you're asleep (collecting dreams to tell when you're awake) ... Talking is a New Yorker's way of showing friendship, especially to strangers.'

Deborah Tannen, Professor of Linguistics
at Georgetown and author of
You Just Don't Understand: Women
and Men in Conversation

The presence of public spaces also means involvement. In some parts of the city – the East Village, for instance – a public space means a meeting of neighbours, a place in which people gather to talk about issues concerning their geographic location, or chat, drink, walk dogs or play dominos.

Social or cultural ties are also created through shared language and interactional routines. One native New Yorker, who comes from a Jewish home on Long Island, has noticed similarities throughout the Northeast: 'Pace, dialect and the use of Yiddish often lead to a connection between Northeastern Jews'.

When people try to imitate a New Yorker they'll usually go for the Brooklyn accent.

New York Talk

- substitute 'k' for 'p': 'He *bunked* into a car.'
- drop articles in certain contexts. Don't 'play the piano', simply 'play piano'.
- d is often deleted mid-word: 'She *dint* come over for dinner.'
- r is a free agent. It appears between certain combinations of sounds: 'My wife's a lawryuh. Linder Rondstadt. He's drawring pikshuhs of pigeons in the park. Gimme a slice-a pizzer anna soder.' Then it disappears when you don't quite expect it: 'Is it down on toidy-toid street?'
- liberally season sentences and even words with the all-purpose 'fuck' – absofuckinglutely. Only in New York and parts of New Jersey is fuck not taboo. It is considered taboo on stretches of Park Avenue.
- greeting rituals include 'How *you* doin'?' or 'Hey, how yous doin'?'

Basic New York Vocabulary

absofuckinglutely
absolutely

attache cases
big portable radios, aka 'boom boxes'

ax
ask

Bed-Stuy
Bedford-Stuyvesant section of Brooklyn made famous by Spike Lee in *Do the Right Thing*

bodega
corner market

bridge & tunnel people
the people who don't live in Manhattan but come in to work or party in Manhattan

The City
New York City. True natives will also say New York, but never New York City. Interestingly when you take the subway from the borough of Brooklyn to the borough of Manhattan you say you're going to New York.

fuck
The 'f-word' is to be used with extreme caution in all parts of the country, including New York, but it does have a special cachet in the Big Apple. It is often associated with the 'toughness' accrued to New Yorkers and thus shows up in a variety of utterances. Just listen and learn. In fact, some people say that the courage to regularly use 'fuck' is the litmus test of a true New Yorker. 'Fuck'n A, we got fucked up on that fuck'n shit. Fuck it maaaan, whadda fuck'n mess. What da fuck, ho-lee fuck'n shit, that fuck-off really fucked up. Fuck that! Don't fuck wid me, you fuckface.'

fuggedaboudit
'forget about it' – an all-purpose expression with positive and negative connotations

gedoutahea
    'get out of here' – please leave now or, more congenially, you're
    not serious: 'Gedoutahea, you're pull'n my leg.'
HOWston
    pronunciation of Houston Street
the Korean
    Korean-owned vegetable stands: 'I'm going to the Korean'
the Ladies Mile
    6th Avenue, between 14th and 23rd streets in Manhattan. Fa-
    bled stretch of opulent department stores catering to women.
landlord's halo
    a bare lightbulb hanging in a New York tenement hallway
no problem
    you're welcome
noodge
    pest or nag: 'Don't be a noodge.'
on line
    in line; you wait on line in New York
or what?
    tag phrase put at end of accusing question: 'Are you blind,
    or what?'
The Orient Express
    the subway (the no. 7 Flushing line) to Shea Stadium, Queens,
    home of many Asian immigrants
pisser
    can mean a real bummer or someone/something that is truly
    great: 'My job's a real pisser.' (I love it)
regular
    cup of coffee with milk, no sugar
schlepp
    to cart or drag around, including oneself
stoop
    a flight of steps leading up to a porch in front of a door where
    people sit, schmooze and play stoopball
take
    have: 'take a haircut.'

Yo!
    greeting; can also mean 'Watch it!'

Local pronunciations you may or may not hear:

da Bronx
    Bronx
dallah
    dollar (Canal Street pronunciation)
lenths
    lengths: 'He went to heroic lenths.'
Noo Yawkah
    New Yorker
ongana
    'I'm going to …'
soder
    pop, soda
soupa
    super: 'We had a soupa time at da fights.'
Stat'n Oi-land
    Staten Island
vanella
    vanilla

UPSTATE NEW YORK

There's a huge difference between upstate and downstate. Those from downstate stick out when they head north into the Catskill Mountains to their vacation homes and ski trips. There's also a big distinction between the flatlands/flatlanders and hilltowns in upstate NY, to the point where you often see bumper stickers saying 'You gotta be tough to live on the mountain. Some make it, some don't' and 'I ain't no flatlander'. Probably the most colourful word used to describe people is 'goobrock'. This term is used by flatlanders to insultingly describe people in the hilltowns as uneducated, lazy, drunk, etc. The same term is used by the goobrocks among themselves with pride.

EAST COAST

NEW JERSEY

The New Jersey accent isn't just about dropping the 'r' on words like dollar or butter. There are distinctions between north and south as well as the south Jersey shore. There are some key words to listen for: 'water' sounds like 'wooder', 'dog' like 'dawg', and 'orange' like 'arange'.

BOSTON

The Boston accent is known for the absence of 'r' in words like park, car, Harvard, smart and yard. Pre-eminent is the use of 'wicked' – a superlative used in the same way as 'very': '*Good Will Hunting* was wicked smaht'. Thus things can be wicked cool, wicked ugly, a wicked pisser (something bad), etc.

Another characteristic Boston expression is 'So isn't it' at the end of a sentence to add emphasis to a position that opposes what another person is saying. Some neighbourhoods have a plural form of 'you' that sounds like 'ya's', as in 'Catch ya's latah (later)'.

Boston is a small city, but most people identify with a certain residential section. A lot of these neighbourhoods have names that the residents use to describe them. It's important to know that South Boston is a very different place from the South End.

South Boston

Also known as Southie, it is a relatively low-income neighbourhood located on the water. In recent years there has been a wave of gentrified settlement in the area with the prospect of a new waterfront development. The area is settled predominantly by Irish Americans.

The North End

A neighbourhood close to downtown and the Fleet Center. The North End is a half-residential and half-business district and has the largest concentration of Italian Americans.

The South End

An area which borders Roxbury, one of the more dangerous areas in Boston, and has recently experienced a sort of resurrection. The South End is home to a significant gay community, and it also features several art galleries, gourmet restaurants and stores.

The Back Bay

One of Boston's ritziest neighbourhoods, the Back Bay was built upon a swampy bay, so the name is a bit misleading as it is nowhere near the water.

EAST COAST

Jamaica Plain

Known by residents as JP, this is a neighbourhood located near the Longwood Hospital area. One of Boston's best loved ice cream franchises, 'JP Licks', started here.

Boston Area Terms

bubbler
water fountain

The Cs
the Boston Celtics (basketball team)

the Cape and the Islands
Cape Cod, Nantucket and Martha's Vineyard

frappes
milkshakes

Fud and Kud
as in Chelmsford (pronounced CHUMS-fud), Medford (pronounced MEHD-fud) and Concord (pronounced KAHN-kud)

go to the packy
go to buy liquor (at the packet store)

Head of the Charles
a big Cambridge rowing regatta held on the city's Charles River

legacy
you're a son, daughter or close relative of someone who has been to Harvard. You may not be qualified to attend, though you most likely will – a term used throughout the Ivy Leagues.

Mass
shorthand way to refer to Massachusetts

Mass Pike
Massachusetts Turnpike

Nor'easter
a storm that comes from the northeast and usually hits the coast with high winds, rain or snow

scratchie
'scratch ticket' for the state lottery (common term in Dorchester and South Boston)

St Botolph
    patron saint of Boston
Shawmut
    original Native American name for Boston
Smoot
    a unit of measurement. In 1958 a drunk pledge at MIT's
    Lambda Chi Alpha fraternity was required by his frat brothers
    to measure the length of the MIT Bridge using his own body
    as a yardstick. Unwittingly, Oliver R Smoot, 5 feet 7 inches,
    became the first human ever used as a unit of measurement.
Subs (for submarine sandwich)
    grinders; in Western Mass, as well as Connecticut, 'subs' revert
    back to 'grinders'.
The T
    refers to MBTA, the Massachusetts Bay Transport Authority,
    which operates buses as well as the subway. Good luck under-
    standing anything the drivers announce. Your best bet is to
    follow your track along with the maps inside the train cars.
tonic
    anything carbonated

JEET? SHOOWA!

As in nearby Massachusetts, residents of 'The Ocean
State' have a unique way of speaking which is characterised by dropping the 'r' from certain words: 'car'
becomes 'cah' and 'park' is pronouced 'pahk'. Rhode
Islanders also insert 'r' after certain sounds, so that 'I
sawr rit' is heard rather than 'I saw it', and 'law'
becomes 'lawr'.
   Some sounds are lengthened and some significantly
reduced: 'shoowa' is a lengthened version of 'sure'.
'Jeet?' could be a way to ask 'Have you eaten yet?'.
Ice cream treats not to be missed include the Carvell
and the 'brown bonnet'.

EAST COAST

MAINE

Mainers themselves describe their way of talking as minimally informative, sometimes subminimally informative. Fishing and lobstering communities have a more pronounced, more traditional Maine accent, which includes adding 'r' to words ending in 'a' (Augustar), and dropping it for words such as 'chowdah' (chowder). Like Bostonians, Mainers themselves make prodigious use of 'wicked' (great, very, totally, awesome), as in wicked good, wicked fun, wicked sharp, something wicked.

Abanaki
'The People of Dawn'. Original settlers on Mount Desert Island before the Europeans arrived.

away
not from Maine in general, or a particular town in Maine

ayuh
the 'yes' equivalent. Can mean 'you betcha', 'that's right', 'hello', 'don't know' or can be used as a transition to a new thought or pause in conversation. Akin to New York City's all-purpose 'Yo!', but it is expressed with the Mainer's characteristic terseness.

black flies
ubiquitous nuisance during Maine spring

crocus sacks
coarse cloth bags

cruncher
hunterspeak for a very large deer

driver
hard worker

from away
unless you and your parents were born and raised in Maine, you are considered to be 'from away,' ie, not from Maine. Similar to 'northerner' or 'foreigner' in Arkansas.

gawmy
clumsy, awkward

green dickies
pants usually found on Maine hunters

grunters and groaners
a groaner is a foghorn with one prolonged tone; a grunter is a two-toned foghorn

guzzle hole
a place along Maine coast where one would find a store that also sold gasoline

jag of wood
a full load

MDI
local acronym for Mount Desert Island, located on the coast of Maine, home of Bar Harbor and Acadia National Park

Massholes
people from Massachusetts

on your beam ends
you're in bad shape, like a shipwreck that rests on the ends of her beams

PFAs
People From Away

punt
blunt-nosed boat, almost rectangular in shape, used to row around harbours and coves in Maine

quahog
thick-shelled American clam (pronounced 'co-hog')

Rockefeller Roads
the 57 miles of carriage roads in Acadia National Park built by John D Rockefeller

rusticators
early term for well-heeled summer folk who came to Maine for a break from the heat and humidity in their home locales

scouse
clam chowdah made without clams

scrid
a tiny portion

shagimaw
fictitious animal that is a cross between a mouse and a bear, allegedly found in remote parts of northern Maine

she goes with her head up and her tail over the dashboard
    a proud person
skims his milk at both ends
    stingy
steamers
    clams, second most valuable Maine salt water crop after
    the lobster
windflagging
    when the white pine (the Maine state tree) shows the direction of
    prevailing winds by sprouting branches on the downward side of
    the tree
wood-eaters
    an old-time name for moose
Yankee
    from the Abanaki word 'yenghi', meaning 'white people of
    New England'

Fishing Terms

Maine, with its ponds, streams, rivers and ocean shorelines, is a
draw for fishing, both saltwater and freshwater. Since it's a fair bet
that fishing may be a key topic of conversation, here are some
terms to get you started.

barvel
    a leather apron used by fishermen when salting down fish
bug
    lobster
canned tuna casserole
    food of Mainers everywhere except MDI. Only those from
    'away' eat fresh fish on a regular basis.
clammer
    he or she who digs for clams
feedy
    fisherman's term for when a fish's gut is so full of food it's only
    good for lobster bait
groundfishermen
    distinct from lobstermen, they go after halibut and flounder
gurry
    fish cleanings

gurrybutts
containers to put empty clam shells and discarded lobster debris. Used by diners in some Maine restaurants.

lobster car
a floating raft in which lobsters are stored at sea

pot
lobster trap

SPEAKING MASSACHUSETT

Massachusett of the Eastern Algonquian language family was once spoken by Native Americans who lived in southwestern New England. Massachusett consisted of different dialects, most of which were extinct by the 19th century. Not surprisingly, the word 'Massachusetts', which means 'at or near the great hills', comes from this language and was originally used to refer to a location smaller than the present US state of Massachusetts.

Today's descendents of the Native Americans who still live in the region use very few Algonquian words and expressions. The phrases meaning 'Good morning', 'I love you', and 'Peace be to you' have been preserved from one generation to the next but there is very little written record of this tongue.

The Massachusett Language Revival Project was initiated by Native Americans and language scholars to aid revival of the extinct American Algonquian phrases. Here are some of them:

mot-tomp-an wu-nee
good morning
nuk-kon wun-neeg-in
it is a beautiful night
a-queen-ee kah nah-hon-nush-shagk
peace and farewell
nock-uskor-at-tit-ee-ah wonk tee-an-uk
let us meet again soon

red tide
> poisonous rust-coloured algae occasionally ingested by clams and mussels, which accumulates in their bodies and can cause permanent paralysis in humans. Not killed by cooking.

warp
> rope used by Maine lobstermen to connect a lobster trap to the surface buoy

MARYLAND

In Maryland, it's customary to insult someone's highway driving by calling them a 'Pennsylvania driver'. Residents allege that Pennsylvania drivers typically drive more slowly and have trouble merging onto the freeway. Meanwhile it's very easy to inflame a Baltimorian by singing the praises of the New York Yankees.

Marylanders refer to taking a trip to the beach as 'going down the ocean'. Pronounced with a Baltimore accent it sounds like 'goowin danny-ayshun'. Speaking of the Baltimore accent, it sounds like Bawlmar (Baltimore) and Merlin (Maryland). The 'o' sounds are rounder: 'phone' sounds more like 'phoune', and the 't' is pronounced in the word 'often'.

An affectionate endearment in Baltimorese is referring to someone as 'Hon' (short for 'honey'). 'Ya know, like' often begins sentences, 'ya know, like, when you're late for a meeting.'

WASHINGTON, DC

The nation's capital marks a boundary between North and South and the language and cultural styles of both parts of the country are visible, sometimes leading to a sense of slow-paced urgency or intense leisure.

the Bank
> the World Bank, headquarters are in DC

inside the Beltway
> the physical area enclosed by the Beltway interstate system; the psychological state of 'being in the right place' amongst the movers and shakers of the Free World – close to the centre of power

the City
  in Washington, DC
freshman
  first-term member of Congress
fundies
  fundamentalist Christians
G-men
  FBI agents
grey ghost
  a Congressperson's top aide
Gypsy Moths
  liberal to moderate Republicans
the Hill
  Capitol Hill
Joe 6-Pack, The Average Joe
  the average guy – the point of reference for many political
  decisions; refers to cans of beer coming in packs of six
Langley
  the CIA (Central Intelligence Agency), which is based in
  Langley, Virginia
oilies
  oil industry lobbyists
PACs
  Political Action Committees
pork barrel
  funding for ostensibly unnecessary pet projects (often in a
  Congressperson's state or district) to please the folks back home
Pravda on the Potomac
  old Republican term for the *Washington Post*, used especially
  after the brilliant investigative work of Woodward and Bernstein
  that helped fell the Nixon presidency in 1974
revenue enhancement
  taxes
revenue shortfall
  need for more taxes
Sagebrush Rebels
  Western Congressmen who keep an eye on public land use issues

EAST COAST

spook
anybody who works for any of the intelligence agencies, especially the CIA

tree hugger
pejorative term for environmental activist

war chest
politician's campaign coffers

web issue
an issue that brings together unlikely political alliances, for example, between right-wing gun freaks and liberals

wiggle room
safety net that politicians create around their public utterances, giving them enough room to alter their opinion, ie, 'waffle'

wonk
public policy nerd, especially one who enjoys debating the more arcane and complicated aspects of public policy

wonkish
to act like a wonk

THE SOUTH

As with the other regions, there is no one Southern dialect. Characteristics vary from state to state and area to area within a state, and according to race and class. A given characteristic or word may appear in different areas scattered throughout the South.

Although some people don't want to admit it, over the past few hundred years of contact, Black English vernacular has influenced Southern English to various degrees, from the sounds of words and grammar features, to expressions and phrases.

Especially within the South, your view of 'Southernness' and how it is expressed through language will vary according to where you're from: Deep South (Mississippi and Alabama), coastal south (Virginia, Carolinas, Georgia, Florida), Delta South (Mississippi, Louisiana) and the Gulf States (Texas, Mississippi, Louisiana). In the South itself, the reference to region is more geographically bounded, referring to the name of the state, or 'the Gulf states' or 'the Charlotte area' or 'the (name) River area', 'eastern Tennessee'. The further away you are from the North, the more 'authentic' the roots.

Some parts of the South don't have the typical Southern accent – New Orleans is a prime example. Nonetheless, where it exists, it has often been socially stigmatised, especially by people from the North. To call a Southerner a 'hillbilly' is deeply offensive. The following are some general features of Southern speaking style:

- People in the South often lengthen vowels when they speak. You may also hear more of a rising or falling intonation with vowels in the South.
- Southern people often change the sound of a vowel, for example, 'thank you' may be pronounced 'thank yew'.
- One thing that makes Southern speech sound different is stress on the first syllable of a word: UM-brella, IN-surance, JU-ly, MON-roe.

- When words end in -ing, the endings are pronounced -in: walkin', travelin', eat'n', parkin', gett'n'.
- The letter 'r' is dropped, often from the end of a word (better is 'bettuh'; car is 'cah'), or from the middle of the word (farm is 'fahm' or 'fawm'; quarter is 'quawtuh').
- The letter 'i' has three different pronunciations: the first two ways, 'eye' and 'ah', are the most common. The third sounds a lot like 'ah', but flatter, and may be hard to distinguish. Southerners do not always pronounce this sound the same way. The further South you go, the more often you will hear 'i' pronounced as 'ah'.

- Much like British or Australian usage, Southerners often add a preposition before articles, such as 'to' and 'at', when they are used for motion or location:

    I'm goin' over to my brother's house.
    She's walkin' up to the mailbox.
    They are sittin' down at the river.

- 'Ya'll' is the plural of 'you'. It refers to two or more people. In Texas, another y'all construction has come about: 'all y'all' – roughly equivalent to 'all of you'.
- If someone calls you 'sugar', know that it's a classic term of endearment, used with people you know as well as those you don't know. It is not meant to be condescending. (In Maryland, the ubiquitous 'hon' fills the same function.)
- When a Southerner asks you how you are, they often genuinely want to know and to start a conversation. Not that this is not true in other places, but it is characteristic in the South.
- You may hear 'well' and 'oh' often in conversation. This word may have a purpose such as filling time when a person is thinking of something to say, but it often is said at the beginning of a comment. This does not mean that the person is hesitating or unsure of themselves. It is simply a habit of many Southern people.

THE SOUTH

Good Ol' Southern Hospitality

The vaunted Southern hospitality comes from its many social rituals. For instance, when Southerners greet it is very much a warm, how-are-you handshake, door-opening and chair-pulling-out kind of thing. They will bring food and insist on serving tea or lemonade.

In some sectors of society there is great emphasis put on privacy and courteousness and there are entire topics that are never addressed, even within families. At the same time, a great deal of the language in terms of personal interaction comes across as blunt.

One aspect of Southern culture that may unsettle visitors to the region, especially given the ritualised aspects of hospitality, is a tone of extreme sweetness coupled with what might be construed as an insult or criticism, as in, 'Bless his heart, he is just as ugly as he can be'. Some people might go straight for colourful Southern bluntness without the linguistic sugar: 'Ooh, Lord, that boy fell out the ugly tree and hit every branch on the way down' or 'Girl, that dress makes your butt look like the broadside of the USS *Missouri*. Don't buy it'.

★ ★ ★ ★ **THE SOUTHERN WAY** ★ ★ ★ ★

The true Southern culture as I see it is a sweet tea-drinking; biscuit, grits and sausage gravy eating; and gossiping on the back porch sort of place – all mixed in with a little African voodoo magic, old wives' tales, magnolias, gardenias, humid and sticky nights, mosquitoes and alligators. A true Southerner won't walk and smoke – they stand still and smoke and talk, or hide the fact that they smoke. A tourist will find that everyone seems sweet, slow walkers and drivers. People smile and say 'good afternoon'. Men usually hold doors open.

– Mary-Denise Tabar

WHAT TO SAY ...

if you are serious:
Girl, I am serious as a heart attack.

if you were very shocked:
I was so surprised I nearly went into cardiac arrest.

if someone is bothering you:
You are gettin' on my last nerve.
Oooh, Sweet Jesus, I am not in the mood for this [cussword of choice] today.

if someone does something excessively, and annoyingly:
That boy is a runnin' fool, an eatin' fool, a singin' fool, etc.

if food or drink is too strong or spicy:
That étouffé was so spicy it like to slap your tongue out your head.
That tea is so strong it could make a dead man sit up and whistle Dixie.

to warn against interfering:
Let them run their mouths while you run your business.

to refer to stupidity or inattentiveness:
She/He don't know shit from Shinola.
She/He don't know upside down from straight across.

to refer to a bullshitter:
Mean as a snake and twice as twisty.

if the weather is really, really frigid:
It's colder than a witch's tit (in a brass brassiere)!

bodega (pronounced 'bo-DAY-ga')
   small grocery store

Can I carry you somewhere?
   Can I take you somewhere?

cuss
   to swear or curse

I didn't know him from Adam's off-ox
   I didn't know him at all; I didn't know him from Adam

mash the button
   push the button (in an elevator, for instance)

she/he doesn't take tea for the fever
   to be upset about something, and refuse to take comfort
   from others

trailer trash
   derogatory term for a lower-income person often with little
   formal education; also used outside the South to signify a
   general style and not a specific type of individual

waiting on you
   waiting for you

FRENCH & SPANISH IN THE SOUTH

In Louisiana, especially the further south you go, you'll hear Creole French, a variety of French influenced by English, Spanish, African and Native American speakers. Many towns in the marshlands near the Gulf of Mexico have public signs in French.

Creole words used in social settings include 'bourrée' (Cajun poker) and 'lagniappe' (something extra). Some words for New World French cuisine are 'étouffé' (to steam or braise), 'beignet' (deep-fried pastry) and 'courtbouillon' (fish soup).

In Florida and Texas you'll hear a great deal of Spanish as it's the native language (monolingually or bilingually) of a large percentage of the population. Public signage is in Spanish and English.

SOUTH FLORIDA

SoFlo is not one language. It's polyglot – part Colonial Caribbean, part Eastern European, part working-class English, part good ole Dixie. There are perhaps a dozen language groups in this part of Florida (not all of them resting beside each other comfortably). Tampa, for instance, is strongly influenced by Cuban and Spanish cultures. In Miami alone you'll find unique lexicons for Little Havana, Little Haiti, South Beach, Coconut Grove and a host of other ethnic enclaves. Here, we've created just two categories – Key West and Miami, and have thrown in a few other examples to help orient you to the Sunshine State.

LIKE A YANKEE

Doing anything 'like a Yankee' is a surefire put down in the South, as Yankees are seen as arrogant, stuffy and insincere. So you might hear something like, 'You talk like a Yankee' or 'You drink beer like a Yankee'. Most important is referring to activities that 'Deep South' Southerners feel they do better than anyone else, like play sports, cook, drink, gamble, etc. It would not be quite as effective saying something like, 'You watch TV like a Yankee' or 'You ride a bike like a Yankee'.

Another somewhat negative term is 'Border Yankees', basically people from the border states like Kentucky, Virginia, etc, who are not 'real' Southerners because they are not from the Deep South. It is always astonishing for people from the Deep South to hear folks from the North refer to people from Virginia and like places as 'Southerners'. Their response: 'You have no idea what you're talking about. Come on down to the Mississippi Delta and we'll show you the real South.'

KEY WEST

The indigenous language here is Conch (pronounced 'conk'), nickname of the locals. But some say there's so much Cockney in Conch that one might rightly call the language 'Conchney'. There's also a heavy Caribbean influence, particularly from the Bahamas, as opposed to the Haitian/Cuban influence in Miami. Many of these words and expressions can still be heard in a conversation with older Conchs raised in Key West.

boatel
  it's not just a boat, it's not just a hotel – it's a boatel. And it's unique to Key West.

bolios (pronounced 'boy-ohs')
  a Key West version of southern hush puppies made with mashed, shelled black-eyed peas instead of ground corn meal

Cayo Hueso
  the original name of Key West; translated it means 'Little Island of Bones' because, as the legend goes, when Spanish settlers arrived on the island they discovered bones left over from Indian battles. Today one of the names of the popular Conch trolleys is the Cayo Hueso Express.

conch (pronounced 'conk')
  a chewy pink-coloured shellfish that comes in huge spiral-shaped shells (without the critter inside you blow the shells as horns or put them next to your ear to hear the ocean). Also the nickname for anyone born in Key West.

conch cruiser
  an old rusty bike with basket, no fenders and high handlebars; or an old beat up car, sometimes stolen from up north

conch houses
  built in the 1850s by original Key West settlers who came from Great Britain via the Bahamas

grunt
  a fish you can easily catch but wouldn't want to unless you were awfully hungry; takes its name from the grunting sound it makes

THE SOUTH

grunt bone alley

 where locals would toss their grunt bones during the Great
 Depression (a time when Key Westers ate only grits and grunts)

how ya doin', cuz?

 familiar Conch to Conch salutation

key lime

 the scrubby key lime tree grows to about 15 feet. Key limes
 (aka 'true limes') are greenish-yellow and are more tart than
 other limes.

key lime pie

 the area's signature dessert, featuring the small limes native to
 SoFlo, a yellow meringue topping and a graham cracker crust

Mañanaville

 Key West. As Jack Moyer of the historic Conch Tour Train
 notes, 'Nobody's on time in Key West. There's nothing that
 can't be put off till tomorrow'.

Margaritaville

 Key West, immortalised in the lyrics to Jimmy Buffet's song,
 'Margaritaville' ('Wasted away again in Margaritaville')

MIAMI AREA

barbacoa

 the original name for barbecue – said to be so-named by the
 Seminole Indians

bodega

 a store specialising in Latin American groceries

cafe Cubano

 very strong black brew, served in thimble-sized cups with lots
 of sugar

cafe con leche
> same as Cafe Cubano but with warm milk – very popular

calle ocho
> SW Eighth in Miami's Little Havana, the street that literally and figuratively divides Miami – Coral Gables to the south and Hispanic, Haitian and African-American neighbourhoods to the north

crackers
> people who were born and raised in the Sunshine State. According to author Joyce LaFray Young, the test of a true-blue cracker is whether they have eaten swamp cabbage, the terminal bud of the Sabal palm. Careful using this term; it's also a pejorative way of referring to white people.

dolfin fish
> don't be misled or confused when you see this for sale in local fish markets. A SoFlo speciality, this plump fish has nothing to do with the marine mammal.

Everglades
> 'pa-hay-okee' or 'grassy waters', according to the native Miccosukee Indians. This 50-mile wide (80 km), 100-mile long (161 km) and only six-inch-deep river of saw grass barely hangs on as America's largest remaining subtropical wilderness.

Palmetto bugs
> cockroaches – huge ones. Another term for Miami politicians.

pan Cubano (Cuban bread)
> famous, long, denatured white crusty Cuban bread

plátanos
> deep-fried, soft, deliciously sweet plantain bananas, served regularly as a side dish

pullmanette
> 1940s lingo for a hotel room with a fridge, stove, sink (and roaches)

Seminoles
> native residents of the land now called Florida; about 2500 of them remain

SoFlo
South Florida; aka Baha New York

Spanglish
the mixture of Spanish and English in a single conversation – heard throughout SoFlo

Tropical Deco
Art Deco in Miami; architectural style unique to SoFlo. Essentially Art Deco adapted to the climate of Miami. Features flamingos, palm trees, alligators etched in glass and nautical elements (ship-like porch railings, porthole windows).

turistas
tourists; aka gringos

Yanquis
Yankees

ziggurat
stairstepping – the lightning flash effect on Art Deco rooflines, particularly on structures from the Med-Deco period of the late 1920s and early '30s

THE MELTING POT

AFRICAN-AMERICAN ENGLISH

Many people think that black English, African-American English
or Ebonics – the names all refer to the same thing – is bad English
or slang, or think that people who use it are uneducated. But no
stereotype could be further from the truth. Although it is not the
same as standard English, the variety of English that has developed
among African-American communities is not randomly different.
On the contrary, it has a complicated and consistent set of
grammatical rules, some of which are the same as those of other
varieties and dialects of English.

For example, saying 'ask' as 'aks', 'that' as 'dat' or 'mouth' as
'mouf' follow clear rules about how to pronounce certain letters
together. Saying 'two dog', not 'two dogs' or 'they house', not
'their house', or 'he run', not 'he runs', are not wrong by the rules
of this well-defined language variety.

The rules for using forms of 'to be' are especially detailed and
allow speakers to make distinctions in fewer words than other
English speakers need. For example, 'She be late' means 'She is
always late' and 'She late' means 'She is late now' – there is no
need to say 'always' or 'now'. Sometimes these distinctions can
cause misunderstandings: 'He bin married' means that 'he is still
married' to most speakers of this variety of English, but most
standard English speakers think that he was married before but he
isn't now. Because these rules are so subtle, it is very easy to spot
someone who is mocking the variety – they get it wrong.

Misunderstandings can also arise with the use of double negatives.
Standard English speakers are taught not to use double negatives
and that, if they are used, they cancel each other out. In this
variety of English, however, they make the negative even stronger:
'Ain't no girl gonna wear that dress' means 'There is no way that
any girl is going to wear that dress'.

Sometimes words and expressions sound like Southern dialects,
reflecting the long history that African Americans have with the
South. For example, stressing the first syllable in 'PO-lice' and

making vowels longer, often for emphasis ('ba-a-a-d!'). (Of course, 'ba-a-a-d!' usually means 'really good'!) Words like 'ain't' are also heard in other English dialects.

Many words and phrases that start out in African-American speech are taken up by speakers of other forms of English, especially by teenagers as a form of slang. Over the years, 'tote', 'jive', 'cool', 'Right on!' 'high-five' and 'rap' have become familiar to non-African Americans.

An emphasis on verbal skill and the ability to play with language is also important. There are many established verbal games and speaking patterns, some (like parts of the grammar) with roots in African cultures and others that developed as ways to cope with the powerlessness of slavery.

The insults that are exchanged in the game often called 'the dozens' (also known as capping, styling and signifying) can be easily misunderstood as serious insults. It's a traditional, stylised verbal game in which the players pile on the insults. It appears to insult family members, especially mothers. But part of the skill is to keep it a game and never cross the line by making people angry.

The active participation of the audience in a verbal event, whether it is a game, a sermon or a speech, may be unfamiliar. People who expect just to listen to a speaker will find that their fellow listeners are far from silent, as they make short comments on what is said, offer words of agreement and encouragement. One example is interjecting at intervals with 'Amen' in church. This is not done in order to take attention away from the speaker or to heckle. Instead it shows that the audience is involved in what the speaker is saying, that they are really listening.

Not all African Americans speak this variety of English, and people of other ethnic backgrounds who grew up in African-American communities usually know and speak it, too. Furthermore, African Americans who speak it usually also speak some form of standard English and switch back and forth depending on the situation and to whom they are talking. Many also choose to use this form of English symbolically, to make a point about ethnic identity and to express a political opinion about racism, power and educational and social opportunity in America.

JEWISH

Contrary to popular belief, not all American Jews live in New York. In fact, you will find many heavily populated Jewish communities in major cities across the United States including Los Angeles, Chicago, Miami and Boston. Unlike some of the stereotypical depictions, Jews come from all walks of life and many different cities, and look and sound and behave differently everywhere. The TV comedy *Seinfeld* has popularised a version of the assimilated stereotypical Jew. The movie *Keeping the Faith* came close to accurately characterising Conservative/Reform Manhattan young Judaism.

Judaism is equally varied, with differences based on theological grounds and cultural and religious practice. There are three different branches of Judaism – Orthodox, Conservative and Reform – which vary according to belief in God, knowledge of the past texts of your tradition, and the practice of traditional rituals and means of commemoration. In all cases words and expressions are fundamental to religious identity.

THE MELTING POT

WHAT'S KOSHER?

Kosher is a term used to define food that is rabbinically allowed to the Jewish people for consumption. Kosher food today is food that has been watched to make sure it does not come into contact with non-Kosher ingredients. Kosher doesn't allow for milk and meat to be mixed together so you will find meat kosher restaurants and dairy kosher restaurants. In Yiddish these are referred to as Milchik (milk) and Fleishik (meat). Smoking is one way of making meat Kosher (smoking and salting meat take all the blood out of it).

Outside the food realm, the word can also be used to refer to the propriety of a situation, as in 'the president's and intern's relationship was not kosher'.

Popular media has been responsible for transmitting Jewish ways of talking to the larger culture. Many popular phrases have emerged from the Jewish population – a large portion of whom immigrated to the USA between 1880 and 1920 – whose vernacular is influenced by both Hebrew and Yiddish (as well as German). Yiddish is a Germanic language with elements of Slavic, Romance and Aramaic – and a language that is considered endangered. Here are some of the more popular phrases, some of which are used more exclusively by those within the community and some of which have become mostly mainstream:

bubbe meisis
> nonsense, old wives' tales: 'Don't give me your bubba meisis.'

Bubeh
> grandma

chutzpah
> audacity: 'I could not believe she spoke to her boss that way – she has real chutzpah.'

fress
> to eat a lot quickly, to gorge: 'He's such a fresser when I make his favorite meal.'

kvell
> an outpouring of pride in someone's accomplishment

kvetch
> complain

macher
> somebody who thinks they are very important or someone who is energetically accomplished: 'When he walks into the room, he acts like such a macher.'

mensch
> literally translated as a man, but means someone who acts properly and with character: 'After the date, he called me like a mensch.' Can also be used for a woman.

mumella
> term of endearment

nebish
  nerd
nosh
  to snack on
Oy gevalt. Oy vey! Oy!
  'oh my gosh', or 'oh no!'
shiksa
  non-Jewish girl
shlep
  to carry, to drag along. Can also be used to refer to a person
  who is dragging you down: 'He's such a shlep.'
shmaltz(y)
  sappy or sentimental
shmatas
  rags
shmootz
  dirt
shtik
  a routine
shukut
  non-Jewish boy
shul
  synagogue or temple
tchochkes
  knick-knacks
tuchis
  behind
Zeyde
  grandfather

The ever-popular Yiddish words, 'shmuck' and 'putz', both refer
to the male anatomy and can be used in the noun and adjectival
form: 'That was a very shmucky thing to do' or 'He can be such
a putz when he's in a bad mood.'

THE MELTING POT

JEWISH HOLIDAY

Jewish holidays are also important and are celebrated throughout the year.

Passover, which commemorates the Jews leaving Egypt 4000 years ago, is celebrated in the springtime. People often go to a Seder, which is a ceremonial meal during the first two nights of Passover.

Other important holidays include: Rosh Hashanah, the Jewish New Year; Yom Kippur, the Day of Atonement; and Hanukah, everyone's favourite, which is celebrated by the kindling of lights on a menorah (candelabra) sometime in November or December. Gifts are also given during the eight days of Hanukah and some lucky children receive one gift every day.

Food

Jewish food is incredibly important to the culture. Besides bagels and lox, some popular Jewish foods are matzo balls and chicken soup, challah (braided bread used on Friday nights to honour the Sabbath) and hamentashen (triangular shaped cookies filled with jam or poppy seeds). While delis are something that people associate with being Jewish, not all delis are Jewish-run or Kosher. Italian delis and Middle Eastern delis often overlap in the foods they carry. Other Jewish foods include cholent – a meat, potato and bean stew made before the Sabbath and left on a low flame on Friday night so you can eat it warm on Saturday after synagogue. Kashe varnishkas is another popular dish – a mix of pasta bow-ties and buckwheat.

US SPANISH

Spanish has been spoken in the Americas as long as Europeans have been coming to the New World. Spaniards brought their different regional dialects to North, Central and South America. Spanish in the New World was also influenced by the languages of the Native Americans. Everyday Spanish in the United States is therefore different from the standard Spanish taught in schools or spoken in other parts of the world. Furthermore, immigration to the USA from many parts of the Spanish-speaking world has led to changes in US Spanish, as these different regional varieties influence each other.

There are also recognisable local dialects in Chicano Spanish, based on the home of the original immigrants. East Los Angeles Spanish has been heavily influenced by dialects of Mexican Spanish, New York Spanish by the Spanish of Puerto Rico and Miami Spanish (until very recently) by that of Cuba, and so on.

Spanish has been maintained over generations in some Latino communities but much of the Spanish spoken in the US today is spoken by immigrants from Central and South America. There is a vibrant Spanish-language media and Spanish is often seen as one's 'home' language.

THE MELTING POT

CHICA-NO O SI?

'Hispanic' is a bureaucratic term for US citizens of Latin-American extraction but it is a term to avoid. Latinos don't like it and use the term 'Latino' or 'Latina' instead. Among all the Latinos are Mexican Americans, also known as Chicanos. The term Chicano (or Chicana), like 'black' for African-American, was once a term of disparagement; its value was inverted when it was adopted in the 1960s and '70s as a signal of ethnic pride. Young people do not use the term much until they get the bigger historical picture; most Mexican Americans become Chicanas/os in their college years.

Many Spanish speakers in the USA are fully bilingual, especially those born here. They often use Spanish at home or among close friends but English in public places such as work or school. When they are with other bilingual speakers they may code-switch, that is, go back and forth between the two languages as they talk: 'Vamos a tu house' (Let's go to your house).

Another result of bilingualism has been 'Spanglish', a mixed speech variety that is basically Spanish in its grammar, but has borrowed a lot of English words, treating them as if they were Spanish words by using Spanish endings (eg, 'park[e]ar' 'to park [a car]'; 'park[e]o, park[e]as, park[e]a' = 'I park, you park, s/he parks'). Other borrowed English words are given a Spanish pronunciation, eg, 'factoría' (factory).

In the same way, the English spoken by Latinos, especially those who identify themselves culturally and sociopolitically as Chicanos, has been influenced by Spanish. For example, a Chicano English speaker may speak primarily in English but use certain Spanish-derived words that mark him as 'Chicano' (or her as 'Chicana') (perhaps even from a particular area, such as a certain neighbourhood).

Many Spanish speakers from Spain or Mexico think that US Spanish, 'Chicano Spanish' and Spanglish are corrupt types of language, and the use of them can be heavily frowned upon. People who speak that way can be perceived negatively. The same has been true of Chicano English. However, precisely because these language types are so characteristic of US Latinos they are often used as proud markers of ethnic or community identity within the American context, especially in contrast to the dominant Anglo-American culture.

YEEEEEE-HAR!

Many Spanish terms for ranch work are used regularly by both Spanish and English speakers:

chaparreras	chaps
encalmar	control cattle
espuelas	spurs
la reata	lariat, lasso
mesteño	mustang
remuda	string of horses
remudero	horse wrangler

Other terms are familiar as adoptions into the English language: bronco, rodeo, corral.

THE MELTING POT

THE MELTING POT

ASIAN-AMERICAN LANGUAGES

Asian-Americans are a diverse group with many subcultures and distinct languages so it is difficult to generalise about any particular dialect or accent. Of the five most spoken languages in the world, three are Asian: Mandarin (number one), Bengali and Hindi (ranked four and five respectively). According to statistics provided by the National Asian Pacific American Legal Consortium, the most spoken languages by Asian Americans in accordance to the population of these groups in the USA are:

1. Chinese (Mandarin and Cantonese)
2. Filipino (Tagalog)
3. Japanese
4. Asian Indian (Hindi)
5. Korean

In the 1990 Census about 2.5 million Asian Americans (approximately 56 per cent) indicated that they do not speak English 'very well'. Moreover, 34.9% of the Asian Pacific American population lives in linguistically isolated households where there is no-one 14 years or older who can speak English well.

Due to continued immigration in the last decade the numbers of limited-English proficient individuals and linguistically isolated households within the Asian-American population have increased. Therefore, most Asian-American communities are against English-only legislation because it is seen as one of the key barriers contributing to the 'glass ceiling' which prevents advancement to prominent positions for those without English proficiency. For many Asian Americans, non-proficiency in English also denies them adequate government services, including health care and equal protection in judicial proceedings.

Language plays a crucial role for a community in the preservation of their identity and culture. Although the gap between first, second and third generations of Asian Americans continues to grow, a major part of culture and identity will continue to be manifested through language, even for those who speak English primarily and their native language secondarily.

There is growing concern in various Asian-American communities that indigenous languages are being lost as younger generations of Asian Americans are losing touch with their mother tongue and adopting English as their primary language. This is part of the process by which immigrants who come to this country lose their native language by the third generation. The Asian-American community feels it is important that language preservation remains an important part of cultural identity among Asian-American families and that the government supports bilingual education and services.

It is an unfortunate fact that there are many racial epithets associated with Asian Americans which have deep-rooted historical origins, starting in the early days of anti-Asian sentiment in the United States at the end of the 19th century. During WWII there were anti-Japanese campaigns, and there was much anti-Vietnamese sentiment in the late 1960s and early 1970s.

Since Asian languages are unique and distinct from one another it is difficult to make any generalised claims. However to many Western scholars, Asians tend to be more indirect with explicit rules of politeness during conversations, synonymous with the notion of 'saving face' in most Asian cultures. In many Asian languages, social status can be denoted within the language, especially when addressing an elder family member or someone in a prominent social class.

THE MELTING POT

HERITAGE LANGUAGES

More than 150 non-English languages are spoken in the United States. The term 'heritage language' has been used to refer to immigrant languages, indigenous languages and colonial languages – like Greek, Spanish, Chinese, Dutch, Yiddish and Navajo – and is predicated on the notion that languages of heritage are valuable and worth sustaining.

There are two main sources of heritage language programs: the heritage language communities themselves, and public schools, community colleges and universities. The formal education system has made only limited progress to date in developing heritage language resources. Recently the Center for Applied Linguistics (CAL) and the National Foreign Language Center (NFLC) launched an initiative to overcome this neglect.

THE MELTING POT

PENNSYLVANIA GERMAN

Pennsylvania German is still spoken by conservative Amish and Mennonite groups in North America. These communities have their origins in the Anabaptist movement of 16th-century Europe. The language grew out of a blend of the different dialects that came into Pennsylvania during the first wave of immigration in the 17th century – from the Palatinate in Germany and surrounding areas like Bavaria, Hessen, Swabia and Wurttemberg as well as the German-speaking areas of Switzerland.

Through a general levelling process the language varieties of these early German-speaking migrants mixed to produce what we now know as Pennsylvania German. The outcome is a language which, in sounds and grammar, resembles most closely the modern German dialect of the eastern Palatinate – Rhein-Frankisch – although Pennsylvania German is now diverging because of increased influence from English. The label 'Pennsylvania Dutch' is a popular English misinterpretation of *Deutsch* (or in their language, *Deitsch*). Speakers have command of three languages: Pennsylvania German, High German and English. Pennsylvania German is usually only spoken and is the language of home and community. High German is (archaic) Luther German – the language of the Luther Bible and hymns with influence from Pennsylvania German. English is read and written and is only spoken when dealing with outsiders – the so-called *Auswendige*. This English is not *verhoodelt* or 'mixed', as is commonly believed, but is remarkably free of interference from the other two languages. Examples like *Ve get too soon oldt un too late schmart* and *Throw Father down the stairs his hat once* occur everywhere in tourist phrasebooks, on beer coasters and tea towels but are nothing more than fictional cliches.

In light of the fate of other immigrant and minority languages in North America, it is exceptional that well after three centuries Pennsylvania German is alive and well. This is one persistent language and the secrets of its survival undoubtedly lie in the deeply religious significance the language has for these communities.

Alldaagsgschwetz (Everyday Conversation)

Guder Daag/Nochmiddaag/Marriye!
Good day/afternoon/morning!

Is es net en scheener/kalder/wieschder/heeser Daag?
Isn't it a beautiful/cold/ugly/hot day?

Denkscht du es gebt heit Regge/Gwiddere/Schnee/Reife?
Do you think there'll be rain/thunder storms/snow/frost today?

Wie bischt du/Wie gehts dir?
How are you/How's it going (with you)?

Mir geht's gans gut/so wie immer/maerrickwaerdich schlecht.
I'm quite well/just as always/remarkably bad.

Was machst du heit?
What are you doing today?

Heit duhn ich mol gar nix!
Today I'm doing nothing at all!

Ich muss geh – mach's gut/bis speeder/schaff net zu hatt!
I must go – make good/until later/don't work too hard!

Hendiche Wadde (Handy Words)

bissli	a little
der Bannet	bonnet
der Frack (die Fracke)	dress
der Gaul (die Geil)	horse
der Hut (die Hiet)	hat
der Peffer	pepper
der Rock (die Reck)	suit coat
der Salz	salt
der Schlidde	sled; sleigh
der Wagge (die Wegge)	wagon
die Aerwet	work
die Gaellesse	suspenders
die Grummbeer(e)	potato
die Hosse	trousers
die Schtrump (die Schtrimp)	stocking
der Schuh (die Schuh)	shoe
Dummel dich!	Hurry up!

eens/zwee/drei/vier/finf	one/two/three/four/five
es Brot	bread
es Buggy	buggy
es Hemm (die Hemmer)	shirt
es Oi (die Oier)	eggs
gut	good
Hock dich anne.	Sit down.
hungrich	hungry
Kumm rei.	Come in.
Mach die Deer zu/uff.	Shut/Open the door.
Nee.	No.
schaffe	to work
Ya.	Yes.

LANGUAGE LOSS

Many languages indigenous to the USA, or imported during the big waves of immigration in the last two centuries, have died out or are in danger of dying out. This process is not going unchecked. From Hawaii to California to the Southwest to Florida and Maine, communities are working to revitalise or renew dormant or dying languages. This takes the form of education programs (the language nests of Hawaii, or Saturday schools throughout the States), one-on-one language development (the master–apprentice program fostered by California Indians) and media (Navajo radio is a prime example).

Even Irish (endangered in its native Ireland) is enjoying a renaissance in the USA, with immersion weekends and classes burgeoning throughout the country. Nearly every Native American tribe has some program in place to honour its language as people realise that language loss also means the loss of rich cultural knowledge and incomparable ways of looking at the world.

CANADA & MEXICO

It's a fact that unless they are living near the borders of Canada or Mexico, the average American doesn't really think often about the neighbours. Of course, visits are in order. Mexico is a popular vacation spot, especially its resorts during the winter. Nearly every tourist to the San Diego area will spend part of a day in easy-to-reach Tijuana. Canada's cities and wilderness make it popular with American tourists, too. But this is an acquaintance on the most superficial level.

Spanish speakers have an easier time navigating Mexico and the border towns throughout the entire Southwest. The visitor with Spanish will, of course, have a more meaningful visit. Despite the role of French in the Canadian linguistic map (with Canadian French influencing the English of Quebec), most Americans tend to pay attention to Canada as an English-speaking country and to be largely unaffected by Canadian speech patterns.

There is more free exchange among Spanish speakers along the Mexican borders, with US Spanish speakers mixing in more English (and then feeling some censure when they visit family back in Mexico), developing a variety known as Spanglish (see the US Spanish section in this chapter on page 253).

Canada's transparency to most Americans is likely due to the prominence of the English language. While Americans are generally oblivious to the subtle differences between US English and Canadian English, Canadians are not. Canadian spelling falls somewhere between British and American models (using the British '-our' as in 'colour' and the American '-ize' as in 'maximize'), but American spellings are regularly rejected.

Canadians are very sensitive about not being identified as US nationals, in the same way Scots don't like to be called English and New Zealanders don't like to be called Australian. Canadian use of the words 'America' and 'American' is very different to that of Brits or Americans. Canada is not part of America. Nor are they Americans. The USA is rarely referred to as 'America' by Canadians; it is usually 'the States' if the usage is informal or 'the US(A)' if it is formal. To generously include all of Canada by the term 'North American' tends to irk the average Canadian.

Among its claims to word coinage is the term 'Generation X' by a Canadian from Vancouver in an eponymous book by Douglas Coupland in the early 1990s.

THE MELTING POT

HAWAIIAN ENGLISH

The language history of Hawaii is rich and multilingual, reflecting the region's interesting social and economic history and varied mix of peoples. The '50th state' (the islands became a state in 1959) has two official languages: Hawaiian, the original language of the indigenous people, and English. But another language variety, Hawaiian English, also needs to be recognised as it is the 'local English', the language you'll hear everyday that unites a variety of people. It is a dialect that has incorporated elements of Hawaiian Creole English (another linguistic cultural unifier), native Hawaiian words, and other languages that have been spoken in Hawaii.

Hawaiian English has become synonymous with Hawaiian Creole English, the English-based language that developed as a result of contact among populations of mixed-language backgrounds on plantations in Hawaii. It started first as a pidgin – a simplified language developed by speakers who don't share the same language – and became a creole when the children of pidgin speakers used it as their primary language.

In 1778, British explorer Captain James Cook arrived in the Hawaiian Islands, and from this time other explorers, adventurers and traders visited Hawaii and impacted not only on the lifestyle and culture of the people, but on their language as well. The Christian missionaries who arrived in Hawaii from New England in 1820 were among the most influential of these visitors. They were of the Calvinist faith and taught the Hawaiians to read and write. Hawaiians were soon writing and publishing newspapers in their own language and the population became one of the most literate in the world, in both English and Hawaiian.

Contact with the outside world continued, and as the missionary families became established, their descendants branched out into other ventures, one of which was the sugar industry. The native Hawaiian population was in decline and a large labour force was necessary for the budding sugar plantations. Therefore, contract labourers were brought to Hawaii from the mid-19th century right up until the mid-1970s, from China, Japan, Portugal, Puerto Rico, Korea and the Philippines. Elements of the languages of all these people helped to develop Hawaiian English.

Although Hawaii's population was a multicultural one, the control of the government, commerce and education was held by the English-speaking Caucasians. In 1893, the Hawaiian queen Liliuokalani was overthrown as the last monarch of the Hawaiian kingdom and the government was replaced by a republic that was eventually annexed to the USA in 1898.

In 1896, the Hawaiian language was banned and replaced by English as the medium of instruction in all public schools. Parents were discouraged from using the Hawaiian language in the home because it would hinder their children's learning of English. This led to the decline of the use and knowledge of the native Hawaiian language.

It wasn't until 1978 that Hawaiian was re-established as one of the official languages of the state of Hawaii. Several educational programs, such as 'language nests', have also been developed to foster the language among children and their parents. These programs, based on programs developed by the Maori in New Zealand, are considered innovative and are used as examples by other communities seeking to revitalise their own fragile languages.

Today, although Hawaiian and English are the official languages in Hawaii, a newcomer will be unlikely to understand the English that is spoken by many local residents, as it will be Hawaiian Creole English.

Here are some examples of Hawaiian Creole English:

I going come your house bumbai.
  I'm going to your house later.
Wat you guys get fo' eat?
  What do you have to eat?
Wat bada you?
  What's the matter, does it bother you?
Eh, you like go show?
  Hey, would you like to go to the movies?
Gunfunit, I said try come on time!
  Darn it, I said to come promptly!

THE MELTING POT

Eh, Daddy dem going come.
  Hey, Daddy (and them) are coming.
Wat time you pau school?
  When are you done with school?

'Bumbai' (by and by) is a term from the language's pidgin stage
that marks future events; *'dem'* marks plurals. You'll hear them often.

Hawaiian English incorporates many words from native Hawaiian,
such as:

aloha	greeting, farewell, love, sympathy
haole	Caucasian (originally a foreigner); pronounced HOW-lay
mahimahi	dolphin
mahalo	thank you
pau	finished, completed
pupule	crazy
wahine	girl, woman, wife
wikiwiki	hurry up

Some local foods and related terms are:

lunch wagon	a van on the side of the road where plate lunches are sold
malasadas	a Portuguese donut
manapua	a Chinese bun with pork in the centre (char siu bao)
mixed plate	a plate lunch with two or more entrees
plate lunch	a paper plate usually with two scoops of rice, salad and an entree

NATIVE AMERICAN LANGUAGES

NATIVE AMERICAN LANGUAGES

① Pueblo	④ Cherokee	⑦ Ojibway	
② Navajo	⑤ Choctaw	⑧ Lakota	
③ Hopi	⑥ Mohawk	⑨ Arapaho(e)	

THE LANGUAGES

Native North America is a continent of great linguistic diversity. At one time the number of distinct languages ran into several hundred, and many of them are spoken to this day.

It is customary to classify languages into families. A family is a group of related languages descended from a single ancestral language. For example, the prayer of communication above is from the Oglala who are one of the seven sub-bands of the Western Teton, all of which speak the Lakota dialect of a Siouan language. These Western Teton are one of the seven bands, or 'Seven Council Fires', of the Dakota (The 'Allied'), which is one of the nations belonging to the large Siouan linguistic family. This linguistic group also includes the Assiniboin, Biloxi, Crow, Hidatsa, Iowa, Kansa, Mandan, Missouri, Ofo, Omaha, Osage, Oto, Ponca, Quapaw and Tutelo.

If we add up the North American Indian languages spoken today and those that became extinct during historic times, we can total at least 60 language families. Some of the families include as many as 20 members, while others are represented by only one language. Linguists have been unable to find any relationship between these language families and languages outside the American continent.

Language can be defined as a system of communication used by people who share a history and culture. Native American people use language for communication with all living things. And all things are alive. When Native American people pray with songs, using words or chants, the language carries hopes, dreams and thanks to the whole of all living things.

> The language becomes a part of the whole earth and sky
> and universe, as all living things are.
> – Ah ho
> **Eagle/Walking Turtle**

ETYMOLOGY

When regarding the etymology of some Indian names of certain tribes and localities, it should be noted that the true pronunciation has been changed by non-Indians who did not understand these words, and consequently their orthography (spelling) is inaccurate. In the following list, we have included some words as they are commonly written (and incorrectly pronounced), accompanied by their etymology and accurate orthography.

Abitibi
Cree: means intermediate water. From *abit* (middle, half) and *nipïy* (water) which makes *ipi* (in composition) whence *abitipi* (water at half distance). The name of this lake comes from its position at the level of the land, between Hudson's Bay and the St Lawrence.

Ayabaska, Atabaska
Cree: means place where there is an amount of high grass here and there

Attikamègues
Cree: from *attikamekw*, 'white fish'

Babiche
Cree: means raw-leather line. Probably from *assababish*, which is the diminutive of *assabâb*, thread

Canada
Iroquois: a village of tents or huts. Some believe that it is derived from *kanâta* or *kanâtan* (Cree), something which is very neat and clean.

Chicago
Potawatomi: from *chicâg* or *sikâg*, 'a skunk, a kind of wild cat', word, which at the local term makes *chicâgôk*

Illinois
Miami: from *iliniwok*, 'men'

Kankakee
Algonquin: from *kâkâkiw*, 'a crow'

Michigan
Cree: from *mishigâm* (pronounced mishigamaw), 'the big lake'

Ottawa
>   Ojibway: *ottawokay*, 'his ear', or *otawask*, *watawask*, 'bulrushes'.
>   The Indians from that part of the country called themselves
>   *watawawininiwok*, 'the men of the bulrushes'.

Québec
>   Cree: from *kepek*, *kipaw*, 'it is shut'. Indians today call the
>   Gulf of St Lawrence Kepek.

Saskatchewan
>   Cree: from *kisiskâtjiwan*, 'the rapid current'

Squaw
>   Cree: from *iskwew*, 'woman'. Note: the word 'squaw' is offensive
>   to Native American women.

Totem
>   Ojibway: from *nitotem*, 'my parent, my relation'

Tomahawk
>   Cree: from *otâmahuk*, 'strike them', or *otâmahwaw*, 'he is stricken'

Wigwâm
>   Munsee Delaware: 'dwelling, tent, lodge'

Winnipeg
>   Cree: *winnipek*, 'swamps, salt water, unclean water'

SIGN LANGUAGE & PICTOGRAPHY

Indian languages value highly figurative and poetic locutions
compared to many others. But nothing gives such a complete insight
into the way of Indian thought and expression as does sign language.

Some speculation exists that there may be a connection between
sign language and pictography. The illustrations here show a
number of similarities in style.

Before the coming of non-Indian people to this continent, sign
language was a very useful means of communication among the
large number of language families in America. Today you will
often hear Indian people say that they are thankful for one thing
that came with the arrival of non-Indians to America: English.
Now we can all talk to each other.

NATIVE AMERICAN
LANGUAGES

NATIVE AMERICAN LANGUAGES

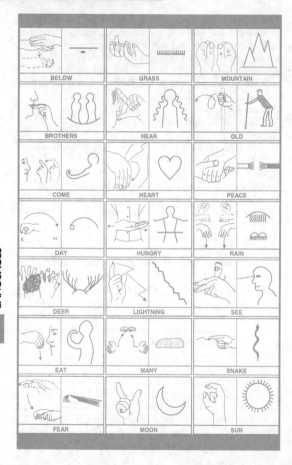

BELOW	GRASS	MOUNTAIN
BROTHERS	HEAR	OLD
COME	HEART	PEACE
DAY	HUNGRY	RAIN
DEER	LIGHTNING	SEE
EAT	MANY	SNAKE
FEAR	MOON	SUN

CHANTING

Chanting is universal amongst all Native American tribes. It is a medium of communication with all life and it is generally used in prayers and songs. It is a connection to the eternal existence. The energy created by voices – vibrations caused by wind from the lungs in their bodies – is the foundation of universal intelligence. When Native Americans chant, the universe is seen to communicate with them in visual images.

Chanting is the primordial history, the distant future and the eternal now, defined as only one existence. This existence, pronounced 'now', can be made good, or healed, through chanting. Any past wrongs, imagined or real, personal or universal, can be made right. Chanting is also an analysis of the people's need for healing.

Native American elders practised chanting to stay focused on 'now'. They also used chants to heal the physical body and to wash and heal the inner cosmic thought. When they sing words or chants, their true meaning is revealed directly to the soul through bodily vibration.

OGALA (LAKOTA) PRAYER

'Oh Wakaŋ-Taŋka (Grandfather, Great Spirit),
    You are and always were. With the help of all things
    and all beings we are about to send our voice to You.

Uŋshe ma la ye (Be merciful to me).

Oh Waŋbli Galeshka (Spotted Eagle),
    You see all things in the heavens and upon the earth.
    Help all those who send their voices to Wakan-Tanka
    through You.

Oh Uŋchi and Ina (Grandmother and Mother),
    You are sacred. It is from You that our bodies have come.
    Help us.

Wakaŋ-Taŋka oŋshimala ye oyate waŋi wachiŋ cha.
    (Oh Great Spirit be merciful to me that my
    people may live.)'

– Oglala (Lakota) Prayer

As the chanter, you are the universe in miniature. You are the same as earth and sky. Your inhale is the sky and your exhale is the earth. Your highest nerve centre is in your voice where the sky and the earth are connected. Your chant sound vibration connects the mind, body and spirit, and makes your physical body whole.

Native American people believe that the physical anatomy of the human being is composed of the infinite self. This is a never-ending existence and refers to our relationship with the universe. Parts of our anatomy are metaphors for this relationship. Visual images of the sky, earth, natural living things and even the whole universe are realised when parts of our own body are chanted. When chanting, the vowel sounds in any word are held for as long as possible. Consonants can be passed over or even left out.

Chanting the elements fire, water, wind, land and wood will bring about the realisation that all are truly one essence. They constantly awaken our perceptions of the one highest order.

When attending a Native American powwow or ceremony, listen to the singer's chants and connect the sounds to the sounds of sky, earth and elements found in the universe. A new meaning of your own life, as well as the meaning of life in the universe, will be your reward.

> Earth, sky, wind, water, clouds;
> Oh the beauty language forms in our minds.
> – Ah ho

Eagle/Walking Turtle

VISITING NATIVE AMERICAN SOCIETIES

When visiting a tribal village or area, be respectful of local customs – as you would anywhere. Request permission to enter a village and take no alcohol or drugs. Don't take photographs or make recordings without permission.

Several tribes welcome visitors to their fairs and powwows but before you go, get information from local tribal councils or visitor information centres. There are ceremonies and areas which are restricted to tribal members – you will simply be politely asked to leave if you happen to come across one.

The publication *Indian America* by Eagle/Walking Turtle provides a detailed guide on how and where travellers can visit Native American tribes, historical sites, cultural centres and so on.

LANGUAGES IN THIS BOOK

The following chapters give you a brief introduction to nine languages. These have been included as the tribes are among those that are most well known in the USA, and because they represent large linguistic families. There are still over 350 tribes in the USA and many other languages could have been included. We just didn't have the space. The reading list in this chapter should help those interested in finding out more about Native Americans, their languages and cultures.

FURTHER READING

Couro, T & M Langdon. 1975, *Let's Talk 'Tipay Aa: An Introduction to the Mesa Grande Diegueño Language*, Malki Museum Press & Ballena Press.

Densmore, F. [1932] 1972, *Yuman and Yaqui Music*, Smithsonian Institution, Bureau of American Ethnology Bulletin No 110, Reprint, Da Capo Press, New York.

Eagle/Walking Turtle (Gary McLain). 1993, *Indian America*, John Muir Publications, Santa Fe.

Hair, WJC (ed). 1983, *Arapaho Language and Culture*, Zdenek Salzmann, compiler, Wind River Reservation.

Heizer, R.F. 1978, *Handbook of North American Indians*, Smithsonian Institution.

Malotki, E. 1978, *Hopi Tales*, Museum of North Arizona Press.

Margolin, M (ed). [1981] 1993, revised edition, *The Way We Lived: California Indian Reminiscences, Stories and Songs*, Heyday Books, Berkeley.

Rael, J with ME Marlow. 1993, *Being and Vibration*, Council Oak Books, Tulsa.

Vera, M. 1993, 'The Creation of Language, a Yowlumni Story' in *News from Native California*: 7(3): 19-20.

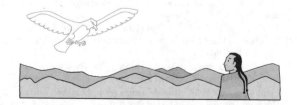

PUEBLO PEOPLE

The Pueblo People live in an area extending from northeastern Arizona to the Rio Pecos in New Mexico and from Taos on the Rio Grande in the north to a few miles below El Paso, Texas in the south. The term 'Pueblo' applies to all people living in compact villages and who are usually not nomadic.

From 1539, when the Spanish explorers first encountered the Zuñi, until 1847, when the Taos People rebelled against the US Government, the Pueblo People were harassed by invading foreign armies and missionaries. In spite of the 300 years of turmoil, the Pueblo People have successfully maintained their lifestyles, ceremonies and languages.

The Languages

The languages spoken by the Pueblo People include Keresan and Tanoan. Tanoan includes dialects of Tewa, Tiwa and Towa. Many Pueblo People describe their language as an ancient tongue and their elders say that the language was constructed according to the different vibratory levels of mother nature.

According to their ancient ones of wisdom, the sounds of all native tongues are in an enormous ball of whirling energy which comes from an existence of goodness. Out of this whirling ball the Creator created the different tongues, each with specific differences, and each made from resonating qualities of goodness. Every single tongue has its own specific vibration that is different from any other.

In Pueblo thought, the answer 'yes' is what created the blood of life. Their people were vibrations constructed by four processes described as descending, arising, purifying and relativity.

Their tongue is the tuner sound that fuses descending and arising light in the crystallised meaning of time. Beyond the tongue, and beyond all sound, is silence. Silence is the root of all tongues, and languages, because it is the pathway to the materialisation of all concepts.

> The Creator made us when He found that form could exist
> from sound. He made vibration, He made form,
> and He made our Mother and Father, the living universe.
> **Eagle/Walking Turtle**

TEWA SONGS

Tewa Summer People's Song

Than sendo i thamu khe winu Yophe k'ewe
P'o sendo wa'a i thamu khe winu Yophe k'ewe
Mba i thamu khe winu iwe ra han O'ke owinge
I thamu khe ho'o tse hwä kwa wi p'o

Sun Old Man be at dawn ready must stand Cactus
    Stalk Ridge on
Moon Old Man also be at dawn ready must stand,
    Cactus Stalk Ridge on
And be at dawn ready must stand thence going San
    Juan toward
He at dawn ready now Eagle Tail Rain Standing Road.

Tewa Winter People's Song

Towa'e tsä'i'i seng K'u seng p'i neri
Mbi thamu khe winu O'ke owinge piye
Kwa wi p'o ge O'ke owinge piye
Agoyo nu khu seng i thamu khe winu
O'ke owinge piye

Little People White Men Stone-Man-Mountain from
You two at dawn ready must stand San Juan
    town towards
Rain Standing Road at San Juan town towards
Great-Star-Dark-Night Man at dawn ready must stand
San Juan town towards.

The People

Most Pueblo villages are divided into two groups of clans, one commonly known as the Summer People and the other as the Winter People.

Pueblo People today follow two paths: one modern, the other traditional.

There are dances every weekend at some Pueblo villages. Since the economic foundation of the people was agricultural, involving mainly corn, many of the ceremonies reflect celebration for planting, abundance, harvesting, etc.

Jobs off the reservations are not too abundant, but many work for their tribe, the Bureau of Indian Affairs or the Indian Health Service. In many ways the Pueblo People may have been more fortunate than other Native Americans. They have been able to preserve their villages, ceremonies, lifestyles and beliefs more effectively because they have remained on their land and, since they were not nomadic and not wholly dependent on the buffalo for subsistence, the invasion of non-Indian peoples did not change them as drastically as it did other Native Americans.

NAVAJO

The Navajo Indian Reservation is located in the Four Corners area of the USA (where Utah, Arizona, Colorado and New Mexico have a common border). Navajo Monument Valley Tribal Park is north of Kayenta. Navajo Nation Visitor Centers are located in Cameron, Chinle and Monument Valley. Kinlichee Navajo Tribal Park is eight miles east of Ganado.

The Navajo Nation is the largest Indian tribe in the USA. The majority reside in Arizona, roughly one-third live in New Mexico and a few make their homes in southern Utah. The Navajo call themselves Diné, 'the People'.

The Language

Some Navajo speak only the Navajo language, and amongst all the members of the tribe, whether they are fluent or not, there is a deep respect for the language. It was used during WWII as a code to confuse the enemy. Kept in utmost secrecy at the time, the Navajo Code Talkers are now famous for their wartime contribution.

Since 1942, the US Government has been working with the experts in Indian languages to develop a popular alphabet which encourages the writing of Navajo. The belief that such a written language would spread more rapidly than English was based upon experience with other Indian tribes.

Navajo belongs to the Athapascan language family, a group of languages which includes Apache. With one exception it is possible to write it using only the letters of the English alphabet.

WATER STANDING STILL

Dííji,
shimá bighandóó ńdii'náh,
shimá haigo bighandóó
Hooghan názbąsgo nástł'ineé bits'ą́ą́ ńdii'náh.
Hooghan 'atníí'gi ko'yęe bits'ą́ą́ ńdii'náh.
Dził̨góó nihidibé dah dadiniilkaad.
Dibé tł'oh dóó chahash'oh
dóó tó
dóó tó danlíníígíí
dóó tó naazkánígíí bá hóló
dziłtahgi.
'Áadi
doo níyol dai
dóó séí 'ádin.

Today,
we leave my mother's hogan,
my mother's winter hogan.
We leave the shelter of its rounded walls.
We leave its friendly centre fire.
We drive our sheep to the mountains.
For the sheep,
There is grass and shade
and water,
flowing water
and water standing still,
in the mountains.
There is no wind
There is no sand
up there.

Pronunciation
Vowels

a as in 'father' *gad* (juniper)
e as in 'bet' *ké* (shoe)
i as in 'pit' *sis* (belt)
   as in 'seek' *diit'ash* (let's go)
o as in 'boat' *doo* (not)

Vowels may be either long or short; the long vowels being indicated by a doubling of the letter. This never affects the quality of the vowel, except that long i is always pronounced as in 'seek'. The hook beneath a letter (*ǫ*) means it is nasalised. In addition, vowels are always nasalised after n.

Diphthongs

ai as in 'aisle' *hai* (winter)
ei as in 'say' *séí* (sand)
oi as in 'joey' *'ayói* (very)

The diphthong oi will frequently be heard as ui (as in 'dewy') in some sections of the reservation. The diphthongs ei and ai are not always distinguished.

Consonants

Most letters in Navajo are pronounced in much the same way as they are in English. The following letters are somewhat different from English:

b like the 'b' sound in 'spoon' *bá* (for him)
d like the 'd' sound in 'store' *díí* (this)
g like the 'g' sound in 'ski' *gah* (rabbit)
zh as the 's' in 'pleasure' *'ázhi'* (name)
ł like 'l' but without the voice, as the 'thl' in 'athlete'. Best to hear this one to get the right sound.
' (glottal stop) *yá'át'ééh* (it is good)

This last sound, the glottal stop, is a sound you often come across in Native American languages. One way to describe the sound is that it's like the voice break by a Cockney who is saying 'better', without pronouncing the 't'. Or, as we all would say 'Uh-oh!'

In Navajo, there are two sounds represented by the letter **h**. The difference is in the intensity or fricativeness. Where **h** is the first letter in a syllable it is pronounced by older people like the 'ch' of German. However, the younger generation of Navajo tends to pronounce the sound much as in English.

gh *hooghan* (hogan – a circular, earth-covered dwelling)

This is the voiced equivalent of the harshly pronounced variety of **h**. There are several other combinations of consonants which have specific sounds, but most require more detailed explanation than we can provide here. However if you stick to the basics as outlined in this chapter, you should be pretty close to the right sound.

Sounds represented by **g, t, k, h, gh, ch**, and **ts** (when heavily aspirated) are palatalised before **e, i**, and labialised before **o**. For example, the word *ké* (shoe) is pronounced as though it were written *kyé*, and *tó* (water) as though written *twó*.

Tones

The common system of writing Navajo (as used in this book) uses the acute accent mark ´ to express four tonal variations.

- the tone is high when a short vowel or **n**, both elements of a long vowel, or a diphthong are marked with the acute:

  azéé (mouth)   high tone

- the tone falls when only the first element of a long vowel or diphthong is marked:

  háadish? (where?)   falling tone

- the tone rises when only the last element is marked:

  shínaaí (my elder brother)   rising tone

- the tone is low when a vowel, diphthong or **n** is unmarked:

  ázee' (medicine)   low tone

The difference between low and high tone in Navajo is similar to the difference in tone of 'do you' and 'know' in the English question 'Do you know?'.

Sentence Structure

Whereas normal word order in English is subject-verb-object, Navajo is subject-object-verb. The possessive pronouns of Navajo are always prefixed to the noun. Thus, *shimá* (my mother), *nimá* (your mother), *bimá* (his mother), but the stem *-má* has no independent form and never occurs on its own.

The structure of the Navajo verb has similar characteristics, but is more complex. The subject of the sentence is always incorporated in the verb. Similarly, affixes are added to verbs to show person, time and mood. Ideas conveyed in English by auxiliaries such as 'will, did, have, might', and so on are expressed by different forms of the verb itself, as they are in most European languages other than English.

Another difference between the two languages is that English prepositions are postpositions in Navajo.

with my elder sister	*shádíbił*
	(my elder sister, with her)
for my mother	*shima bá*
	(my mother, for her)

Whooooooo ... So, now you know how to pronounce all the sounds in Navajo so you can speak the language real gooooood. (If only you had a Navajo dictionary.) Just kidding; as Indians say *ai eeeeee* when they are pulling your leg and they get afraid that you might know that they are pulling your leg and be offended by it and then they chicken out and make sure you know that they are pulling your leg so you can laugh, too.

For myself I never chicken out ... *ai eeeeee*.

Eagle/Walking Turtle

The People

Most Navajo People today speak English, especially around the places that tourists visit on the 'res' (reservation). Just be friendly and respectful and you will do fine. There are special ceremonies known as 'sings', dances and 'medicine ways' healing ceremonies but it isn't likely that you will come across one. If you are asked to leave an area, just do so and everyone will appreciate your courtesy.

Many of the Navajo continue to live in hogans and keep sheep, in a way of living that gave rise to the poem at the beginning of this section. Beautiful rugs are woven from the sheep's wool and the sheep also provide a source of food. But the culture has expanded now to include the 'American culture'. Many Navajo work off the reservation for the Bureau of Indian Affairs, the Indian Health Service and in the public economy. The tribal government employs some and there is employment in many Navajo-owned enterprises.

The Navajo spiritual understanding and their creation story are somewhat complicated and mysterious, making for very interesting reading and study. And the sound of their language adds to the mystery and beauty of the People, the breathtaking desert landscapes, the loneliness of the isolated hogans in a violet sunset or the chilling sound of a distant coyote's cry.

HOPI

The Hopi Indians, who live in villages on several mesas in northern Arizona, are the most western of the Pueblo agricultural society which dominated the southwestern USA for 2000 years or more, prior to European settlement. Geographically isolated from non-Indian peoples in the centre of the Navajo reservation, many of the Hopi still live on their original homeland.

Although their way of life was altered ffom 1540 when they became enslaved to invading Spaniards, and later in the 1800s when smallpox, brought by the Europeans, ravaged the population, the Hopi have been able to preserve their cultural heritage and language remarkably well.

The Language

A total of 21 symbols represent the sounds which occur in the dialect of the Third Mesa villages. Most of these are from the English alphabet; one is borrowed from German orthography (the umlauted ö; while an apostrophe is used to represent the glottal stop). (See page 279 for an explanation of a glottal stop.) Stress and the falling tone – the latter occurring in conjunction with long vowels, diphthongs and certain vowel-nasal sequences – occur in speech but are not normally written.

Hopi vowels can be long (indicated by a double vowel) or short. There are a number of diphthongs with a 'y' glide. That is, they are pairs of vowels which end in a 'y' sound. For example, *tsay* (small, young), *uyma* (he has been planting) and *ahoy* (back to). There are also diphthongs with a 'w' glide, that is, they end in a 'w' sound. For example, *awta* (bow) and *pew* (here, to me).

There are many difficult sounds in the Hopi language, including a falling tone, nasal **m** and **n**, and glides which can precede or follow the vowel. If you'd like to learn more about the sounds, the best thing to do is to get hold of a language tape.

Useful Terms

The following glossary of Hopi terms will also present information on the culture of the people.

Angaktsina
the long-haired Kachina who is beautiful and sings with beauty. *Anga* means 'hair'.

Dart Game
mötöplalwa (dart game) was a game for boys only. No longer practised by boys, members of some women's societies practise a similar game during autumn spiritual ceremonies.

Demon Girl
masmana, or demon girl, has supernatural powers that allow her to come back to life. She is a sexually attractive seductress of men. She is evil.

Hasookata
he steals from the People and traps them into gambling with him for their lives, which they always lose

Hopi
the sounds of the word *Hopi* imply a gamut of positive character traits and qualities, such as moral uprightness, unobtrusive behaviour, poised disposition, non-agressive conduct, modesty and many more. One connotation from its core meaning of 'good in every way', has led to the popular interpretation of Hopiit as the 'peaceful ones'.

Kachina

(correct pronunciation, *katsina*) is one of the most important aspects of the Hopi culture. The spiritual ties related to this figure bind the people together. When the human dancer dons the mask of the spirit he becomes, in essence, *the* spirit. All good things the spirit can do the impersonator can do as well. The spirit kachinas are not worshipped; they are personal friends.

Kiva

Hopi term for the underground spiritual celebration chamber

Kooyemsi

the Hopi version of a Zuñi kachina. The popular name is Mudhead. He may carry a drum *(pusukinta)*.

Kwikwilyaqa

translates literally as 'Striped Nose', this kachina is never seen in a line dance. Always behaving in a clownish manner his image is unmistakeable.

Kwingyaw

the 'Chief of Cold', *Kwingyawmongwi* is the one responsible for cold weather, winds and snowstorms

Maasaw

the owner and keeper of the underworld; he is thought of as the one who will save the world from wickedness

Mixed Hunt

this *neyangmakiwa* rabbit hunt is participated in by unmarried girls as well as men and boys. This event provides opportunity for amusement and courtship.

Oraibi

this is the Third Mesa Village, properly called *orayvi*. Probably the oldest, continuously inhabited settlement in the USA.

Pik'ami

this cornmeal dish is delicious but it requires a lot of work to prepare. The contents include wheat sprouts *(ngaakuy-vani)*, often a sweetener and corn husks.

Piki

pronounced *piiki*, this bread is very nutritious and eaten during special festivities, such as weddings or ceremonial events.

Pöqangwhoya & Palöngawhoya
　　the little demigod brothers that live at Poqangwwawarpi, north
　　of old Oraibi. They are the grandchildren of Spider Woman,
　　and since they live with her, linguistic reference is frequently
　　made to the trio. Today the brothers have the difficult task of
　　keeping the gigantic water serpent in check, to prevent it from
　　destroying the planet with floods and earthquakes.

Shinny
　　the Hopi stickball game is extinct today. It was played after
　　the *Powamuy* ceremony in February.

Sikyaqöqlö
　　this Hopi Kachina comes during the *Powamuy* ceremony in
　　February. His mask is painted yellow, hence his name, 'Yellow
　　Qöqlö'.

Somiviki
　　the Hopi food for special occasions; this one is made from blue
　　cornmeal and sprouted wheat (*ngaakuyvani*) as a sweetener

Sosotukwpi
　　this guessing game is no longer played among the Hopi. It was
　　not uncommon for players to play all through the night about
　　100 years ago.

Spider Woman
　　(*Kookyangwwuuti*) has divine powers, wisdom and an all-en-
　　compassing knowledge. She is always ready to intervene, assist,
　　counsel, guide and save.

Tiikuywuuti
　　this female is ugly, terrifying and powerful. Said to be the owner
　　of all world game animals, she grinds corn at night and is
　　related to Maasaw.

Totolospi
　　this checkerlike board game is popular among the Hopi today

Tsorwukiqlö
　　this name identifies the giver as a member of the Bluebird Clan

Witch, Witchcraft
　　Powaqa is the concept of black magic. Either sex can be associated
　　with this evil entity.

The People

The Hopi People are friendly and courteous, but you should contact the tribe for a guide before entering the villages.

Since the Hopi are village people, not nomadic, and traditionally dependent mainly on agriculture to survive, their culture is in many ways very typical of the cultural ways of other Pueblo People. However, as you have seen from some of the definitions in the preceding glossary, their spiritual lives have been and are very complicated. The Hopi prophesy for the future is very interesting reading.

Of course, the people have been forced to walk two roads, as most Native Americans have. Today those who can find employment work on and off the reservation. Modern America has found its way to Hopiland as it has to every other place.

Enjoy your visit to Hopiland.

– Ah ho
Eagle/Walking Turtle

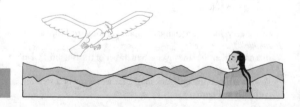

OJIBWAY PEOPLE

The *Otchipwe* language is commonly known today as Ojibway with such names as Algonquin, Chippewa, Ottawa or Odawa, and Saulteaux used in English. Its speakers call themselves Anishinaabe and the language is called Anishinaabemowin. It is related to about 25 other languages in the Algonquian language family, including Blackfoot, Arapaho(e) and Cree.

One of the most used of North American languages, Ojibway, is spoken today in Michigan, Minnesota, North Dakota and Wisconsin. In Canada, it's spoken in Manitoba, Ontario, Saskatchewan and Quebec. In numbers of speakers it is probably the fourth largest Native American language. Recent estimates approach around 50,000 speakers. In the USA and southern Canada, it is spoken mainly by people of middle age and older; in many communities only the elderly are fluent. In parts of Canada, it is spoken by Anishinaabe of all ages and still learned by children as their first language. Some communities use writing, radio and TV as media for the language, and most Anishinaabe communities ensure that the language is taught in their schools or community centres. Its survival is threatened by the immigrant's languages: English and French.

Ojibway is not a single language. It is a chain of connected dialects or local varieties. Each local variety differs from adjacent ones in pronunciation, words and grammar. For example, the word for 'table', usually given as *adopowin* (pronounced 'adoopowin') can also be heard in different places as *doopwin*, *wiisiniwaagan* or *achigan*. Speakers of one local variety can usually be understood by their neighbours, but small differences pile up across distances so that people from one place may have a great deal of difficulty understanding or communicating with people from somewhere distant.

The main dialects are those that were spoken 150 years ago on the south shore of Lake Superior. However, nearly all the basic patterns of the words and the meaningful building blocks in them are the same across the whole language. Individual words have been left behind as ways of life have changed; few today will use *agwingweon* (cradleboard bow) or *nandobani* (goes on a war party).

Some words have changed or added meanings; for example, *odâbân* (sled) now has the added meaning of 'car'. New words have developed for a wide range of modern activities and objects from 'wear lipstick' to 'computer'. All languages change slowly and imperceptibly in the sounds they use, and sound changes in Ojibway are no exception. A process called syncope has shortened words by dropping out certain short vowels: the Ottawa word *assiponigan* (scissors) is now pronounced without the first and third vowels as *ssipnigan*.

The following names have been changed by non-Indians. Included here are the meanings and true orthography of these words.

Abénakis
'land of the east'. Probably comes from *wâban* (daybreak), and *aki*, or better, *ahki* (earth) which produces *wâbanahkiyak* (the people from where the sun rises).

Manitoba
from *Manitowaba*, 'the strait of the spirit(s)'

Milwaukee
milw-ahki, 'earth, land, the fine land'

Mississippi
misi-siipi, 'the big river' (siipi means 'river')

Moccasin
mahkisin, 'shoe'

> Our People of the lakes and streams and trees still live in the USA and their songs, prayers and voices willalways be over this land. Join with them to honour the everlasting spirit of celebration for all life.
> – Ah ho
> **Eagle/Walking Turtle**

MOHAWK

Mohawks were first seen by the French Explorer, Samuel de Champlain in 1609 in the Mohawk River Valley in New York. Around 1670 many began to migrate northward, eventually settling at the present-day sites of Caughnawaga and Oka, near Montreal. Around 1750 some Caughnawagans moved upstream to St Regis. Most of those who had stayed in the Mohawk Valley sided with the British during the Revolution and soon afterward they moved to the present Six Nations Reserve in Ontario. Others fled toward Montreal and ultimately to the Bay of Quinté, now the Tyendinaga Reserve. In 1881 some Oka Mohawks moved on to Gibson, Ontario.

The Language

The earliest Mohawk vocabulary recorded by a Westerner was written in a journal kept by Adriaen van den Bogaert, a surgeon at Fort Orange (Albany), in l634-35.

Mohawk is spoken today by about 3000 people living at Caughnawaga and Oka in Quebec, St Regis, Cornwall Island, Snye, Deseronto and Brantford in Ontario, and Hogansburg, Buffalo, Rochester, Syracuse and Brooklyn in New York state. Dialectal variation is discernible from one community to the next. Some children are learning Mohawk as a first language, but it is not spoken by many under 30 years of age.

**NORTH &
NORTHEAST**

atòokv⁾	axe
kanàataro	bread
ohryòokv⁾	chipmunk
yothóore⁾	cold
okàara⁾	eyes
okũhsa⁾	face
yosnóore⁾/yostóore⁾	fast
otsista⁾	star
kv́tsyū	fish
wisk	five
ahsì:ta⁾	foot
yo⁾aríhv	hot

The People

The Mohawk are part of the Iroquoian confederacy, a group of tribes which was originally set up in the 16th century with the aim of establishing peace among themselves. The tribes involved are the Mohawk, Oneida, Onondaga, Cayuga, Seneca and the Tuscarora. They continue to operate as a confederacy.

The people of the Iroquoian confederacy have done well to maintain their culture, arts, dances, songs and spirituality against the encroachments of modern society.

Listen to the sounds of Indian America and enjoy their languages at celebrations throughout the northeastern USA and southeastern Canada. You can hear the beauty in the wind.
– Ah ho
Eagle/Walking Turtle

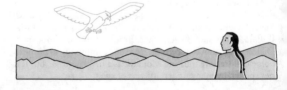

NORTH CENTRAL LAKOTA PEOPLE

Next to the Algonquian, the Dakota (Sioux) form the most populous language family north of Mexico. The Dakota live in North and South Dakota, Montana and Nebraska.

The name Lakota is taken from a term applied to the largest and best-known tribal group or confederacy belonging to the Dakota family. This band of Lakota are typical of the Plains Indians of America. Nomadic in nature before the coming of non-Indians, they followed the buffalo and lived free on the plains.

While it is not possible to make general statements about the habits and customs of these people that will be true for the entire group, we can say that all the eastern Siouan tribes and most of the southern Siouan tribes raised corn, but the Dakota (except some of the eastern bands) and the Crow depended almost entirely on buffalo and other game animals, the buffalo being the basis for economic and spiritual life of all the tribes of the Great Plains.

In the east, they lived in bark and mat wigwams but on the plains, earth lodges and buffalo-hide tipis were used. Formerly they had no domestic animals except dogs, which were used to transport tipis and all other family belongings, as well as children (the *travois*). The introduction of horses constituted a new epoch in the life of all Plains tribes, facilitating their migratory movements and the pursuit of the buffalo, and contributing largely to the Sioux's ability to conduct warfare against intruding non-Indians.

The Language

The Dakota language is spoken in four dialects, Santee (often referred to as Dakota) and Yankton (Nakota) by the eastern groups, Teton (Lakota) by the western, and Assiniboine in the northwest. They are all mutually intelligible, although there is a greater difference between the Assiniboine and the others than there is among Santee, Yankton and Teton.

The Teton (Lakota) dialect has the greatest number of speakers.

THE GREAT PLAINS

Pronunciation

After each letter, the nearest approximation to the sound in an English word is given, followed by an example of the sound in a Lakota word.

Vowels

a	as in 'father'	*na*	(and)
e	as in 'bet'	*pte*	(buffalo)
i	as in 'keen'	*hi*	(to arrive)
o	as in 'over'	*ho*	(voice)
u	as in 'rule'	*tuwa*	(someone)

ŋ   occurring only after the vowels a, i and u, it indicates that the preceding vowel is nasalised. Not a sound in itself.

aŋ	*waŋji*	(one)
iŋ	*najiŋ*	(to stand)
uŋ	*yaŋkᶜaŋ*	(and then)

Diphthongs

Diphthongs only occur in a few exclamations, as in the man's word of greeting, *hau* (like English 'how'), and a woman's exclamation of surprise, *haiye!* (with the 'ai' like that in English 'aisle').

Consonants

Several sounds are similar to those in English. However, the way they are written may be different. Here are some sounds that may cause difficulty.

The glottal stop is a consonant. It occurs between vowels, and as an integral part of seven other consonants. For an explanation of the sound, see page 279.

p	as the 'b' sound in 'spot'	*pahi* (to pick up)
pᶜ	as in 'pot'	*pʻa* (head)
pʾ		*pʾo* (fog)
k	as the 'g' sound in 'ski'	*kakʻiye* (yonder)
kᶜ		*kʻigle* (he went home)
kʾ		*kʾuŋ* (definite article, 'the', in the past)
t	as the 'd' sound' in 'stop'	*takuni* (nothing)
tᶜ	as in 'tea'	*tʻi* (to live)
tʾ		*tʾe* (dead)
c	as in 'attach'	*caȟota* (ashes)
cᶜ	as in 'chew'	*cʻaŋ* (tree)
cʾ		*cʻicʾu* (I give you)
h	as in 'horse'	*ho* (voice)
ȟ	as in the Scottish 'loch'	*ȟoka* (badger)
j	as in 'pleasure'	*waŋji* (one)
š	as in 'sugar'	*ša* (red)
sʾ		*sʾe* (as if)
šʾ		*akišʾa* (to shout)
ġ	like ȟ, but voiced	*kaġe* (to make)
g	as in 'go' when	*gli* (to arrive back here)
		followed by a consonant

The People

When you attend powwows and ceremonies among the plains of Dakota, you will hear the people speaking their native tongue and even the announcers will be speaking Lakota over the loud speakers. It has a beautiful, musical, haunting sound. And when the singers sing in Lakota, the chills will run up your spine and you may even feel your whole body float above the ground.

Today the Plains people are shut upon little islands surrounded by land where a flood of non-Indian inhabitants settled. The buffalo are gone, except for a few here and there in reserves or on private ranches.

Neither the people nor the buffalo are wild and free to roam the prairies and to enjoy the natural opportunities that the universe offered to them. But they still celebrate those times of freedom and those times of beauty. Sweat lodges, Sun dances, powwows, Peyote Meetings and other ceremonies still voice the sounds of their heart in prayer, song, chant and drumbeat across the plains of the USA, and the language of that heart of the people will never die.

THE GRASS MOUNTAIN MICE

Ħe P'eji It' unkala Kin

Tuwe oyas' in it 'unkalakin,
    slolwic' ayapi in c'initunkala kin
    ohiniya' unpi kin he' un.
it' unkala owe'okt'okca ota
mak'oc'et' okt'okca ec'ekc'e ot'ipi
na c'ajet'okeya kin nakun
t'okecapi ho tk'a hecenaš it' unkala hec'api.

The Grass Mountain Mouse

Everyone knows about mice
    because mice are everywhere
Different kinds of mice
    live in different kinds of places
    and have different front names,
    but they are mice just the same.

ARAPAHO(E)

The Arapaho(e) language belongs to the Algonquian family, one of the largest in North America. It extends from Labrador and the northern Atlantic coast to Montana. Two languages of northern California – Yurok and Wiyot – are considered to be distantly related to it.

Among the tribes sharing the Algonquian tradition are the Delaware, Natick, Narraganset, Penobscot, Abnaki, Malecite, Passamaquoddy, Micmac, Shawnee, Miami, Fox, Menomini, Potawatomi, Cree, Ojibwa, Cheyenne, Blackfoot and Arapaho(e).

The Arapaho(e) are typical of the mounted Indians of the Great Plains. The Northern Arapahoe consider themselves to be the direct descendants of the mother Arapahoe tribe and keep in their possession several sacred tribal articles, the Flat Pipe and the responsibility of conducting the annual Offerings Lodge (Sun Dance) ritual. They have managed to retain their cultural identity through the Arapaho(e) language. However, today's younger people use English almost exclusively and, to a very large degree, are deficient even in passive knowledge of their native language. Tribal leaders have succeeded in introducing into the curricula of the Wind River Reservation area schools some oral instruction at both elementary and secondary levels.

The Language

A project, sponsored by the National Endowment for the Humanities, has produced a dictionary, indication of the strong efforts to preserve the Arapaho(e) language for future generations.

Since the Arapaho(e) language requires its own alphabet, which is based on the principle that each distinctive sound unit (phoneme) is represented by only one letter, no Arapaho(e) word may be spelled as it might be spelled if it were an English word.

The entire alphabet is written as **b, c, e, h, i, k, n, o, s, 3, t, u, w, x, y.**

Vowels are **i, u, e** and **o.** Consonants with a 'stop 'sound are **b, t, c, k** and **'** (glottal stop); fricative consonants are **3, s, x, h.** The **n** is nasal.

The Arabic symbol for the number 3 was selected because the English word 'three' begins with the same sound and the symbol is found on the typewriter keyboard.

Refer to an Arapaho(e) dictionary for a more detailed explanation of length, stress, pitch, and one diacritical symbols.

céeséy	one
niis	two
néésó	three
yéin	four
yoo3ón	five
sesínónó	ache, it is aching
wonotónó	ear
cebtéenocoo	fried bread
bésonon	neck
woo'téenoowu'	coffee
hinén	man
he3	dog
ho3	arrow
wó'oo3	foot
hó3o	star
sítee	fire
nec	water

The People

Our People, Blue Sky People – their names for themselves sound as descriptive and as beautiful as their language.

Once proud to roam the plains following the buffalo, the Arapaho(e) today live in the confines of areas surrounded by non-Indian people. True to themselves, they have maintained some spiritual identity with the past and enjoy knowing who they were and who they are in their songs, arts and lifestyles.

> Beauty is still their path.
> – Ah ho
> **Eagle/WalkingTurtle**

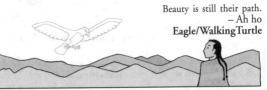

CHOCTAW

The Choctaw People were the first tribe on the Trail of Tears, as early as 1831. The Trail of Tears is the name used to describe the removal of several Indian tribes (some 100,000 people) from their land to a country set aside for them beyond the Mississippi. The Indians made the move on foot and many lives were lost. Today the Choctaw live in both Mississippi and Oklahoma because of their forced removal by the US government from their traditional homelands in central and southern Mississippi.

The Choctaw were once one of the largest tribes in what is now Southeast USA. They had strong democratic government institutions and a productive, agriculturally based community.

The Language

The language of the Choctaw, of the Muskogean family, is preserved through use by the people. Muskogean was a major linguistic family in the Southeast, and it includes Chickasaw (closely related to Choctaw), Creek and Seminole.

ačaaffah	one
tookloh	two
tooččiinah	three
ooštah	four
tałłapii	five
haannaaliih	six
ontookloh	seven
ontooččiinah	eight
čaakaali	nine
pookooliih	ten
nakna	man
tayik	woman
hakčoma	tobacco
šukba	blanket
paska	bread
poskoos	child

nantaho	what is it?
sabanna	I want some
babišali	friend
inakfiš	half brother
itibapiši	brother
tali	metal, stone
tali holisso	money
nanih chaha	mount or hill
lowak	fire
pinilowak	steamboat or fireboat
okahomma	whisky
kapassa	winter, cold weather
čokma	good
fihna	very
mahoba	I think

The People

Choctaw People of the Mississippi have been on their land so long that their origin is understood from legends of landmarks. Nanih Waiya Mound, near Preston, Mississippi, is both the creation focal point and the place of destination from a long migration from another place.

The first Europeans to have contact with the Choctaw were Spanish gold seekers. In 1519, Alonzo Pineda entered Choctaw territory lands that today are called north central Alabama and central Mississippi.

The Choctaw were farmers and hunters. They lived in log houses in villages along the rivers, and the natural circumstances of their lives suited their desire for happiness.

In 1540, Hernando de Soto and his armies enslaved and killed Indian people throughout the southeast. But even though the Choctaw were driven from their lands, they returned around 1700 with the French and English. The Mississippi Valley was rich and much coveted and the Choctaw were caught in the middle of non-Indian struggles to obtain the land.

By the early 1800s, the US Government had decided to allow US citizens, not Indians (who had no recognised citizenship), to hold land. Some Choctaw managed to stay in their traditional homeland but most were removed to Oklahoma. Hardship, heart-break, disease and death were the consequences many suffered on the journey.

Out of the 8000 who managed to remain in Mississippi, only about 1200 survived by 1910.

The Choctaw always allied themselves with the USA and the structure of the US Government itself was modelled after many Native American confederacy organisations.

Visitors are welcome in Choctaw country, be it Mississippi or Oklahoma. The people are friendly and hospitable and you may have the chance to join them in honouring all things that live. If you are able to attend one of their public ceremonies you'll enjoy their sense of humour, their colourful costumes and their wonderful food.

CHEROKEE

As far as we know the first North American language to be recorded was Iroquoian, the family of languages which includes Cherokee. As early as 1534, words were transcribed from Iroquoian-speaking people encountered by the explorer, Jacques Cartier, in the Bay of Gaspé. From that time to the present, missionaries, philologists and linguists have continued to wonder about the intricacies of these languages and their interrelationships. Much still remains to be discovered.

When Europeans first arrived in North America, Iroquoian people lived as far north as Quebec, as far south as Georgia, from the coasts of Virginia and the Carolinas west to Ohio, Pennsylvania, and Ontario.

The Iroquoian language family consists of two divisions: a south-ern division, represented by the Cherokee, and a northern division. Northern Iroquoian is composed of several sub-divisions: Huron-Wyandot, Laurentian, Tuscarora-Nottoway and the Five Nations languages, represented by Cayuga, Mohawk, Oneida, Onondaga and Seneca. Several other Northern languages are known to have had speakers including Andaste, Erie, Neutral, Petun and Wenro.

Since the Trail of Tears in the 1830s, when many Native Americans were moved from their lands, the Cherokee People have been divided. The Cherokee Reservation in North Carolina is in the proximity of the original Cherokee area of residence.

CENTRAL &
SOUTHEAST

As a federally recognised tribe, this Eastern Band of Cherokee Indians is a sovereign unit of government in its own right. Other Cherokee People, whose ancestors were removed by force by the US Government, live today in communities near Tahlequah, Oklahoma.

Much of the culture of the Cherokee remains, including the production of fine arts and crafts but principally consisting of ancient folklore and customs. Most, if not all, Cherokee speak or understand English, but the Cherokee language is taught in the homes and elementary schools. The language is spoken today by about 10,000 people living in eastern Oklahoma and by another 1100 in western North Carolina. At least six different dialects are presently used.

The first contact with Europeans probably occurred during de Soto's expedition in 1540. In the 17th century, the Cherokee inhabited the southern Appalachian region of Tennessee, North Carolina, Virginia, South Carolina, Georgia and Alabama. From 1838 to 1839, the majority of the Cherokee were forced to walk to Oklahoma, but several hundred people hid in the North Carolina mountains until 1849 when they settled on land bought there on their behalf.

The Language

Estimates of the number of speakers of Native American languages are only approximations. Degrees of linguistic ability are difficult to assess. Abilities range from storytelling and formal oratory to passive comprehension only. Because the majority of the speakers of these languages can also speak English, French or Spanish, and often choose to do so, members of a community are sometimes unaware themselves of the linguistic skills of their neighbours. Furthermore, an indeterminate number of speakers have moved to cities.

Pronunciation & the Alphabet

The Cherokee alphabet was invented by Sequoyah, a celebrated Cherokee chief, in the early 1800s. Sequoyah's syllabary, which uses symbols of sounds instead of letters or words, has made it possible for this language to be written and taught from text.

The following is transcribed using Roman letters to indicate the appropriate sounds.

Vowels

a as the 'a' in father, or short as the 'a' in rival
e as the 'a' in 'hate', or short as the 'e' in 'met'
i as 'i' in 'pique', or short as 'i' in 'pit'
o as 'aw' in 'law', or short as 'o' in 'not'
u as 'oo' in 'fool', or short as 'u' in 'full'
v as 'u' in 'but', made nasal, nearly as if followed by the French nasal *n*. This sound is not found in the English language.

Consonants

d represents nearly the same sound as in English, but close to that of 't'
g is nearly the same as its hard sound in English, but close to the 'k'

The letters **h, k, l, m, n, g, s, t, w** and **y** are as in English. The letter **q** is invariably followed by **u**, as in English, with the same sound. The sounds of the other Roman consonants never occur.

Those syllables which are written with the consonant **g**, except *ga*, sometimes have the sound of **k**. *Do, du, dv* are sometimes sounded as *to, tu, tv*. Those written with *tl*, except *tla* (pronounced *dhla*), sometimes vary to *dl*. Instead of *ts*, this might be written *ds*, but the distinction is not very perceptible. A German would write them with sufficient accuracy as *za, ze,* etc.

Each character expresses a syllable by itself, with the exception of **s**. Since the alphabet is syllabic, and the number of syllables is so small, the task of learning to read the Cherokee language is much easier than that of learning to read English. When English scholars remember tedious months occupied in learning to read, they may regard it as astonishing that an active Cherokee can learn to read his or her own language in a day, and usually only three days is required.

a-sga-ya	man
a-ge-hya	woman
u-do-da	father
u-ji	mother
a-yoh-li	child
u-do	brother, sister
u-wev ʾi	river
u-gv-wi-yu-hi	king, emperor
go-da	earth
e-qua	great
ga-lv-quo-di	holy
a-do-ni-sg	priest
u-wo-du	fine
ju-li-chv-ya-sdi	valiant, brave
so:kwa	one
tha:li	two
tso-i	three
a-jaʾ-di	fish
ʾv - ʾv	yes

The People

There are Cherokee reservations in Oklahoma and North Carolina, although most Cherokee now live outside them. Many Cherokee still cling to their ancient lore and customs. They sing old hymns in their own musical language. Some of the older women wear long full dresses and a bright kerchief tied on their heads. Occasionally you will see a baby tied on the back of a Cherokee woman.

Visiting the Cherokee is an adventure in fun and learning. To respect them is to gain their respect for you. Visitors are welcome.

Eagle/Walking Turtle

HAWAIIAN

INTRODUCTION

Hawaii is at the northern apex of the cultural area known as the Polynesian Triangle, which extends south-west to New Zealand and south-east to Easter Island. The languages spoken within this area, including Samoan, Tongan, Tahitian, Rapanui and Maori, to name a few, belong to the Polynesian language family. This group includes languages such as Malagasy which is spoken as far away as Madagascar. Settled some 1500 years ago by Polynesians from the central Pacific, Hawaii was isolated from the west until the arrival of Captain Cook in 1778.

In 1820, missionaries arrived in Hawaii and, in an effort to spread Christianity, began teaching Hawaiians to read and write. Through time, Hawaiian was replaced by English as the commonly spoken language in Hawaii. In 1896, Hawaiian was banned as the medium of instruction in Hawaii's public schools, which led to the further decline of the language.

In the 1970s and 1980s, a resurgence of interest in Hawaiian culture, history and language began. In 1978, Hawaiian was made an official language of the State of Hawaii, along with English. In the 1980s, the Hawaiian language immersion movement began with total immersion in pre-schools, like that established by the Maori in New Zealand. Total immersion grade, middle and secondary schools followed.

Although English is spoken everywhere in Hawaii, a visitor has a greater chance of hearing the Hawaiian language being spoken today than they would have had 20 or 30 years ago. Hawaiian used to be heard mainly among elders or in isolated communities but today can be heard on the street, in shopping centres, hotels and playgrounds. Hawaiians are very proud of their language and are actively working to assure its survival (see also Hawaiian English in The Melting Pot section).

ALOHA

Aloha, the traditional Hawaiian greeting, can mean 'love', 'welcome' or 'goodbye'.

PRONUNCIATION

A Hawaiian alphabet was established in 1826 and is very similar to that of other Polynesian languages. Two basic rules of Hawaiian spelling are that two or more consonants never appear next to each other, and that every word ends with a vowel. Hawaiian isn't difficult to pronounce, and your effort to pronounce it properly will be appreciated.

Vowels

There are five vowels in the Hawaiian alphabet, which sound similar to their English equivalents. Each vowel has both a short and long pronunciation. Long vowels are indicated by placing a macron over the vowel (ā, ē, ī, ō and ū).

a	as in 'father'
e	as in 'egg'
i	as in 'ski'
o	as in 'home'
u	as in 'blue'

Consonants

Hawaiian has eight consonants – h, k, l, m, n, p, w and ʻ. The consonants are all familiar to the English speaker, except perhaps the ʻokina, or glottal stop (ʻ). The use of the ʻokina is crucial because it can indicate a difference in meaning. The name Hawaii itself is pronounced with a glottal stop in the Hawaiian language, as Hawaiʻi. Native speakers don't use the ʻokina when writing because they know the meaning by context, but the second language learner will benefit by the inclusion of both macrons and glottal stops in this chapter.

w	like 'w' or like 'v'
ʻ	glottal stop (ʻokina), like the sound between the words in 'uh-oh' or the Cockney pronunciation of 'butter'

MEETING PEOPLE

Hawaiians are usually friendly and enjoy meeting people. The first Hawaiian word you may hear is aloha (hello/welcome). You may be presented with a lei (garland), with or without a kiss. Although a kiss is not a traditional gesture, it has become common practice for people to embrace and exchange kisses on the cheek, especially if they're good friends or related.

Greetings & Goodbyes

Hello.	Aloha.
Good morning.	Aloha kakahiaka.
Good day. (midday greeting)	Aloha awakea.
Good afternoon.	Aloha 'auinalā.
Good evening.	Aloha ahiahi.
Goodbye.	Aloha a hui hou.

Useful Words

Yes.	'Ae.
No.	'A'ole.
Please.	E 'olu'olu.
Thank you.	Mahalo.
Excuse me.	E kala mai ia'u.
Sorry.	E kala mai.

Body Language

When meeting someone or passing someone on the street, you might notice that they raise their eyebrows at you. Don't be alarmed, it's a non-verbal greeting found in Hawaii and elsewhere in the Pacific. Eye contact in Hawaii may be different than in other English-speaking countries. People, especially strangers, may briefly glance at you, then turn away. If you stare at a Hawaiian, they may interpret it as a challenge and ask you what you're looking at. This is in direct contradiction to Westerners' belief that honesty is shown by looking someone straight in the eye.

HAWAIIAN

Family

The basic Hawaiian family unit is the 'ohana (extended family).
Because genealogy is an important aspect of Hawaiian culture,
Hawaiians take pride in being able to identify relationships. At
times it can seem that most Hawaiians are related when just about
everyone they introduce you to are relatives.

Deities

akua
> major Hawaiian god; when capitalised, Akua usually refers to
> the Christian god

'aumakua
> ancestral guardian gods which take animal forms such as sharks
> (manō), owls (pueo) and eels (puhi)

Hi'iakaikapoliopele
> Pele's favourite younger sister

Hina
> Polynesian goddess; wife of Kū, one of the four main gods

Ka'ahupahau
> benevolent shark goddess of Pu'uloa (Pearl Harbor)

Kamapua'a
> demigod, half man-half pig; rival and lover of Pele

Kanaloa
> god of the oceans; winds

Kāne
> god of creation; life

Kū
> god of war

Laka
> patron deity of the hula

Lono
> god of agriculture

Māui

pan-Polynesian demigod who performed feats to improve the quality of life of his people. He raised the sky so that his mother's kapa (bark cloth) could dry, and fished the islands out of the ocean when his fishhook snagged the ocean floor and he tugged with such force that the islands of Hawaii were yanked to the surface. They would have been one mass except that someone looked back and the line snapped.

menehune

a people believed to perform miraculous feats overnight, always evading capture. According to legend, they built many of Hawaii's fishponds, heiau and other stonework.

Papa
earth mother

Pele

goddess of fire; volcano. There are several proverbs that link Puna, the easternmost point of the Big Island, with Pele. To express anger, someone might say Ke lauahi maila o Pele ia Puna, 'Pele is pouring lava out on Puna'.

Wākea
sky father

FOOD

Hawaiians cook food in a variety of ways and especially enjoy delicacies from the ocean. Food and eating have a special significance in Hawaiian culture. Many activities culminate in a lū'au or feast (formerly called pā'ina or 'aha'aina). A child's first birthday, a wedding or a graduation all warrant a celebration.

Getting together to prepare food for any occasion is a time for family and friends to help each other, catch up on the latest news and just enjoy each other's company. You'll have many opportunities to attend commercial lū'au, which are modified for the non-Hawaiian palate. However, if you do have a chance to attend a private lū'au, by all means go for it – it'll be a very pleasant experience.

HAWAIIAN

GETTING AROUND
Geographical Terms

ahupua'a	land division from the upland to the sea
'āina	land
ala	pathway
hana/hono	bay
heiau	ancient Hawaiian place of worship
honua	earth
i kai	to head toward the sea
i uka	to head inland
kai	sea/saltwater
ko'a	fishing shrine
ko'olau	windward side of an island
kona	leeward side of an island
Kū'ula	fishing god
luakini	type of heiau dedicated to the war god Kū and used for human sacrifices
ma kai	seaward
ma uka	inland
mauna	mountain
moana	ocean
moku	land district; island
pali	cliff
puna	spring
pu'u	hill
pu'uhonua	place of refuge
wai	freshwater

SHAKA SIGN

Hawaiians greet each other with the *shaka* sign, made by extending the thumb and the little finger while holding the other fingers to the palm. The hand is then held out and shaken. This greeting is as common as waving.

HAWAIIAN

Placenames

Hawaiian placenames are often descriptions of the geographic feature they represent, or are references to historical events. The descriptive words or adjectives follow the nouns they modify. For instance Mauna Kea is 'white mountain', Punahou is 'new spring' and Ala Moana is 'ocean pathway'.

HAWAIIAN SIGNS

Kapu, meaning 'taboo', is part of the ancient Hawaiian social system. Today the word's often seen on signs meaning 'Keep Out'.

The word *kokua* means 'help and cooperation'. *Please Kokua* written on rubbish bins is the equivalent of 'Don't litter'.

Ala Wai	freshwater canal or waterway
Haleakalā	house of the sun
Halekūlani	house befitting royalty (hotel)
Halemaʻumaʻu	fern house
Haleʻiwa	house of the frigate bird
Hanalei	crescent bay
Honolulu	protected bay
Kailua	two seas
Maunaʻala	fragrant mountain
Puʻukapu	sacred hill
Puʻukoholā	whale hill (heiau near Kawaihae, Hawaii island)
Puʻuloa	long hill
Waikīkī	spurting water
Waimānalo	drinking water
Waimea	reddish water (as from erosion of red soil)

HAWAIIAN

In the Surf

To Hawaiians, the ocean is a source of food and entertainment. Surfing and canoeing are favourite pastimes for people of all ages. Experienced surfers make surfing look so easy, but novices should beware – waves are very powerful and caution should be taken even when you're standing on the beach.

kahakai	beach
kaha nalu; he'e umauma	bodysurfing
wa'a	canoe
ama	outrigger
hoe	paddle
papa	reef
one	sand
papa he'enalu	surfboard
he'enalu	surfboarding
nalu	wave

WHAT WAS THAT?

While visiting Hawaii you might catch a quick glimpse of a small, brown, weasel-like creature dashing across the road and disappearing into the brush. It's the mongoose, a native of India that was brought to Hawaii by the sugar growers to help with the battle against rats.

The only problem was that the rat is nocturnal and the mongoose is diurnal, thus they each did their own thing at different times of the day.

The mongoose has no natural predator in Hawaii so its population has grown virtually unchecked. It has caused problems for farmers because the mongoose loves eggs and young fowl. On occasion you might see them at rural visitor stops running to retrieve bits of leftover food.

HAWAIIAN

HOLIDAYS & FESTIVALS

Aloha Festivals
> celebration of Hawaiian culture with parades, contests, canoe races and Hawaiian music. Festivities take place in September and October on every island.

Kamehameha Hula Competition
> one of Hawaii's biggest hula contests held in Honolulu near the end of June

Ka Molokai Makahiki
> modern-day version of the ancient makahiki festival Celebrations include traditional Hawaiian games and sports, a fishing contest and Hawaiian music and hula. Held in Kaunakakai, Molokai in mid-January.

Lei Day
> May Day (1 May) is Lei Day, celebrated with a lei-making competition

King Kamehameha Day
> on 11 June, or the nearest weekend, the statue of Kamehameha is decorated with long lei and a parade is held through Waikīkī, ending at Kapi'olani Park where Hawaiian crafts are usually demonstrated

Merrie Monarch Hula Festival
> Hawaii's longest running hula competition is held in Hilo, on the weekend after Easter

Molokai Ka Hula Piko
> held in Molokai in mid-May. Celebrates the birth of hula, with traditional dance performances, Hawaiian food and visits to sacred sites.

Prince Kūhiō Day
> 26 March, birthday of Prince Jonah Kūhiō Kalaniana'ole

Prince Lot Hula Festival
> hula exhibition held in July at Oahu's Moanalua Gardens

HAWAIIAN

THE HULA

Hula is the traditional dance of Hawaii. The hula is taught in hālau or hālau hula, which means 'school' or 'dance school'. In ancient Hawaii the hula accompanied oli (chanting). Today that style has been joined by a new style of hula that accompanies contemporary Western-style music. When watching the hula remember to try to keep your eyes on the dancers' hands because the hands tell the story of the chant or song. There are many hālau hula and they often enter competitions to see who are the best at their craft.

LETTER WRITING

Dear Sir/Madam	*Aloha kāua*
Humbly yours	*'O au iho nf me ka ha'aha'a*
Sincerely; Yours truly	*'O au iho nf*
With love	*Me ke aloha*
With warmest regards	*Me ke aloha pumehana*
With never-ending love	*Me ke aloha pau'ole*

HAWAIIAN

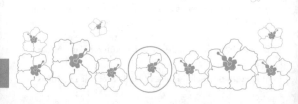

COMPLETE LIST OF LONELY PLANET BOOKS

AFRICA Africa on a shoestring • Cairo • Cape Town • East Africa • Egypt • Ethiopia, Eritrea & Djibouti • The Gambia & Senegal • Healthy Travel Africa • Kenya • Malawi • Morocco • Mozambique • Read This First: Africa • South Africa, Lesotho & Swaziland • Southern Africa • Southern Africa Road Atlas • Tanzania, Zanzibar & Pemba • Trekking in East Africa • Tunisia • Watching Wildlife East Africa • Watching Wildlife Southern Africa • West Africa • World Food Morocco • Zimbabwe, Botswana & Namibia

AUSTRALIA & THE PACIFIC Aboriginal Australia & the Torres Strait Islands • Auckland • Australia • Australia Road Atlas • Bushwalking in Australia • Cycling Australia • Cycling New Zealand • Fiji • Healthy Travel Australia, NZ and the Pacific • Islands of Australia's Great Barrier Reef • Melbourne • Micronesia • New Caledonia • New South Wales & the ACT • New Zealand • Northern Territory • Outback Australia • Out to Eat – Melbourne • Out to Eat – Sydney • Papua New Guinea • Queensland • Rarotonga & the Cook Islands • Samoa • Solomon Islands • South Australia • South Pacific • Sydney • Sydney Condensed • Tahiti & French Polynesia • Tasmania • Tonga • Tramping in New Zealand • Vanuatu • Victoria • Walking in Australia • Watching Wildlife Australia • Western Australia

CENTRAL AMERICA & THE CARIBBEAN Bahamas, Turks & Caicos • Baja California • Bermuda • Central America on a shoestring • Costa Rica • Cuba • Dominican Republic & Haiti • Eastern Caribbean • Guatemala • Guatemala, Belize & Yucatán: La Ruta Maya • Havana • Healthy Travel Central & South America • Jamaica • Mexico • Mexico City • Panama • Puerto Rico • Read This First: Central & South America • World Food Mexico • Yucatán

EUROPE Amsterdam • Amsterdam Condensed • Andalucía • Austria • Barcelona • Belgium & Luxembourg • Berlin • Britain • Brussels, Bruges & Antwerp • Budapest • Canary Islands • Central Europe •Copenhagen • Corfu & the Ionians • Corsica • Crete • Crete Condensed • Croatia • Cycling Britain • Cycling France • Cyprus • Czech & Slovak Republics • Denmark • Dublin • Eastern Europe • Edinburgh • England • Estonia, Latvia & Lithuania • Europe on a shoestring • Finland • Florence • France • Frankfurt Condensed • Georgia, Armenia & Azerbaijan • Germany • Greece • Greek Islands • Hungary • Iceland, Greenland & the Faroe Islands • Ireland • Istanbul • Italy • Krakow • Lisbon • The Loire • London • London Condensed • Madrid • Malta • Mediterranean Europe • Milan, Turin & Genoa • Moscow • Mozambique • Munich • The Netherlands • Normandy • Norway • Out to Eat – London • Paris • Paris Condensed • Poland • Portugal • Prague • Provence & the Côte d'Azur • Read This First: Europe • Rhodes & the Dodecanese • Romania & Moldova • Rome • Rome Condensed • Russia, Ukraine & Belarus • Scandinavian & Baltic Europe • Scotland • Sicily • Slovenia • South-West France • Spain • St Petersburg • Sweden • Switzerland • Trekking in Spain • Tuscany • Venice • Vienna • Walking in Britain • Walking in France • Walking in Ireland • Walking in Italy • Walking in Spain • Walking in Switzerland • Western Europe • World Food France • World Food Ireland • World Food Italy • World Food Spain

COMPLETE LIST OF LONELY PLANET BOOKS

INDIAN SUBCONTINENT Bangladesh • Bhutan • Delhi • Goa • Healthy Travel Asia & India • India • Indian Himalaya • Karakoram Highway • Kerala • Mumbai (Bombay) • Nepal • Pakistan • Rajasthan • Read This First: Asia & India • South India • Sri Lanka • Tibet • Trekking in the Indian Himalaya • Trekking in the Karakoram & Hindukush • Trekking in the Nepal Himalaya

ISLANDS OF THE INDIAN OCEAN Madagascar &Comoros • Maldives • Mauritius, Réunion & Seychelles

MIDDLE EAST & CENTRAL ASIA Bahrain, Kuwait & Qatar • Central Asia • Dubai • Iran • Israel & the Palestinian Territories • Istanbul • Istanbul to Cairo on a Shoestring • Istanbul to Kathmandu • Jerusalem • Jordan • Lebanon • Middle East • Oman & the United Arab Emirates • Syria • Turkey • World Food Turkey • Yemen

NORTH AMERICA Alaska • Boston • Boston Condensed • British Colombia • California & Nevada • California Condensed • Canada • Chicago • Deep South • Florida • Great Lakes • Hawaii • Hiking in Alaska • Hiking in the USA • Honolulu • Las Vegas • Los Angeles • Louisiana & The Deep South • Miami • Montreal • New England • New Orleans • New York City • New York City Condensed • New York, New Jersey & Pennsylvania • Oahu • Out to Eat – San Francisco • Pacific Northwest • Puerto Rico • Rocky Mountains • San Francisco • San Francisco Map • Seattle • Southwest • Texas • Toronto • USA • Vancouver • Virginia & the Capital Region • Washington DC • World Food Deep South, USA • World Food New Orleans

NORTH-EAST ASIA Beijing • China • Hiking in Japan • Hong Kong • Hong Kong Condensed • Hong Kong, Macau & Guangzhou • Japan • Korea • Kyoto • Mongolia • Seoul • Shanghai • South-West China • Taiwan • Tokyo • World Food – Hong Kong

SOUTH AMERICA Argentina, Uruguay & Paraguay • Bolivia • Brazil • Buenos Aires • Chile & Easter Island • Colombia • Ecuador & the Galapagos Islands • Healthy Travel Central & South America • Peru • Read This First: Central & South America • Rio de Janeiro • Santiago • South America on a shoestring • Santiago • Trekking in the Patagonian Andes • Venezuela

SOUTH-EAST ASIA Bali & Lombok • Bangkok • Cambodia • Hanoi • Healthy Travel Asia & India • Ho Chi Minh City • Indonesia • Indonesia's Eastern Islands • Jakarta • Java • Laos • Malaysia, Singapore & Brunei • Myanmar (Burma) • Philippines • Read This First: Asia & India • Singapore • South-East Asia on a shoestring • Thailand • Thailand's Islands & Beaches • Thailand, Vietnam, Laos & Cambodia Road Atlas • Vietnam • World Food Thailand • World Food Vietnam

Also available: Journeys travel literature, illustrated pictorials, calendars, diaries, Lonely Planet maps and videos. For more information on these series and for the complete range of Lonely Planet products and services, visit our website at **www.lonelyplanet.com**.

LONELY PLANET

Series Description

travel guidebooks	in depth coverage with backgournd and recommendations
	download selected guidebook Upgrades at www.lonelyplanet.com
shoestring guides	for travellers with more time than money
condensed guides	highlights the best a destination has to offer
citySync	digital city guides for Palm TM OS
outdoor guides	walking, cycling, diving and watching wildlife
phrasebooks	don't just stand there, say something!
city maps and road atlases	essential navigation tools
world food	for people who live to eat, drink and travel
out to eat	a city's best places to eat and drink
read this first	invaluable pre-departure guides
healthy travel	practical advice for staying well on the road
journeys	travel stories for armchair explorers
pictorials	lavishly illustrated pictorial books
eKno	low cost international phonecard with e-services
TV series and videos	on the road docos
web site	for chat, Upgrades and destination facts
lonely planet images	on line photo library

LONELY PLANET OFFICES

Australia
Locked Bag 1, Footscray,
Victoria 3011
☎ 03 8379 8000
fax 03 8379 8111
email: talk2us@lonelyplanet.com.au

USA
150 Linden St, Oakland,
CA 94607
☎ 510 893 8555
TOLL FREE: 800 275 8555
fax 510 893 8572
email: info@lonelyplanet.com

UK
10a Spring Place,
London NW5 3BH
☎ 020 7428 4800
fax 020 7428 4828
email: go@lonelyplanet.co.uk

France
1 rue du Dahomey,
75011 Paris
☎ 01 55 25 33 00
fax 01 55 25 33 01
email: bip@lonelyplanet.fr
website: www.lonelyplanet.fr

World Wide Web: www.lonelyplanet.com *or* AOL keyword: lp
Lonely Planet Images: lpi@lonelyplanet.com.au